Here's what people are sayi

"*Stand-Up & Heartbreak* i ... f a "funny girl" into a full-fledged workin ... hen she unites love and comedy, however, our heroine is confro... with painful choices she can't laugh off. This is a humorous, courageous memoir that takes you from the ups and downs of the seedy comedy club to a high-style romance only to reveal secrets you didn't see coming. You won't be able to put it down!"

- Janet Lombardi, author of the memoir *Bankruptcy: A Love Story*

"Mrs. Maisel is alive and well and living in 1980's New York City!
And this time she's for real!
With biting humor and naked honesty, Arlene Schindler recounts the struggles of a comic's coming-of-age in one of entertainment's toughest corners, as she prepares for the most challenging gig of her life - marriage to a duplicitous sex addict."

- USA Today Bestseller Julie A. Richman

"If you thought it might be a hoot to be a standup comic, you definitely want to read Arlene Schindler's memoir, *Stand-Up & Heartbreak*. It's the chronicle of what hell it was in 1981 to be a woman (then called "girl") with a dream to be a standup comic, who had to navigate the myriad of obstacles thrown in her path. It was a man's world in a big way. So why was it so hard for her to meet the right man? *Stand-Up & Heartbreak* delivers."

- Cathy Ladman, comedian, actress, writer

"Arlene's page-turner tale tells it like it was for us women in comedy in the late 70's. I rue how true to life her writing is as she captures the times, the jokes, the clothes, the sexual manipulations, the steep learning curve of trying to fit into a man's world while breaking new ground for funny females. Her struggle to succeed as an audience-pleasing standup, while fighting her way free of the need to please the wrong guy, resonates keenly."

- Melanie Chartoff, Actor ("Rugrats" "Seinfeld" "Newhart" "Parker Lewis Can't Lose" "Fridays")

"Arlene Schindler's seriocomic contribution to Women Under Scrutiny added exactly the spice the anthology needed. Her work is a joy to read."

- Randy Susan Meyers, author of Waisted.

"Arlene Schindler is full of heart, full of wit, and full of incredible stories! I love that she shares openly about her adventurous life."

- August McLaughlin, host of Girl Boner Radio

"This memoir is not only funny but immerses the reader into a cauldron of emotions. It is a story of laughter, heartache and growth. Arlene Schindler gives us an intimate look at what drove her as a comedian and what drove her in her relationships plus all the ups and downs that followed. *Stand-Up & Heartbreak* gives the reader a true insight into the world of comedy which can also lead to a world of struggles and choices many comedians can't laugh their way out of. An engrossing memoir."

- Brian Kiley – comedy writer, stand-up comic and author of The Astounding Misadventures of Rory Collins and Maybe Kevin.

"*Stand-Up & Heartbreak* has everything I look for in a memoir... You know what? It actually has everything I look for in any story...a protagonist I'm rooting for, memorable characters, relationships, transformation, and an inspiring, hopeful ending. Arlene Schindler is hilarious and unsparing in telling her story. This is a wonderful book. Don't miss it."

- Heidi Mastrogiovanni, author of the Lala Pettibone series

Dear Terri,

Love + Laughter

Stand Up & Heartbreak:
a comic and a sex addict walk into a marriage…

Arlene Schindler

Arlene Schindler

Cover: Design by Mark Christopher Harvey
Author Photo by Dennis Apergis

Published 2019 by HumorOutcasts Press
Printed in the United States of America

Disclaimer:
This is a work of nonfiction. The events, conversations and experiences detailed herein have been faithfully rendered as the author has remembered them to the best of her ability. Names, identities and some circumstances have been changed or compressed to protect the privacy of the individuals involved.

ISBN-10: 0-9600085-3-5
ISBN-13: 978-0-9600085-3-7

Acknowledgements

A tremendous debt of gratitude to the many who helped make *Stand-Up & Heartbreak* a reality, especially the following people for many varied reasons:

Arlene Phalon Baldassari, Barbara Bottner, Melanie Chartoff, Jackie Hoffman Chin, Susan Cuscuna, Terry Delsing, Kathleen Garrett, Debbie Kasper, Bob Keenan, Catherine Leach, Meg Livesey, Janet Lombardi, Heidi Mastrogiovanni, Grace Miller, Jill Rothenberg, Carol Schlanger, Linda Schwab, Dan Staroff, and MK Timme.

Thank you to my best girls for being funny, kind, constructively creative and supportive.

Special thanks to Elaine Silver, for her guidance, support, and cheerleading that helped me arrive at the finish line.

Table of Contents

CHAPTER 1:

DAY JOBS DON'T HAVE PUNCHLINES

I never said the word vagina in public until my parents were dead. That's why you probably never heard of me.

Center stage: Comedy U, down-town Manhattan. Spotlight on me and my jokes.

"Some people have stage presence. I have stage absence. In school, I was voted most likely to be forgotten. The teachers called me "Um."

Thrilled to be in front of an audience, I felt the hot lights on my face. As the crowd laughed long and loud, it seemed as if the room had embraced me in a loving hug. Nothing like a great set to make me feel fearless. Afterwards, taking compliments and congratulations from well-wishers, I grabbed my coat and left the club after midnight.

On nights like tonight that ran late, I'd ask a fellow comic if I could go home with them and sleep on their couch, then train home to Brooklyn in daylight. But after a few months of that, I'd now run out of couches.

I had to take the subway. Walking alone through the chilly April wind, my adrenaline surged as my heart beat kept pace with the clickety-clack of my spike heels on cement. One foot, then the other, echoing a half block away as I race-walked the five blocks to the urine-scented subway for a 45-minute ride home on the F train.

I was 25, with big permed hair and enormous shoulders thanks to the oversized pads I tucked into every garment. It was 1981, the most violent year for crime in New York City. A mugging was more common than a celebrity sighting. I may have had a big mouth and big dreams for a comedy career, thinking nothing could harm me when I was on stage, but my courage shrank on the streets. And with the spin of the subway turnstile, I went from fearless to fearful.

Old muggers don't die; they just steal away.

My orchestrated plan to avoid muggers was dressing in my "Ugly-Up-Get-Up" the shabbiest of coats over my nice club outfit, appearing to have the fashion sense of a bag woman. Carrying all money inside the coat, with no purse in evidence, I sat in the middle car of the train, near the conductor. Solo on the desolate ride, if anyone approached me, I'd start singing loudly about the solar system (*Moon Over Miami* was my favorite song/rant, encompassing both) so potential muggers would think I was insane.

The near-empty train chugged along the tracks as I worried about my safety, always anticipating the worst.

While my F train lingered at the West 4th Street station, waiting for it's D train connection, I replayed the evening's show in my head. How did I get to be in a smelly subway car around midnight after loitering in smoke filled comedy clubs with wacky guys?

My mother blamed my dad, a former comic, for my pursuits. In an era before Tina Fey, Lena Dunham, the Amys (Poehler and Schumer) or Ilana Glazer and Abbi Jacobson, my ambitions to write, direct, and star had but one role model: Elaine May. After an accomplished career in nightclubs, comedy records and TV, May was an idol to every funny girl my age. In 1963 Dad used to wake me up close to midnight to see the comedy team of Mike Nichols and Elaine May on *The Jack Paar Show* on our black-and-white television. A sleepy, pajama-clad second-grader, I was mesmerized watching her. Whip-smart, in a little black dress, May caused the all-male cast on the show to roar with laughter. Daddy had no idea that during our special times in front of the TV, when we were bonding in comedy, I was also setting a goal for my adult life.

When I was twelve, Dad and I saw *A New Leaf,* a movie in which Elaine May starred, wrote, and directed, on one of our cherished Saturday afternoon movie-and-a-meal dates. Although Dad's comedy career ended in his twenties, his knowledge and opinions about the comedy business shaped my own.

Afterwards at a Chinese restaurant, he said, "You're funny, kid. You saw what she did on screen. You could do that, too."

Those words were emblazoned on my psyche for years. Dad neglected to mention, however, that I'd need lots of other people, bags of money, and most of all, unrelenting chutzpah—to turn my chubby, funny self into a funny girl onscreen.

Sadly, I was the roundest and most graceless in Madame Benet's ballet class, where each girl had to leap into the air and then effortlessly tumble. Madame stood tall, inscrutable, black leotard, toe shoes, and that bun pulled painfully tight at the top of her head. She tapped her long wooden pointer as every girl began her tumble, counting the beats, "a one, two, three," until each girl stood again.

Not me. Flat on my ass on the floor, legs in the air, I couldn't get my chubby legs over my head. I was mortified as my body veered to the left or right, never quite overhead.

"Again, one, two, three." Madame insisted. My legs were unresponsive. "One, two, three." My body heated up with tension and embarrassment as my classmates stared at me. Just then, Madame Benet, and her trusty pointer, pounded down on the hardwood floor, again, again. Still, I was hopeful that on the next try, my legs would swing over my head. Meanwhile, Madame hit her pointer so hard, her impeccable bun was starting to unravel, as was she. After about five minutes of watching me fail, she retreated. "Let's just move on."

I told Mom about this, hoping she'd put a stop to my humiliations.

"It's important to get rid of your klutziness. Ballet can turn you from a klutz into a swan."

My dad tried to be sympathetic in the only way he knew how—with corny humor.

"A chubby girl doesn't wear a two-two. It's a four-four," he said.

Compared to that, telling jokes in front of a roomful of strangers on a brightly lit stage didn't seem scary. And years later, after hearing so many stories about my Dad performing in clubs and my watching Jack Parr, *The Ed Sullivan Show*, Woody Allen movies, and comedy everywhere, I decided this was my dream.

Meanwhile, still sitting in a blindingly bright subway car, trying not to be nervous or look at anyone, I ate raisins one at a time, like a chipmunk, to appear insane, and be left alone.

Two young punks running through the car, slowed to look at me. Fearing getting mugged on the train, head down, I struggled out loud with new jokes.

"I used to be so fat, they called me a Behemoth babe the size of a BUICK. Behemoth BABE the size of a Buick. BEHEMOTH babe the size of a Buick."

The punks laughed, gesturing that I was crazy. Then they exited the car. Relieved, I stopped eating raisins. Just four more stops.

Finally at my train stop, I rushed up the stairs of the desolate station to the street. Gusts of wind swirled through trees as I passed gated storefronts and groups of men congregating on the corners along the barely lit Church Avenue to home. As a chill brushed my cheek, the memory of my show's laughter warmed me when a room full of strangers adored me. Now, I wished there was someone at my side to walk with me. Turning the corner to Ocean Parkway, house keys in hand, the warmth waned. This was the part of stand-up I hated—the profound after-show loneliness—the emotional crash of life alone in my studio apartment.

I hated being solo, with my inner voice screeching unrelenting criticisms.

"You idiot, you're not funny enough. You blew that punch line. The neurotic guy with the mother issues, his set three comics before you, he could have saved it. He's a crazy jerk, hungry for more stage time than you. He's out six nights a week. Do you want this badly enough to keep coming back night after night? Can you do it all, clown girl?"

#

After the death of disco, New York City was a hotbed of new comedy—and male comedians (geeks, nerds, misfits, and man-children). The club scene was a man's world where "girl comics" were allowed to participate, but not be taken seriously. Small clubs and restaurants needed performers yearning for stage time.

I'd worked my way through school writing jokes for other comedians, with plenty of gags to spare, but I wanted to tell my own. Dad, my comedy cheerleader agreed. When I'd started college, he'd waltz into my room early on Sunday mornings carrying a brown paper bag brimming with hot bagels, shaking the bag under my nose to rouse me, stirring the smells of fresh garlic and onions, saying, "Get out of the rag business. Become a comedian, your true calling. And don't forget to find a husband." He called this "bagel hypnosis."

Dad was a Catskills comic in his early 20s, in the 1940s. His agent, Rose, also booked gigs for him at dinner theaters and supper clubs in Brooklyn and Manhattan, like Leon and Eddies, where food was served on fine china with cloth napkins and waiters wore tuxedos. That sounds worlds classier than working in dive bars, like me. Rose had two other comedians she booked on the circuit; Irwin Alan Kniberg, who became a comedy success as Alan King and Leonard Hacker who had a great comedy career as Buddy Hackett. In that era Jews either changed their names or their noses or both, to be accepted in the Gentile world. Rose revised Dad's name too, from Al Schindler to Hal Chant. Sadly, neither Hal nor Al was as successful as Alan or Buddy or his other contemporaries Stubby Kaye, who went on to star in the original *Guys and Dolls* or Sammy Shore, comedian, club owner, and father of Pauly Shore. But Dad was happy, telling jokes in his comedy life, until his father made him quit and get an "adult job." Former comedians may stop performing, but they don't stop being funny. He hoped someone, somewhere in his world, would work in comedy and he was banking on me. So for me, performing was the natural progression of my comedy education, the way the son of a dentist goes into the family business.

"As I look into your faces, I see your faces need looking into." That was a line from Dad's act in the Catskills, years before I was born. Goofy to me, but he said it sparked laughter.

#

My first night onstage was at an open-mike night at a club called Good Times. The room brimmed with underworld bravado, like an early Scorsese film. Dark, ugly faces appeared interesting. I had a hard—or should I say, flat-out impossible—act to follow, the kind of "talent" many comedians have nightmares about. The comic, a guy dressed in one of those shiny, printed Huckapoo disco shirts from the late '70s—same era it was last washed—jumped on the dimly lit stage, cleared his throat and began reading from a small box in his hands.

"For relief of occasional constipation or bowel cleansing before rectal examinations." Then he opened the box and continued reading. "Lie on left side with knee bent, arm resting comfortably." He assumed the position. Curled up on his side, when he said the word *insert*, the crowd went wild. Maybe his comedy hero was Andy Kaufman, that was my only justification for why someone would read enema directions *as* their act. How could the audience find this funny?

"Why can't I follow someone who has actual jokes?" I whispered to another comic for validation and a consolatory smile. There's fight or flight. I chose a third way: complain.

Up next, I had no choice. I thought, "I should get in a cab right now." Heart pounding, I paced the back of the room, longing to flee. Nervously running fingers through my hair, I mumbled my jokes to myself like a Buddhist chant till his set ended. It felt like forever.

Finally, Paul, the MC said, "Next, we have a girl from Brooklyn. Welcome, Arlene."

I took the stage. The spotlight prevented me from seeing faces in the audience. Looking to the back of the room, I saw myself in a mirror, looking sleek in a black jumpsuit and low-heeled lace-up boots, pleased my hair had cooperated and didn't frizz, just this once.

"Hey, that's me!" said my little-girl inner voice in amazement.

"That's me?" said my doubting inner critic. I almost froze from the thrill of being somewhere I'd always wanted to be. After practicing jokes as a girl in my bedroom, this was my moment. "I only wear designer clothes," I said into the microphone, unaccustomed to the echo, my mouth too close to the mike. I pulled back. "My favorite designer is final sale."

A few people chuckled.

The sweating began. I felt it drip down my sides and back. My scalp under my permed hair heated up slowly, then fiercely, feeling like a tin of Jiffy Pop popcorn cooking on top of my head. Was I pursuing comedy at the wrong time in a world where timing is everything?

In spite of my discomfort, somehow more jokes tumbled from my mouth, in a surreal out-of-body experience akin to being underwater, (which would have been refreshing). Everyone's favorite joke from my set was, *"I'm a procrastinating bulimic. When I'm ready to purge, it's already turned to fat."*

I didn't kill that night—but I didn't bomb. I was hooked.

#

I quit a good job as a copywriter at an ad agency to become a *gal du jour* temp secretary, so I'd be available for auditions, cattle calls, and other forms of soul-crushing that entertainment hopefuls endure.

Think *American Idol* in a blender, with the top off.

Working odd jobs for sporadic paychecks at buttoned-down corporations around midtown Manhattan provided a small income. Writing new material, juggling appointments and a budget that never balanced, trying to maintain calm, my life was in turmoil. At the time, I didn't realize I was living my dream, maybe because I thought I was supposed to have another goal, something stable. Fantasizing about being onstage at night while I licked envelopes and made copies, all I wanted to do was perform and then go to sleep. It was all exhausting.

"Hey Vinnie, how about another Seven and Seven?" I asked the bartender one night. "Sorry, girlie, just one. A second would not be a good idea." As I leaned over the bar to try again, a guy pinched my ass. At first I thought I had imagined it, but when he passed the bar again, he pretended to reach for something next to me—and got my tits.

Nights like these made it uncomfortable being in a club by myself. Plus, it's scary to be onstage at the mercy of strangers' approval. In retrospect, rather than feeling brave, I saw pursuing comedy as an alternative because I didn't think I could get and keep a "regular" job (and didn't want one). Onstage, I was queen of my universe, star of my show, writer, designer, music arranger, leader of my life. I liked that part.

Mornings, bleary eyed, sandwiched between other rush-hour subway strap-hangers on their way to work, I was a mere peon in the job world. Sometimes I was a temp copywriter at marketing companies, composing copy for catalogs and brochures, even dinner menus: "Succulent roast beef, piled high with mashed potatoes." Remember that one? That was mine. Other times, I got to use my eight years of art training. I had attended the High School of Art and Design and Parsons School of Design, a prestigious art college in New York City, only to be faced with a recession in the clothing industry due to the over-use of polyester. Once, I designed an ad for cellulite cream that involved hours of poring over photos of models with cottage-cheese thighs. The ad ran in *Harper's Bazaar* for six months.

Mostly though, I was a receptionist: answering phones, taking messages, and doing "lite" typing. I didn't have a business card or know what to say when people asked, "What do you do?" I couldn't sum up my catch-all career as copywriter, comic, girl Friday, and one other thing— itinerant overeater. Sure, I'd lost my post-adolescent emotional eating weight by putting a padlock on my dorm refrigerator (12-18-32). But anxiety led me to believe I was just one mood swing away from consuming enough food in one evening to gain it all back … and more.

When I turned 25 my parents put a sign in front of their house: Last girl before freeway...plus Salad Bar.

I had hopes for a romantic future, in spite of my pitiful romance-less present. The dating life of stand-up comics was laughably unglamorous, low-rent, and sometimes dangerous. One night, a lecherous fellow performer, asked me, "You live in Brooklyn? I can drive you home."

I asked, "Where in Brooklyn do YOU live?"

"It doesn't matter." he tossed off.

I immediately pictured myself screaming and struggling to get out of a locked car trunk. A ride with a drunken, wild-eyed, ax-carrying hitchhiker would be safer than getting in the car with this guy.

Usually, I was the only woman on the bill. If there were others, many were either unattractive, anorexic, wore overalls, got their hair cut with a bowl on their head or were just plain freakish. As for me, I'd lost 40 pounds in my last year of college. Still thrilled that I could choose clothes that weren't pastel polyester in a size 18, I wore slinky black jump suits, secretly hoping I was channeling a sleek, sophisticated Audrey Hepburn or Marlene Dietrich. I looked pretty onstage, I was told. Not a good thing for comedy. Audiences watched the first few minutes of my show, nodding and smiling, thinking this was the singer's intro patter. When they realized I was the comic, my set was over. Maybe I'd dressed too prettily for the job.

I spent my 20s in a holding pattern. Was it marriage or a career? I wasn't sure … but I was waiting. While I waited, I bought "good-enough" sheets along with make-do furniture, dishes, and pots and pans. My first apartment and all of its contents were like a training bra for my adult lifestyle. When this "thing" I was waiting for came, then I'd buy my dream house and fill it with the best. Hopefully I'd have a spouse, soul mate, or life partner to share it with too.

I have a new way to sexually satisfy my wife. I let her sleep.

That was my joke! I sold it to a Catskills comic when I was 25. I had no idea it would be the prophetic punch line for my future, riskier than a fearless vagina joke.

CHAPTER 2:

MY FIRST MISTAKE

"What's the only difference between a job interview and a first date? At the end of the date you could be naked." —Jerry Seinfeld

The first time I met him I thought he was the slimiest man I'd ever seen.

"Rupert Santo," he said, cheerfully. "Call me Rupert. I'll call you Arlene."

I shook his hand and smiled because I had to: he was my new temp boss of the week at BBS News in New York City. It was a lingering handshake; not my choice. He apologized for having a sweaty palm, and chuckled sinisterly, like Peter Lorre. Staring at me, with the sneering smile of a guy checking out a pole dancer, I sensed that he found me attractive. Pulling my hand back and discreetly wiping it on the side of my blue cotton skirt, I wished I could take a shower that very minute. A hazmat shower.

His desk was neat and orderly. A photo from a recent film was pinned on a board nearby; the actress looked just like me. "I'm his type," I noted to myself.

Rupert was a news man, with thick horn-rimmed glasses, an aged linen shirt with rolled up sleeves, and his black hair was oily and pasted to his head. Shorter than me, at 5’5” he looked like a shrunken, sweaty, Clark Kent.

“I think you’ll work out just fine.” His low, modulated theatrical voice was often heard on the radio; on the BBS late night news show he wrote and produced. Yet now that voice had the slick sleaze of an obscene phone caller.

We walked from his office to the barren cubicle just outside, where there was a desk, an IBM Selectric typewriter and phone. He held the chair for me like a well-mannered waiter. “All you need to do is answer the phone. It won’t ring that much. There are pens and paper in the drawers…” he explained.

“Do you need anything to be typed?” I asked, nervously. I’m a slow typist.

“No, there’s not much of that. My secretary is out on a medical leave, so I needed someone to sit in, just in case anything happens. But I don’t expect anything to happen.” He was stretching his time with me, and studying me. I felt my skin crawl, knowing his eyes were all over me. The phone rang.

“Don’t worry, I’ll get it,” he said, running into his office.

I sat down and snooped around the cubicle, searching for some clue, trying to figure out how to play his secretary’s role.

Over my shoulder I heard, “Have you read today’s paper?” I looked up and it was him, with the energetic enthusiasm of a

Chihuahua greeting its owner. He handed me *The New York Times* and walked back to his office.

My new boss just gave me permission to read the newspaper at my desk. I was being paid for a week to read and answer a phone that he said would never ring. Apparently when it did, the boss himself ran into his office to get it. Cool.

This meant I could focus on my real job, writing comedy. Maybe I'd glean some political jokes for my next show from the newspaper. The phone rang. As I moved towards it, I heard him say, "I'll get it." Less work for me. Great boss. Glad he found me appealing, giving me freedom to work at not working. I considered writing jokes about my new non-job. I'd heard of women in the White House, hired as secretaries, but paid not to work. How many women like me were hired in television news? After I'd been there two hours and done nothing for BBS News, I heard a bell announcing the arrival of the coffee cart.

"Would you like coffee?" I looked up. It was him.

"Shouldn't I be getting YOU coffee?" Women did that in those days.

"Let me please, it's my pleasure," he insisted, bolting off to the coffee cart.

He returned like an obedient child. "Here's your coffee. I wasn't sure how you like it, so here's milk, cream, sugar and artificial sweetener."

"Thank you," I offered, reaching for my purse to pay him.

"No, please. Put your money away," he insisted, still looking at me, as if he were waiting for me to dismiss him. Rupert's piercing stare was jarring and intriguing; a gentlemanly leer, repulsive and intoxicating with alternating breaths. I looked down at his feet. Small for a man. He wore well-kept Gucci loafers. I flashed to Mickey Mouse's feet, small and round. Can I write jokes out of working for this weird creepy guy? My new boss, Mr. Mouse Feet? Busy thinking about how to mine this situation for comedy, I didn't realize the long silence. Dazed by his attentiveness, I was dazzled that a suit wearing grown-up found me appealing.

"Well, I guess I'll go back to my office," he chimed.

"Let me know if I can be of assistance," I added, guilty about the free ride.

"Just knowing you're here is great." He turned and walked to his office.

I worked for Rupert for a week, hardly lifting a finger. By the end of that week, he still seemed slimy but, hey, I've known comedians who are slimier. Besides, scallops are slimy and people gobble them up in restaurants. Odd as it was, something about Rupert intrigued me.

CHAPTER 3:

THE MARY TYLER MOORE OF BROOKLYN

"Laughter is the most fun you can have without having to shower (unless there's a prop comic involved.)" —Arlene Schindler

I hated living in Brooklyn, mostly because I grew up there.

My Brooklyn—in the 1980s—was crack and crime ridden, not the hipster haven of farm to table restaurants and poetry slams that it is today. I'd tired of its gritty underbelly, urine smelling train stations and bohemian charms, so close to one of the greatest places on earth, yet worlds and seven train stops away. Everything in Manhattan seemed better and more exciting. I envied people who lived there, sheltered in their apartments and their relationships. To me, that life was a goal embodying success. My studio apartment on Ocean Parkway was a mere twelve minutes' drive, without traffic (otherwise it could take two hours), to the Promised Land. Most nights I was lulled to sleep by the sounds of fast cars whooshing by on the parkway, speeding into the city. I knew why they were going so fast, wishing that I too was on my way there, never to look back.

What would it take for me to live in Manhattan? My treadmill: Look for work. Keep my spirits up in hopes that someone would hire me. Find a job. Work hard to keep that job. Go to work, come home, make dinner, write jokes. Go to sleep. Get up and do it again for the rest of the work week. I spent weekends writing jokes, doing laundry, grocery shopping, seeing parents. I'd talk to friends on the phone. We'd make plans to get together the following week. Those plans would get cancelled and fall away, 'cause they were on their own treadmills to success. I repeated this week after week as the seasons changed. Everyone's too-busy-ness fed my loneliness and my late-night consolatory ice cream binges.

Finally, one of my get-togethers with a friend didn't get cancelled. My best pal from high school, Josie called. We'd lost touch during college, different schools in faraway states.

"I phoned your house and your mom gave me this number," she began. "I miss you. Come see me and my new place!" Josie blurted eagerly.

"Where are you living?" I was intrigued.

"Upper West Side, near where I grew up." Her voice sounded elated.

"You have your own apartment in Manhattan? Cool!"

"Not as sparkly as it sounds. It's in a residential hotel. Singers, musicians and artists live here. I had to audition to get an apartment. Let's have a sleepover!"

Josie was a painter, specializing in oils and acrylics, with a talent for getting me out of my own head and into the real world. Envious and eager to see her Manhattan pad, anticipating glamour and gloss, I was thrown when her space ended up being a dark, tiny, hotel room. It was just light enough to see water damaging the buckling ceiling, and walls that were in need of painting. I guess her audition didn't go that well. It was scarcely large enough for a bed, desk, easel and a hot plate plus a half fridge for a makeshift kitchen. Cozy meets claustrophobic.

After a day of shopping for the perfect jeans, we plopped our purses and shopping bags on the bed. Josie opened a night table drawer, pulling out menus.

"Find something you want to eat, and the food will be here in 20 minutes," she announced. This was how dinner was served at her place. She was right. Chinese food arrived in less than a half hour; a brown bag brimming with crisp white cardboard cartons, delivered by a skinny, anemic looking guy.

"Willie!" Josie hugged him. "Without you I'd starve. When is your band playing?"

"Josie honey, without your tips, I'd starve. Tuesday night, that club on 14th Street. Bring friends. Who is she? Bring her."

They exchanged more hugs, money, and Willie was gone.

"You didn't introduce me. Is he your delivery man, or someone you dated?"

"He is my type, the skinny musician type, but we haven't dated."

"Or slept together? If he was coming to my apartment all the time, I'd find another kind of delivery," I joked.

"Would you like to date him?" Josie arranged, plates, chopsticks, and a bottle of wine.

"He barely noticed me. Guys never see me when you're around."

"Don't say that. I can introduce you."

"You've got man magnetism that makes them jump and bark and kneel at your feet. I'm like the scoop of rice or side salad *with* the hot and spicy dish."

"You're a dish, my spicy sister." Josie giggled. We dined cross-legged facing one another on her queen-sized bed.

While piling a plate with food, my self-conscious comic took hold. "But without a mister. I would like someone, but I think Willie is all willy, plus skin and bones." I was eating, overfilling each forkful, then stuffing it into my mouth, ferociously. "I do spend too much time alone. I have enough voices in my head for a party platter."

"Is it a pity party?"

"Are you asking if I feel sorry for myself? I just wish there were more voices in my life, on the outside of my head, you know."

"What about dating and relationships?"

"I wish I had someone now. This past year, a brief fling here or there, more brief than fling. There was Bob when I was 19. We talked and wrote when I was at college. When school ended, that did too."

"Anyone since Bob?"

"The next person I dated after Bob, I guess I trusted him a little too much."

"Why do you say that?"

"I thought he'd be kind and gentle as Bob. But he was forceful and violent. You know when you say no, and then they laugh and just pound you anyway."

"Arlene, were you raped? Is that what happened?" Josie spoke tenderly, visibly shaken.

"Yes, that's what happened."

"What did you do afterwards, did you call the police?"

"This guy said, 'The more you scream the more I know you want it.' I just felt awful and angry with myself for being vulnerable. I trusted him enough to invite him into my apartment and I undressed, and got him excited…I blamed myself for what happened. I'm more guarded now." Realizing I'd just jostled a painful moment, I robotically shoveled food, faster, into my mouth. "I'm trying to move past it," I mumbled, mouth full of rice.

"I understand why you haven't dated. You must be so scared." As she chomped on crunchy eggrolls, Josie asked, "So you're not dating anyone, but you're out in bars every night?"

"I'm working. It's comedy."

"Are they paying you?"

"Open mike nights are showcases. People see what you can do. If a bartender likes you, you get free drinks. When you do well, then come the weekend gigs. That's the money."

"Aren't you scared to get onstage?"

"Aren't you afraid we'll spill Chinese food on your bed?" I fired back.

"Crummy blanket, too many disgusting things happened on it. Very few were food."

"Oh baby," I giggled. "I remember sleepovers at your house, you'd talk in your sleep, moaning, oh baby. Sex dreams about Gregg Allman, right?"

Allman was Josie's rocker crush when we were in high school, maybe because he looked like the male version of her.

"I've been trying to forget that. Let's get back to you. Just the thought of standing in front of a people telling jokes. I'd be afraid. You must be fearless."

"Me fearless?" I blurted, almost spitting moo shoo pork on the navy and white bed spread. "It's not like I have anyone to go home to at night. My life is about managing fear."

"I'm afraid too."

"When I'm onstage, that's the only time I don't feel alone. I could flop or die up there! But the exhilaration makes me forget I'm alone."

"Sounds exhausting. Pass the rice." Josie filled her plate with more food. "Which would you rather have, a great career in comedy or a boyfriend?"

"Ideally, I'd like both," I offered, reflecting.

"Do you think you'd have time for a guy? I've seen you fall for people who were charming but fake."

"You mean the two guys I dated in 11th grade who turned out to be gay?"

"And Bennie and Sal in 12th grade too," she said, stifling a laugh.

"What do you expect from an arts high school? Where's *your* boyfriend tonight? I hoped I'd meet him."

"He's traveling on the road, bass guitarist, for a disco golden oldies band. They had a top 10 hit: *Shame*. He's the only white guy in the band."

"When do you see him?"

"When he's not on the road, I tune out the world and see only him."

"You two become inseparable? I haven't felt that way about someone."

"Wait until it happens to you. You'll do the same thing. Love and sex become some kind of cocoon you won't want to climb out of."

"Really?" I was surprised. "Not even for friends?"

"When he's out of town, working, that's my social time. Like now."

"Do you think he's the one?" I quizzed.

"You mean Mr. Right? He's Mr. Right now. Musicians' lives have too many ups and downs. Now is good. We go to movies, walks in the park, eat Chinese food."

"And get back in bed?"

Josie nodded, giggling. "Sometimes *with* Chinese food. Whoever invented takeout…I really have to thank them."

Josie had a boyfriend, all the time, even in high school. I envied that about her, as she has a funny nose and a high-pitched laugh. If she could get guys, I should be able to also. "How do you always have a boyfriend, Josie?"

"It helps that there's tons of single guys living in this building, sort of a captive audience. He saw me in the laundry room, was out of soap…the next thing I knew we were washing my sheets together…a lot."

"More wine?" The bottle was on the floor near my side of the bed.

"Just a little, the bus is back tomorrow. I have to get back into greeter girlfriend mode," she said, now cleaning up the dishes and the containers.

"What does that entail?"

"Change the sheets, straighten the apartment. Shave my legs!" Josie now, task completed, curled up on a pillow, closed her eyes and fell asleep.

I finished the bottle of wine, fluffed my pillow, and turned off the light wondering if I'd ever find the cocoon she was experiencing.

#

I worked at the BBS Broadcast Center for three more months, floating between temp assignments in other departments: sports and music.

One day, I saw Rupert in the cafeteria. I caught his eye and waved, trying to be friendly, yet indifferent. He wore a crisp linen fitted shirt, revealing strong shoulders and muscular arms. His hair was clean and soft: a confident nerd.

He looked at *me* smiling, delighted, as if someone had surprised him with a birthday cake, lit candles and all. No one ever looked at *me* that way, so thrilled to see me. As the daughter of a fashion model/showgirl/glamour girl, I was unlike most of the women in my family, who were knockouts or movie star look-alikes. I always felt like their invisible understudy…until now. A glow simmered inside me—sort of a giant grin throughout my being.

Insisting I put my cafeteria tray down, and join him for lunch, Rupert escorted me to the elevators. We waited in an awkward silence that was measured as seconds, but felt like minutes. I kept my head down while I studied him out of the corner of my eye; he wore a blue and grey striped silk tie, with jeans and a grey tweed Ralph Lauren jacket with suede detailing. I'd seen it in a full-page ad in *The Sunday New York Times*. Eleven years older and a successful news producer, he was a serious, adult-minded fellow, unlike the goofy comedians of my world. So proper in an old-world way, I bet when he talked to himself he referred to himself as "Mr. Santo." Energized by his attentiveness, if I'd never been assigned as his temp secretary, our worlds would never have met.

He held the door for me and led me into the BBS executive dining room. As we passed high-powered gentlemen in elegant suits on the way to our table, he nodded and smiled to his business associates. I couldn't believe I was in the BBS dining room with a BBS executive.

Sitting at a table with fine linen, cloth napkins and crystal glassware, I was worlds away from the cafeteria tray lunch I'd planned. Rupert studied my hand as it caressed the delicate stem of the water goblet.

"You have very graceful hands. I know temps have other lives. What do you really do?"

"I'm a stand-up comedian."

"That's great. So what's it like to get up onstage and tell jokes?"

"It's what I do. I try not to think about the process." I said nonchalantly.

"Why not?"

"Being onstage, telling jokes is the easiest part of the job." He looked at me, enthralled. This just made me more animated, gesturing grandly as I said, "First there's the sitting at home alone writing jokes, hoping they're funny, and hoping I have enough bits to fill a seven, ten or fifteen-minute set."

"I know how hard it is to write the news, especially with tight deadlines. But I don't have to make it funny. That must take hours."

"Yes. Then, in order to perform at a club, if you're not a regular there, you have to go and get your 'spot.' That means standing in line outside of the club, like I did last week, trying to get a spot at the Improv."

"I've heard of that place—it's in the theater district, right?"

"Yes. When I got there, I was seventh on the line. I stood there for over an hour. The line got longer, maybe 20 or 30 people. Then it started to rain, first a little, then a lot. I scooched to be under the awning, but the raindrops still dripped down my back, past my umbrella."

"I would have gone home," Rupert said.

"Finally, some guy holding a top hat exits the club, walking along the line. He got to me, shoved the hat in my face and said, 'Pick one.' There's a bunch of tiny crumpled pieces of paper in there. I stuck my hand in and pulled one out, then unfolded it. The number "14" was scrawled in blue pen."

"What did you win?" Rupert was eager and wide-eyed.

"I'd get to go onstage that night as the fourteenth performer. Some people who waited all afternoon on line pulled a blank piece of paper, no number: go home, come back next time."

"So what did you do?"

"They said to come back that night at 7:30. I did. Have you ever seen thirteen comedians perform, one right after another?"

"Can't say that I have," he chuckled.

"Yeah, most people leave after eight or ten. I got assigned a time slot so late, I performed for drunks, idiots or people who want to impress their dates and didn't want to hear me anyway."

"It sounds difficult and discouraging."

"I caught a cold that night too."

"But you keep at it?"

"I try…I get dejected."

"I think it's admirable," he said, smiling. "I think you're funny. I'd love to come see you sometime."

"I don't think I'm ready for you to see me."

"When will you be ready?" He asked me a lot of questions about myself, keeping the conversation moving and lively with every morsel of his sensible salad. Whenever I queried him, Rupert politely skirted personal issues, bringing the focus back to learning about me. I saw this as eager interest, rather than avoidance of disclosure, though in hindsight . . .

I noticed that whenever I looked away, he'd zero in his gaze on me, studying my face, neck, and shoulders with great scrutiny. I felt both flattered and slimed. After dessert, I looked around the room, noticing all the other patrons had left and gone back to work. I forgot what I was eating, and where I was, surprised by how much I enjoyed spending time together.

The next Monday, Rupert called me at 9:05AM. Certain this was the first phone call of his new work week, it gave me a little thrill. Getting to know him better, the sleeze factor of his voice had melted into soothing, seductive tones. Over the phone he appeared handsome.

"Arlene, I'm calling to find out when in your busy schedule you'd have time to get together," he cooed. I was charmed by his complimentary insistence.

"You're the one with the busy schedule." I said, flirtatious enough to surprise myself.

"I have tickets for Wednesday night at Lincoln Center. Riccardo Muti is conducting. It looks to be a great concert."

Wow, I thought, hanging up the phone after the date had been set. I was lying on the couch, remembering my last time at Lincoln Center. The music and the majestic expanse of the concert hall carried me to a place I hadn't visited in quite some time: my childhood.

Since my mother was a trained concert pianist, she showered me in classical music from an early age. I played piano, we went to young people's concerts, and I saw my first opera when I was eight years old. Nightly, after dinner, Mom sat at the piano for an hour and banged out Chopin and Rachmaninoff concertos. When other mothers were playing Mah-Jongg, mine was helping me discern Beethoven from Schumann. When other kids had posters of Beatles or Monkees on their bedroom walls, I had Liszt, Caruso and the dreamy-looking Frederick Chopin. I was groomed to be a classical music geek.

This was one of the few pleasures I shared with my otherwise emotionally absent mother. But soon the door to live classical music at home slammed shut. She became crippled with arthritis, her hands too pained and tight to play. The concertos stayed with me, never forgotten. Now I'd get to hear them with a full orchestra, live!

Wednesday night when Rupert and I arrived at Lincoln Center, the lights surrounding the courtyard fountain sparkled like a diamond necklace. Richly dressed patrons clustered together, edging their way towards the theater entrance. Rupert wore a well-tailored grey pinstriped suit. I liked it. Guys I dated didn't even own suits. I dressed in a black, figure flattering outfit from the back of my closet, glad it fit, thanks to control-top panty hose.

Inside the opulent theater, the usher took our tickets, smiled, and walked us to our seats. I glided down the aisle's plush burgundy carpeting, all the way down to the second row! Best seats in the house! We sat so close to the action, I could see when the handsome conductor Muti had hair in his eyes. The evening commemorated the music and birthday of one of America's greatest living composers, Aaron Copland. The orchestra was exhilarating. I wished I felt the same about my adoring date.

Thrilled to be at Lincoln Center, sitting so close to the conductor was an adrenalin jolt that would have brought my mother to ecstasy. That night I visited a world I hadn't seen in more than a decade. I decided that Rupert could be the conductor of my classical music future, if only I could embrace his kindness. I still wavered between highly flattered and uncomfortable. Flattery was winning at high speeds and evolving to endearment and caring.

Halfway through the program, Muti acknowledged Copland, stating, "Let me present the true Maestro of the evening, Mr. Aaron Copland." The octogenarian, seated in the 15th row, stood and waved to the adoring crowd.

As for me, out for a night on the town with a cultured adult who liked me; no jokes here. Maybe he's not a slime ball I can make fun of. I guess I'll have to let down my defenses. Impressed that Rupert had procured better seats than Aaron Copland; this made the short man at my side seem taller in my eyes, or at least someone to whom I should give my full attention.

CHAPTER 4:
FLATTERY WILL GET YOU EVERYWHERE

"My boyfriend is a slob. His apartment is decorated in early summer camp, with bunk beds and an outhouse. The kitchen is full of antiques: A 1947 refrigerator, with the original dust. I don't know if he has rats in his apartment, or his socks are trying to escape. He's trying to be cleaner. Last week he washed the paper plates." —Me

My jokes came from my dating life. Before Rupert, all the men I'd known were colorful, penniless, immature comedians. Take for instance the illegal alien, living in an illegal loft, stealing electricity from his neighbors, a couple of 20-year old strippers. You know, when you have to steal from strippers…

From then on Rupert and I lunched once a week. Even our dates were mature: an upscale restaurant or a play. Once while we were visiting a French restaurant he ordered in French. Impressed, I hoped it was something I'd eat. When I saw the escargot, I shuddered. "Slugs," my mind whispered. He even ate slimy food. I was pleased to see the "hamburger avec pomes frites" that he'd ordered for me. Actually, during this time his sliminess had all but disappeared, so my slime-o-meter was relaxing. I became more aware of what we ate than how I felt. I knew I liked the ways in which he took care of me. I delighted in his inquisitive, animated interest in me, and his passion for cultural things. I wanted him to like me because he was the only serious-minded adult I knew. Rupert was always so gentlemanly, formal and proper, so I didn't really think we were dating, more like socializing. I enjoyed our time together because, in his presence, my Brooklyn feistiness was drained away.

After a month of lunches, I went to Florida to spend a week visiting my mother. Rupert insisted on meeting me at the airport when I returned, stating, "It's a wonderful feeling to be met by someone at the airport, coming home after a tiring trip."

He was right. Seeing Rupert's beaming face at arrivals, I threw my arms around him and hugged him warmly for the first time. When I'd realized what I'd done, I pulled back, politely thanking him. We walked to his car. He placed my bag in the trunk, walked to the passenger side, and opened my door.

Before he started the car, he turned to me and said, "Welcome home. New York hasn't been the same without you. Here are some homecoming gifts." He smiled eagerly and nervously presented me a half dozen long stemmed roses and a small gift-wrapped box. I was surprised and thrilled. The gift box looked like it might contain jewelry, which would have been uncomfortably too personal for me. I unwrapped the box, a bottle of fine perfume, *Chanel #22*. I'd never received perfume from a man before.

I was enchanted by his persistence. "Thank you, this is all so lovely," I said, kissing him on the cheek. He gazed at my mouth, touched my lower lip with his thumb, and we kissed. He leaned into that kiss so intently, I kissed him again. His mouth was warm and responsive. The next thing I knew we were locked in a long lingering kiss that grew with intensity and passion. Tenderly caressing my chin with his hand, I heated up inside. Or was airplane fatigue feeding my vulnerabilities? Minutes later our lips parted. Our kissing had fogged up his glasses.

Rupert started the car, we clicked into our seatbelts, and the ride began.

When we arrived at my studio apartment in Flatbush, there was no street parking to be found. I thanked him for the ride, retrieved my bag and went into the building. As he drove away, I thought: Was the kiss an emotional fluke? Or was something brewing here? On all of our lunch dates, Rupert's maturity made him seem almost too old to consider for a physical relationship. That's why we'd never kissed until now. Besides, in this era of pre-AIDS recreational sex, while most of my friends were ready for the heat of the moment or spontaneous sex, I was more premeditated. I'd never had a one-night stand. I thought about sex more than I acted on it (that fat girl thing, I guess). So for me, a kiss meant a lot. In kissing I tasted hope, future, and promise. Tonight's kisses surprisingly brimmed with all three. Confused and tired, I went to sleep.

The next morning while I was drinking coffee and working on my "to do" list, Rupert called. A minute into the conversation he excused himself and put the phone down. Hearing muffled screams, I held on a few minutes, too concerned to hang up. When he returned to the phone, I asked, "What happened?"

"There was a little upset with an employee. But security is handling it now." Without skipping a beat, he said, "Lunch tomorrow?"

I was curious to find out about the incident, but I decided to let it drop.

The next day, at the Stage Deli, Rupert had an open-faced turkey sandwich. I had a grilled Ruben. Lunches felt like friendship, that was fine with me. I put the kiss out of my mind. At lunch, I told him, "I'm having my first television appearance as a comedienne next week."

"You'll have to tape it, we can watch it together," he gushed. "An evening date."

Later that day I called Ella, the associate producer of Rupert's show. Her desk had been next to mine on Rupert's floor. I liked her well enough to lunch with while working at BBS, and we became friendly. I called her to find out about the upset in the office.

"I'd never seen anything like it," she whispered excitedly into the receiver. "Our department's secretary went into his office, screamed at him, and ran down the hall. Then she was taken away in a strait jacket. Rupert was calm the whole time, no emotion."

"Really? He wasn't sad or upset? Were they close?"

"He's private. I have no idea how close they were. He has lunches and dinners with people…women…but doesn't talk about anyone."

"Really?" Rupert's world became more intriguing by the minute. "Do you know who any of these women are?" I was asking to see if she knew about us.

"I occasionally answer his phone. Mainly colleagues, women who work here at BBS, middle management."

Probing, prying, inquiring, "Do you ever meet any of these women?"

"Like I said, he's very private, meets them at restaurants. 'Colleagues' is a word he uses a lot," she said.

To myself I said, "Maybe he's not a dull little man. He's got a harem at his job. He's full of surprises."

I wondered about the woman and what happened to her, but I didn't have time to delve into it because something great happened to me. I got to be on television!

A few days later, another comedienne, Laurie, and I spent three hours at NBC studios at Rockefeller Center, telling jokes and clowning around with the local news team. We'd been selected because we both performed "Yenta-grams" where we dressed up as little old ladies performing customized jokes for events at private parties for birthdays, anniversaries and other special occasions. While waiting to film our segment, we had coffee in costume in the NBC commissary. Sitting at the table next to us was Paul Shaffer, wacky bandleader of *The David Letterman Show*. He stared at me, so I smiled and said, "Hello." Next thing I knew, we talked about my costume. I had him and his pals laughing. I felt cool and gutsy for speaking with him.

Laurie agreed, stating, "I can't believe you talked to Paul Shaffer!"

I shrugged it off, my familiar pose when good things happened, "I was in costume, it wasn't the real me."

Later, on camera, I told the lead anchorman, *"The body is the temple of the soul. Yours looks like a 99-cent store."* Then I pulled a rubber chicken out of my purse and told him how chicken soup cures everything. Our antics were a five-minute segment on the NBC New York local evening news that night, titled "Give the Gift of Laughter." It was a Valentine's Day news story that generated more work, greater visibility, and made me feel special.

I received a copy of the tape from the technicians and raced to meet Rupert at his office. He took the large boxy studio master-tape and we walked down long corridors to the newsroom, where a technician quickly transferred it to VHS so we could watch it on a home television.

As we walked, he told me he'd just moved into a new apartment the day before, and needed some stuff from his old place. He asked if I could go with him to pick up a few things, and then watch the show at his new apartment. I agreed, hoping that seeing where he lived, I'd learn more about him.

We entered a luxury doorman building on East 87th Street, just off of 5th Avenue. The apartment decorated with Scandinavian-style furniture was stiff and uncomfortable. I looked around, but not too intensely. I was afraid I'd appear too nosy, which I was.

"Still a lot of furniture here," I said, confused.

"My new place is fully furnished. I'll be subletting this one."

I nodded, satisfied for the moment. "Nice typewriter. Are you taking it?"

"Typewriter? No, I won't have much need for it."

"But you're a writer," I reminded him. He seemed suddenly agitated, nervously pacing as I walked around.

"I have another typewriter up at my weekend place. I'd love for you to visit. It's by a lake," he added proudly. "Let's get out of here." He swiftly steered me to the door. "I want to show you my new place."

I wandered past the living room, towards the bedroom, uncomfortable about peering inside. All I could see was an unmade bed with white sheets.

"May I use the bathroom?"

"No!" he blurted, then more calmly, "We'll be at the new place in a few minutes. Please wait until then." He rushed me into my coat, lifted a few boxes and we were out the door. I was surprised that he wouldn't let me use the bathroom. Initially, I wasn't bothered by it because he seemed in a hurry. I figured if it was really important, we'd discuss it later. Our cab moved slowly down 5th Avenue. As the traffic crept, my bladder beckoned. Now I really regretted not using the bathroom. I wished I had been more insistent for what I needed.

We arrived at 5th Avenue and East 64th street, a neighborhood inhabited primarily by millionaires. There was a house on the corner that I knew was owned by Rockefellers. Next to it was a diplomat's residence. The cab stopped at the next brownstone, the new place where Rupert was to live. He didn't have the entire place, it had been newly renovated and broken into six apartments. When we walked into the building, I smelled the scent of fresh paint and new carpeting. We walked upstairs to a charming pied-a-terre. He opened the door and eagerly waited for me to inspect the place. I raced through the kitchen and living room, furnished with chintz by some New England doctor's wife. The bedroom door was closed. As we spoke I thought I heard a scratching, scuffling coming from inside the closed door, sounding like a radiator.

"It's small but cute," I said, then wished I hadn't said small. Whenever I was around Rupert, I was self-conscious about that word.

"Let me take your coat and we can watch your show. I can't wait to see you," he said, the way a five-year-old looks at a candy bar, eager to unwrap it.

I took the tape out of my purse and moved to the television. On top of the set was a piece of paper stapled to a charge slip, a receipt for a new television and VCR. I was shocked to see this here.

"Did you just buy this TV and VCR?" I asked, realizing I was being way too nosy.

"Uh yes, I wanted to see the tape of your show. I figured if I had a television here, maybe you'd want to visit." The moment was flattering, bordering on creepy. Had he really spent hundreds of dollars just to see five minutes of me on a videotape he could have watched at work? I didn't understand.

"This is a special occasion; you on television, me getting a new apartment. Let's open a bottle of champagne and celebrate," he exclaimed. He gave me a glass and took one for himself as he moved closer to me. "To new beginnings and to a wonderful, talented woman."

"I'll drink to that," I said as he inserted the tape, turned on the TV and the picture began to roll. The newsman announced the segment, talking about funny women in New York…blah blah blah and …"Today we have Arlene Schindler, brilliant actress and star of tomorrow…"

"Did you hear that? Did you hear what he said?" asked Rupert, delighted. Watching the tape together, he held my hand. Rupert laughed heartily whenever I was on camera, almost too loud, as if to say, "See? I think you're funny, I really like you, please like me more." When the tape was over he said, "They think you're a star of tomorrow, and so do I." He gave me a long hard kiss. I heard a dog bark. It seemed to be in the next room! The scratching, scuffling sound I'd heard earlier got louder. The bedroom door opened. I'd never heard him mention a dog. Seconds later, the dog, an aging Irish setter, jumped on me, as if to push me away from Rupert.

Rupert sprang up, horrified, "Peaches, stop this right now. You're a polite girl." Upset, barking fiercely, she jumped on the couch and firmly wedged her furry body between us, as if to be a doggie chaperone. "Just let her smell you. Give her your hand."

"I didn't know you had a dog." A secret had been withheld from me. Giving her my hand, she growled at me, clearly not happy I was kissing her master.

"Go back into the bedroom," he commanded, pointing like a drill sergeant. She glared at me before jumping off the couch and scampering back into the bedroom. As soon as she was gone, Rupert leaned in, "Now, where were we?" While we kissed, the phone rang. Rupert ignored it, too enthralled with smooching his "star." As the message recorded, I was astonished he didn't break away from the lip lock once we both heard who was calling. It was a famous New England Senator, with a strong, easily recognizable Boston accent. His message was, "I'm planning to run for the presidency, and wanted to speak with you about working on my campaign and being my press secretary. I think we'd both look good in the White House."

Kissing Rupert, magnetized with exhilaration, yet still sane. I sensed he felt the same. He ignored a call about working in the White House to keep kissing me?

The way his lips enveloped mine, tenderly, yet with a gentle power, spurred my desire to know him better. Devouring each kiss as if reading the pages of a mystery novel, I felt the more my lips caressed his, the better I'd know him. So we kissed for hours that night, just there on the couch—cozy, warm and familiar, without becoming sexual. My self-consciousness melted, and reformed into a trust of the man I was with, something my body and soul sorely needed. A week earlier I told Rupert I'd dated someone in the recent past who'd become violent with me, and I was still recuperating. Too embarrassed to talk about my date rape incident, even though it was two years earlier, I'd hoped my vague statement about the forceful event would reveal Rupert's gentle side. I believed Rupert's affectionate, non-threatening interlude was his way of honoring my needs, and getting me to like him more.

By midnight, both too tired for me to leave, Rupert offered me a T-shirt and the option to sleep on the couch or with him. We spooned all night. I wasn't ready for anything sexual. He was a perfect gentleman. I appreciated his restraint. In the morning, I hoped he'd tell me more about Ted Kennedy. I was too shy to ask, and he didn't offer.

CHAPTER 5:
SUPERMAN OF THE BEDROOM

"The walls of my apartment are so thin, when my neighbors have sex, I have an orgasm." —Linda Herskovic

I decided not to ask about the White House. I hoped the subject would come up again. A week later, Rupert told me his new apartment on millionaire's row was merely a sublet, and he was in the market to buy a place. Would I spend a Saturday co-op shopping with him? I asked myself, "Why not? House shopping would be fun."

So on the first Saturday morning of autumn we drove to the suburbs of Westchester (New Rochelle, Larchmont and Tuckahoe) to look at new developments of town homes. Mortgage rates were a high 14-16% so any situation was rather costly. He wouldn't tell me prices, just asked my opinion about rooms, kitchens etc. When we came to a place we both really liked, he asked, "Can you see me living here?"

"That's for you to decide." At one model home, I saw him looking wistfully out the window at a man-made lake. His sadness frightened me. The look on his face made me ask myself, "Why would a man take you house-hunting and ask your opinions unless he wanted you to live with him? How do you feel about Rupert?"

My feelings for him had changed. I no longer saw him as the slimy little man I'd first met. His perseverance and respectfulness charmed me. Now I saw him as sweet, attentive, inviting me to do interesting, cultural things that I could never afford on my own. I admired his intelligence and view of the world. He was the only real "adult" in my world. I thought I should be with an adult rather than the comedic man-children I had collected. Yet I didn't particularly like adults; they seemed dull and commanded maturity from me. My feelings for him were conflicted, which always made me hungry. "Lunch?"

At a quaint hideaway restaurant in a cottage somewhere in New Rochelle, Rupert told me he lived in this town years earlier—when he was married. This was the first thread of his personal life he'd shared with me. I pulled on the thread gently, eager for him to unravel more of his story.

"I met my wife shortly after she recuperated from a devastating car accident. She'd received one of the largest settlements in history from the insurance company, but most of the money went for therapy and rehabilitation. One leg is shorter than the other. She wears a brace when the pain gets to be too great." he offered, coolly and detached.

I was taken aback by the story and his placidity in telling it. Opening his wallet, showing me her photo, a plain looking girl with straight light brown hair—it seemed weird that he still carried her picture. Vague about why the marriage ended, he offered that she was now remarried and lived in Washington D.C.

"Speaking of Washington," Rupert said, "Senator Kennedy is running for President…and I may work for him," This last bit was added modestly.

"That's exciting. What happens next?" I asked, not mentioning I'd heard Kennedy's message on Rupert's phone the night we were at his place.

"He'll be in town this week, we'll meet and talk," he said, changing the subject.

Later, back in Manhattan, we saw apartments that cost three times as much as the ones in Westchester. We viewed a place that overlooked Central Park, with an equally eye-opening price tag. I stood in the living room twirling around in the spaciousness. Rupert walked into the room, delighted to see me happy. "You like it here?"

"Can you afford it?"

"Whatever you like I will seriously consider. You're right; this is a little too expensive. Let's see a place near Lincoln Center. You like it over there?"

Why did my opinion matter so much? Didn't he have friends to help him make these decisions? We'd hardly kissed. Shopping for homes I could never afford, I felt flattered, exhilarated and frightened, like running in the rain to hide from lightning. We drove into the circular drive of a luxury-hi-rise building that was walking distance from Lincoln Center and Rupert's office. The rooms were spacious and easy to furnish. He considered putting in a bid. Then he learned that the current owner was a leading newscaster at a competitive news station. This made the buy even more alluring. He asked the broker to give his bid to the seller, but not before he asked me once more, "You like it here, right?"

By evening, both exhausted, we drove back to his place, went upstairs and plopped on the couch. As I pressed my head back to relax, he leaned into me and we spent the next hour kissing passionately. Then he led me into the bedroom. As we undressed, he revealed himself to be muscular, with Mediterranean toned skin and a silky blanket of chest hair. His hands and mouth devoured me, a sensory electrical shock. After four months of friendly lunches, a concert or two, and a series of heated smooches, this was sex worth waiting for —almost as if our relationship was an opera—with third act crescendos and curtain calls. The thrill was compounded by the fact that his suit and tie persona was the opposite of the wild man before me now. This nerdy looking, polite Clark Kent had become Superman in bed. It's like he was fighting for truth, justice and the American woman's orgasm.

CHAPTER 6:
THE MAGIC PENIS

"Ever have a day that feels like it's three days long? I've had dates like that. Sitting in a restaurant, sooo bored, I wish I were in a dentist's chair...with the drill on."

I said that, as I put the microphone back in its stand and walked off stage. Not one of my better sets, I felt defeated and unfunny. Monday night crowds were tough, I thought, slinking out of the club with barely a good-bye to anyone.

Afterwards, I stopped off at Rupert's. That day he'd gone back to the co-op for a second look and to talk with the owner, newscaster LeAnn Fletcher. Rupert told me he had been a fan of her reporting and was excited that a newswoman, someone who understood his business, was so cute. He said buying that apartment was like owning a piece of LeAnn.

When I arrived at Rupert's, he greeted me in the doorway with hot kisses, pressing me against the wall, his chest against mine. Breathless heat and hunger, I tingled with excitement and desire. Quickly we were lying side by side in his candle-lit bedroom.

"I went to the apartment. It was as lovely as when you and I saw it together. The rooms were a good size. I like the views. LeAnn made tea and offered me cookies. We sat on the couch together. After talking about our mutual news colleagues, she leaned towards me and asked if I knew anyone she could date. Then she kissed me on the cheek. I'm taking the apartment."

I couldn't imagine the scene as he'd painted it. The beautiful newscaster was cozying up to Rupert? Did she want the sale that badly? I knew some of her co-workers and had heard that she was a nice person on top of her good looks. So why would she be asking Rupert for a fix-up? Did this really happen? Why was he telling me? Did he think that if an attractive newscaster expressed interest in him then I'd find him more desirable? Was I thinking like a teenage girl, or was he? His story bordered on the absurd and was highly implausible. It was the first time I questioned his living on the line between fantasy and reality. But in seeing him with caring eyes, I took his statements at face value. I held him close and tried not to think about it.

In the morning, he handed me the keys to his apartment. "I want you to be comfortable here, to come and go whenever you please."

"Thank you, but our relationship is still very new. Keys are for serious relationships." We'd shared a season of friendly lunches, a few weeks of smooching and three nights in bed; hardly a key-worthy amount of time.

"I seriously want you to have them. I don't like knowing you are taking the subway home at night after shows. You are precious to me. I want you to be safe," he added, putting the keys in my palm. "When you have a show, please don't go back to Brooklyn. Come here."

"You're very kind."

"I love sleeping next to you and waking up with you," he said.

He was offering me stability and safety. Something I always thought I wanted. But I couldn't wait to get back to Brooklyn. I had a show to do.

#

The rehearsal space where I spent all day Sunday, anxiously preparing for a ten-minute club spot that night, was my studio apartment with all of its (two) windows open onto one of the busiest and noisiest Brooklyn streets—Ocean Parkway. Horns honking and disgruntled cabbies arguing just outside my window prepped me for my night's drunks and hecklers.

I stood in front of my mirror and contemplated what to wear. Back then, it telescoped what kind of woman you were, or so I believed men thought.

I tried a short black skirt—but not too short. It did show my knees, which to me with their lumps and dimples resembled bald men crying. That didn't work. Jumpsuits with big shoulder pads were all the rage then, and I liked the one-outfit pulled together look. But the problem was if I needed to use a nightclub bathroom to pee, I had to remove the belt and entire top. It was easier to jump out of an airplane.

I finally decided on that New York uniform of black jeans and a blousy top that didn't show my bra straps or highlight my boobs—good trick, go find them, they were so small. I wanted to be seen as funny, but not as a clown.

The body-shaming portion of my preparation took almost as long as the try-ons. With bittersweet affection I referred to it as the BS hour, short for body shaming—and bitch screaming, usually in my mother Betty Schindler's voice. First was her greatest hit, "You're wearing that?" followed by shrieking out every figure flaw—it was her voice but my thoughts—saddle bags, flabby thighs, and an ass that looked like a peach had been smashed against a wall.

I believed my body was divided into two parts, from two different women. Luckily my above-the-waist self had fewer flaws or flab—just small breasts that could hide in a padded bra so as to be any size for my many outfits or boob moods. Meanwhile, below the waist, I was convinced I resembled a Slavic farm-frau.

Trained by Mom to try and always look my prettiest, Dad assured me that pretty wouldn't work in comedy. "You don't have the looks for comedy," he'd say, as a compliment. "The famous funny broads are not great beauties."

Some might say this era was the second wave of feminism. That's what got me to the club and onto the stage in the first place.

Career and marriage were both necessities that I grasped for, uncertain of how I'd handle them once they were within reach.

In the days before Rupert, when I was in the shower I made sure I shaved my legs, in case I might "meet someone"—my girlfriends' code for a one-night stand. I put on my sexiest panties for the same reason. I had never met anyone at the club, but I felt confident knowing I was ready. I was too self-conscious to really be ready, but through some miracle, if a lifetime's inhibitions were to melt away, I didn't want to let hairy legs and granny panties slow me down.

My permed hair did not need hot rollers or a styling wand. It may have been poodle soft, but I fought like hell to not look like a standard poodle when my curls wanted to do nothing but frizz in the New York humidity. Next came makeup and my beauty regime of Erno Laszlo products, which were obscenely expensive and popular with movie stars and high-powered female executives. I justified the big-ticket items because my best feature was porcelain skin, which I worked tirelessly to maintain. I started by lathering up with Laszlo's Sea Mud Cleansing Bar (as seen in the movie *Annie Hall* when Woody says, "What are you doing, joining a minstrel show?") followed by twenty splashes of gunmetal gray soapy water. Now I'm looking in the mirror, running my lines out loud.

My opening line: "I come from a long line of miserable people. Mom has the worst opinions about everything. I don't wear jewelry. Maybe because my mother says, 'A girl without an earring, I think it's a sickNESS.'" It's a funny word. If I could time it perfectly, I'd get a laugh, I hoped. I waved my mascara wand around. "A SICKness?" Punch lines during mascara application always killed, to my audience of me.

If I could succeed in comedy, maybe Mom would ease her criticisms of me. Are you crazy? Now that's a joke only funny to me. Doing well would impress Dad. All the years he groomed me to be funny would have paid off—for both of us.

Walking the six blocks to the subway, I hoped the early evening wind didn't mess my hair-sprayed, well-coiffed do. I was in kitten heels from Macy's, not exactly walking shoes. Finding a spot on the train where I felt safe, I was in the middle car. Sitting, rehearsing, "SickNESS, sick…ness, SICKness." Trying not to look like a crazy woman while talking to myself. Was this line even funny? Men won't like it. Getting off the train, I climbed subway stairs, and walked to Thirty First Street and Third Avenue on dark streets, stores shuttered without a soul in sight.

Finally, I arrived.

By the time I opened the club door, my exhilaration fizzled. Fatigued from my primping ordeal, all I wanted to do was slip into pajamas, crawl into bed and grind my mascaraed eyes into the pillow. I had to gently slap myself in the face.

Walking into the club, my eyes adjusted to the darkness then, darting from patron to patron seeking friendly faces I could win over for laughter, I spied a group of six women, with two pitchers on their table. Birthday? Bridal party? I could play with them. Chubby men at the back tables draped their arms around their dates like heavy fox stoles.

There were men who came to the club alone, dripping in gold chains and musky cologne, their heads ping ponging back and forth, as if watching a tennis game. More interested in who they could nail later than who was onstage, they were on skank patrol. Some of my fellow female comics and I called them the "three G men." But instead of the three G's of exploration: God, Gold and Glory, we saw them as Guidos, Goombas and Gangsters (not Gangstas.)

I told myself that the glowing candle on each tiny table illuminated the room to resemble a giant birthday cake—my celebration, a great set tonight.

I knew I should mingle with other comics. Too caught up in my own anxieties my mind raced for something warm and witty to say. "Are you going to Pip's this week? It's better than that bowling alley in Flushing, or Uncle Knuckle's Chuckle Hut." I asked one guy, "When's your spot?"

"I'm ninth, it sucks," he said.

"I thought I was ninth," I replied, concerned about my own place in the show.

After a deep exhale, I strode to the king of the room, the bartender, offering a soft hello, "When's my spot? I thought I was ninth? Am I on sooner?" Maybe a girlish smile will help.

"Nah, Eddie needs to catch the last ferry to Jersey. So you're on 12th."

"Will anyone be here besides the dishwashers?" My smile sunk to a frown.

"I'll be here to see you."

I forced a smile and walked away, needing to pace my energy and adrenaline as my part in the show would not get into gear for a few hours. After watching the club fill up, this seemed like the best time to go to the restroom and freshen up. Returning to the main room, I saw patrons ordering second drinks, guys eyeing me, licking their lips, or walking past me, too close for comfort. Most of the evening I waited thru bad comics sets and others so good I felt I had no business pursuing the same stage. While smiling at other comedians, I wondered if I should have that second glass of wine? More performers, hecklers, drunks, people walking out.

Exasperated, the ordeal of waiting for my time to go onstage felt like I was in a crowded waiting room at the dentist's office. Even when it's finally my turn, I'm not relieved. It's easy to see why so many comics develop drinking problems—something to do during endless hours of waiting to go on stage.

In those days, clubs had ashtrays on every table. People smoked cigarettes—sometimes a lot. All the comics cursed when some asshole lit up a stinky cigar. Every club was a smoky room. Most comedians spent a small fortune dry cleaning their stage outfits, never quite removing that divey nightclub stench.

It was now the second half of the show. The audience seemed fatigued. Me too—it was an hour past my bed time, and I was still waiting to go on. I knew this was the paying-your-dues part of comedy. That's what kept me here. Once I could move past this, there would be better spots, and better clubs out of town. Plus, like junkies who spend an entire day trying to cop their drug, I knew my high was almost here.

Coughing from the smoke, I rubbed my burning eyes.

Out of my tired reverie, I heard: "And now, is everyone ready for the comedy stylings of Arlene Schindler?"

What? The MC called my name.

Showtime.

"When you're over 25 and unmarried, parents see you...as a burden for life. After you're married, your spouse is a burden...till death."

Somehow, thankfully, this show was better than a few nights ago. Maybe new jokes, or the crowd had more to drink. Gauging an audience's reactions is always a crap shoot. Sometimes bombing, killing, or doing just okay is mystifying. I got laughs from the audience, *and* the other comics, which is rare. I even got a thumbs up from the bartender! Pleased with myself after the show, I went to Rupert's. He'd gone to dinner with a friend, so I used my new key, came in, kicked off my shoes and turned on the television. I saw LeAnn on TV and thought about Rupert's story and how disturbingly silly it seemed. I changed the channel to *The Honeymooners*. I watched Ralph and Alice bicker about a broken stove. Laughing, I heard a key in the door.

Rupert entered, glanced at the TV and sat next to me. I kissed him quickly and warmed his ears from the cold night's chill. But my eyes were glued to the screen.

"Why are you watching this old piece of crap? This show has no relevance to real life!" he bellowed. Rupert stood up, turned off the television, walked into the bedroom and slammed the door.

I was shocked by his first burst of anger—and he condemned one of my favorites, *The Honeymooners,* to boot. I wasn't sure which of these two new discoveries disturbed me more. I sat frozen on the couch. Finally, I got up and went into the darkened bedroom. Trying to calm him, I climbed onto the bed where he was lying on his side. Putting my arms around him, he curled closer to me. I felt flooded with frustrated, angry feelings I didn't know how to articulate. Instead, using my mouth with forceful, rough nibbles and bites, I screwed him hard, quickly and silently. He enjoyed my probing, aggressive heat, began moaning and biting me too. Having a passionate and exciting sex life, I thought this meant I was in a significant relationship, which appeared to skyrocket my creative energies and self-esteem. So I was eating less, feeling braver onstage, and appearing in more shows each week. Performing with greater frequency, I felt more agile onstage, and got bigger laughs. Club owners started taking me seriously, calling me by name. I got better, earlier spots in shows. I'd go onstage at 10 p.m., when audiences were revved, ready to laugh, and their two drink minimums had kicked in.

Early in their careers, most young comics get the late spots. If I went onstage after midnight, most of the audience had paid their checks and were already home in bed by the time I said my first punch line. No one knew if I was funny; my voice was drowned out by busboys scraping chairs as they stacked them up on tables, before mopping the floors. The only laughter was the echo of the three drunks, half asleep in the back of the club.

Now I was having killer shows and glorious nights, leaving the stage before 11 to the sound of laughter and applause. It was a captivating cocktail, swirling through my senses, energizing and fueling me with joy and hope. As soon as I exited the club and cool night air whipped through me, I liked running in at the end of an evening after a good set in a club to spend the night in the arms of a warm, loving man. I found myself spending those nights at Rupert's apartment. Performing in a club that was just a short trip from his place, I told myself it was convenient, easier than taking a long, grueling train ride back to Brooklyn.

While Rupert laughed at my jokes, comments and sarcastic asides during dinners, I didn't want him to see me perform in clubs. Although I talked about rooms I appeared in and shows I did, I never told him where I'd be appearing on any given night. I didn't feel "ready" for his grown up, newsman professional scrutiny, afraid if he didn't like me onstage, it would hamper our relationship. My being funny was very necessary to me, so I withheld the nightclub part of me from him.

Meanwhile, one night Rupert secretly visited a club where I regularly performed, sat at a small table in a dark corner to take in the scene, experience the room and check out the other comics. I wasn't there, but that night the MC was my ex who preceded Rupert. One of his jokes was, "When a woman breaks up with me, she races right out and loses her virginity."

How do I know this happened? Rupert called and told me who he saw and heard, and how much fun he had. It seemed creepy that he snuck around to learn about the comedy world. I felt that he looked down on all of us because we worked in bars in the dark—kind of like pool players in pool halls, only with snappier patter and sarcasm. I wondered if he'd ever seen me in a club, but didn't say anything, 'cause he didn't think I was any good. I was afraid to ask.

Why was I so reluctant to have Rupert see me perform? He'd seen me naked and survived that. Surely, he'd still love me on a night I might have bombed. (Is that my optimism?) Until he actually saw me onstage, I'd have the mystique of an entertainer; the unknown is sexier than the known. Also, I didn't feel my level of comedy writing was worthy of his attention. He laughed at *New Yorker* cartoons, which frankly I never got. Rupert saw me on television and enjoyed that. He didn't insist on seeing me onstage. I was fine with that. With these reasons amongst others, I still wanted to keep my work life and relationship separate.

Late spring of 1982, our days and nights together felt like those silly love songs about sunshine, lollypops and rainbows. Or in our case, long lunches in expensive restaurants with obsequious wait staffs, crisp linens, fine crystal, and lots of French wine.

One day, when I thought the meal was done, a waiter, presenting yet another silver tray, announced, "Your chocolate soufflé has arrived."

"We didn't order a chocolate soufflé," I said with certainty.

Rupert watched me, smiling. "You don't want him to take it back, do you?"

"It is pretty…"

"And sweet, like you. Get your spoon and try it, no wait." His spoon dove into the heavenly looking creation, then poised for my eager mouth. We both smiled. "I ordered this yesterday, as a surprise, hoping it would please you."

Yup, drinking French wine, screwing in the afternoon, I was in my own romantic mistress/lover fantasy. At 25, my hope-filled self didn't know there was such a thing as the honeymoon phase of a relationship. I wanted to believe this could be our life together, a month, a year, a decade from now.

In public Rupert was a book-wormy looking nebbish. Behind closed doors this adventurous, ardent lover amused me greatly, as my sexual secret. More days he played hooky from work for leisurely romantic lunches, holding hands, then to his apartment. Frequently, there would be a gift box for me on the bed—jewelry, lingerie or chocolates. Our life together seemed like a romance novel that kept getting better and better. It tickled me to my core.

A famous comedian was once asked, "Is sex dirty?"

"It is if you're doing it right," he responded. That's the sense I got from Rupert: it was dirty, prohibited, and, therefore, all the more exciting. The best part of sex was when he acted like it was so forbidden. His urgency in bed seemed like that of a man's last lay before going to the electric chair.

Sometimes I'd race through an evening of conversation, hoping we'd get to the sex sooner. Desiring to be naked with him again, I wanted his cock and mouth, his strong hairy chest pressed against me. Sex with Rupert was wonderful in so many ways, medicinal almost, healing the hurts from my past, curing the silences, the Band-Aid for all disagreements and problems.

Sex with Rupert was a mystifyingly magical experience because this starched shirt, buttoned-down guy was willing to do anything to thrill and excite me. He'd spend hours stroking, licking, and kissing parts of me that no one had ever touched before. Toes, arm pits, the back of the knee were new sensuous discoveries for me with Rupert as my sexploration guide. His gentleness healed the fat, friendless, Friday nights of adolescence, when I thought no one would ever want me. I'd never felt this desired before. During sex, I released all of my unpopular-chubby-girl demons, and gave myself to him over and over, melting like an ice cube at a summer garden party. I felt catered to, cared about and elated. My senses crackled with delight, as my body shuddered with ecstasy. After lovemaking, I felt numb and lightheaded. Rupert was the best lover I'd ever known—he could fuck me stupid.

His uncircumcised penis, which curved to the left, had an inexplicable hold on me. It resembled a basketball player's thumb, draped in a flesh sombrero. I was fascinated by the way the skin surrounding the head slid back and away, like a screen door, revealing the oh-so-sensitive tip. One lick from me sent Rupert quivering and moaning, complimenting me on my sensuous techniques. When his hard cock thrusted deep and repeatedly, the sensation of the foreskin sliding in an opposite motion, made his member seem all the more magical. Deep inside me, it felt like there were two penises in a frenzied passion dance, racing to rocket me to orgasm. Never before or since have I felt anything so mesmerizing or addictive. His cock became the heroin of my existence.

During dinners, I made sure he had an extra cocktail, to guarantee he'd be relaxed and eager for sex by the end of the evening. At restaurants, I'd scan every man in the room, envisioning their penises and sexual techniques; convinced that my man had the hottest cock of all AND that he was the last guy anyone would imagine having a magic missile in his pants. Thinking I possessed a secret weapon further fueled my excitement. So intoxicated was my mind, body and spirit, I was deliriously *infucksiated.*

One night after sex he turned to me adoringly. "You're the first woman I've ever wanted to marry."

Considering he'd had a previous wife, I found this statement astounding. I replayed it in my head… "You're the first woman I've ever wanted to marry," …

"But you've had a wife," I reminded him.

"She wasn't like you."

"Is this a proposal?"

"I think so," he mumbled, uncertain.

"Can I sleep on it?"

We both rolled on our sides and closed our eyes. I didn't consider myself as being in a reality-based relationship with Rupert. Instead, I was in a trance-like fantasy that involved dress-up dinners, opera galas, and orchestrated sex. I was in a well-costumed play. Meanwhile, it seemed Rupert was falling in love.

The following morning, he went to work and I stayed in bed. By late-morning I dressed, ready to go back to my Flatbush studio. But was I really ready? My Brooklyn was a gritty place, the opposite of Rupert's pristine, glamorous Manhattan.

Brooklyn dreams, for most girls of my generation who were born there, are to leave. Walking out his front door I saw four limousines, double parked. Heading to the subway, I noticed Happy Rockefeller walking her Chihuahua. Rich women, cozy in fur coats, collars caressing their chins, chatted with their crisp uniformed doormen.

Back in Brooklyn, stomping up the long staircase exiting the subway station, I felt I was time traveling to a coarse, other planet.

Walking home, I passed the 99-cent store, the OTB parlor, a one-toothed drunk camped out in the schoolyard, and three guys begging for money. No Rockefellers in minks here. My hour-long train ride took me back to my real world—a studio apartment filled with make-do furniture, financial struggles, and bums in the street.

Feeling like Brooklyn's Cinderella, was marriage the glass slipper? Did it fit, I wondered? Or was I shoehorning myself into it? If Rupert was trying to seduce me with New York City the way other men use tequila, his plan was working.

CHAPTER 7:

WITH FOOD AS MY FRIEND

"The secret to a happy marriage is still unknown."—Henny Youngman

Rupert's proposal made me reflect on my main marriage barometer: my parents. My sense of their marriage was that of a unique cartoon of role reversals and emotional avoidance. They married in the 1950s, both in their mid-thirties, because it was the cultural norm to be wed. Neither of them wanted a spouse or a child; they were just accessories of a normal life, like wearing fashionable clothes. And within this scenario, I viewed myself as my parents' shiny possession, like a new car or a frost-free refrigerator.

My suspicions of being a thing my parents possessed were confirmed in my fifteen-year-old mind when we visited family one Sunday. They were standing outside when we drove up to their house in our shiny new silver *Buick Regal*. Dad proudly got out of the car first. He opened a door for Mom. As he opened the door for me, he said to Uncle Arthur, "Whaddaya think?"

As I got out of the car, thinner than my last visit, wearing ripped denim, my rebellious teen finery, Uncle Arthur said, "She looks great. Thinner, taller…quite pretty."

"Not the kid—the car!" Dad shot back.

Feeling like a rejected object, overshadowed by Dad's newest toy, I spent that afternoon eating, then overeating and finally gorging, away from the adults.

For some, food is a crutch. In my case, it was a mini-van. My lifelong journey with food frenzy was a difficult road with a whole series of forks in it. Enough forks for a dinner party.

#

Mom was the first working mother in our Brooklyn neighborhood in 1964. I was a latchkey kid; angry, outraged and eight years old. I hated heading home from school to a dark, lonely house. Once inside I closed the door behind me and became enveloped by the soundless emptiness of the place. The air felt thick. Alone in the dark, I moved methodically towards my favorite spot in the house—the refrigerator. When I opened the door, the light went on, like the gleeful smile of a familiar friend. Planting myself in the doorway, basking in the light and cool air, the hum of the *Frigidaire* motor greeted and comforted me. I tasted everything: peanut butter, pickles, a fingerful of mayonnaise. Any food consoled me, for a minute.

As early as elementary school, food and I were hand-holding best friends. My favorites—the after-school grilled cheese sandwich, followed by a half sleeve of Oreos, pounded down before mom came home from work—made me the unpopular chunkster of my grade. Confident my consumption had reached Olympic proportions, these days ignited my twisted love affair with food, eating away at my loneliness. Always an under-achiever, in spite of my rapidly growing girth I was voted *second* fattest in my class. *I couldn't even excel at overeating.*

Meanwhile, my mother was a career woman, who worked in finance, or as she said, "I go to business." A former runway model, she was a walking style magazine of clothes and accessorized perfection that I could never match.

Many a morning I'd watch her dress, cutting the tags off a brand-new suit, sliding the garment on, always a perfect fit. The sight of this made me want to hug and hold her close, as if her flawlessness could rub off on me by mere contact.

"Don't touch Mommy now, you'll wrinkle her suit."

Coupled with her aloofness, mom's display of fashion made her more of a meticulous mannequin than a nurturing mommy. And within this display, I was another accessory: her daughter, who should be well mannered, well-coiffed, and well behaved.

"Is that what you're wearing?" was her most frequent comment whenever I dressed. Instead, I heard, "My daughter is a walking disappointment."

My tenacious mother, with sculpted cheekbones, long tapered fingers, a tiny waist and a perfectly heart-shaped behind with thin thighs—she had one of those figures that clothes fit flawlessly. Who ever heard of a Jewish woman of Eastern European extraction with a small ass and thin thighs? Never exercised, never dieted. I didn't understand how she was born that way, or how I could possibly be related to her.

Mom's dark hair, brown eyes and olive complexion were nothing like my fair freckled face, red hair and green eyes. At age seven, I was so in awe of how different she looked, I asked if I was adopted. She fired back, "What do you think?" I thought I was. Then I found a photo of her seven months pregnant in a baggy dress, obviously with me, since I was an only child.

When I was around eight years old, we went clothes shopping for school. I was being rewarded for skipping third grade, and I was promised something extra. As I was trying on outfit after outfit, Mom told me they all looked too tight. Then, in response to one outfit, she said, "Let's buy it. It will fit…if you wear a girdle." "A girdle," she confided, "will give a smoother line to your clothes and keep your chubbiness from showing."

That day, Mom got me my first girdle. My clothes weren't bought to fit my body; my body was contorted to fit my clothes. None of the subtext was lost on me. This was no optical illusion.

A girdle *looks* a lot smaller than an actual body. If a city was a girdle, and a country was say, the size of my behind. Now imagine taking a country—that tush—and stuffing it into a city, my girdle.

What a challenge it was. I'd step into it, dance it up to my waist, sort of limboing like my life depended upon it.

That's how I started my day, every day…getting ready for fourth grade.

If this happened today, and not in 1964, this torture might be labeled child abuse or, at the very least, child beauty pageant syndrome. Child Protection Services would be contacted, and years of having Lycra cramp my legs might have been avoided.

Wearing something that tight and hard to get in and out of, I didn't really want to take it on or off during the day, till I could take it ALL OFF, meaning—I don't think I ever went to the girl's bathroom my last three years of elementary school. I was too girdled in to pee, I just held it in. Then there was how the girdle made me feel, squeezed into my clothes, uptight. I became quiet and hardly spoke in school…my mind and personality became restrained too.

Over-elasticized, I became one of those shy girls who sat in the corner, tugging at her clothes to keep them smooth. With a petite, girdled in voice. A tightly controlled, inflexibly molded, tushy-torturing girdled existence, I lived a constrained life…afraid of moving too quickly, nothing rowdy, no dancing. I won't dance, don't ask me.

After a few years of wear and laundering, my girdle got a bit stretched out. I experienced an ounce of freedom, and increased mobility. I developed a sense of humor. I was 10. I went to parties. I still didn't dance. But I might be caught swaying to the music, or occasionally head bopping. Dare I look at a boy? Wouldn't he know I was a girdle wearer? Right before pantyhose was invented—I remember this well at the sixth-grade dance—there were garter belts with itchy stockings that didn't feel comfortable or sexy. By seventh grade there were pointy bras….it all hurt. The architecture of torture.

Then came the unprecedented news—not unlike the tearing down of the Berlin Wall – girls could wear pants to school. Yay, ninth grade. Girdle off, jeans on. Now cool jeans were skin tight. And though I still had to lie down to get them on and zip them up, I felt freer…and comfortable enough to use school restrooms. As teens, girls went to restrooms in two's like swim buddies, every chance they could, for gossip and camaraderie—especially me, since I'd stopped wearing girdles, and felt more like one of the girls and not a product of my mom's creation. I was still shy and inhibited, only now I was shy and inhibited in denim.

Years passed. Like my stretched-out girdle that had lost its elasticity, I too, loosened up with time. Even though I no longer wore one, the girdled life was always on my mind—and in my drawer.

By fifteen, I didn't fit in juniors or, as they used to say, "missy" sizes. Food was my best friend and comfort. Desserts soothed away feelings of loneliness, filling me up with something sweet and warm to buffer against the cold that was my Mom. And though I had an overcrowded closet of clothes, I still carried my girdle mentality, as my mother denied my need to wear a size 16 or 18. So, my brimming closet was filled with unworn too-tight 14's, and there was unspoken pressure to eventually squeeze into them. Mom bought me most of the size 14 dresses, these reflecting her more sophisticated style in the hopes that I'd be transformed into a lady, resembling her. I remember one such dress, a turquoise mohair sheath that wouldn't look good on anyone bigger than a pencil. Not only could I not zip it up, but the two sides of the zipper appeared to be in different time zones determined never to meet. Meanwhile, Mom wore a perfect size six, from her closet full of designer suits and dresses I envied.

Pressured by Mom into following a new diet every other week—the grapefruit diet, the watermelon diet, and the string bean diet (which gave me so much gas I lost interest in resembling a string bean)—I was a poster child for calorie counters, fat shamers, and food kvetchers. Mom's insistence on physical perfection fed my feelings of being a lonely, lumpy outcast. A thousand sensible salads would never make me as beautiful as her.

Mom was a model in the 1940s—first glamorous runways, later a designer's studio or showroom fit model—in other words, a human mannequin, stuck with pins while garments are perfected and reviewed; often standing in a busy room in her underwear, touched by handsy showroom sales people. She complained about getting groped too much in the workplace, saying "Lay off buster." Ultimately, modeling got too full of slimy gropes for her to continue. Decades later, as I took the stage pounds lighter than my adolescent self, clad in form-fitting pants and a filmy black top, I had passed the gauntlet of men at the bar who reached for a squeeze as I walked by. Mom and I had more in common than I thought.

Burying raging emotions of feeling unwanted and being treated like a naggingly disappointing accessory, I overate, bit my nails and picked away at anything in my path or on my person. To win Mom's love and acceptance (and wear her fabulous clothes), I had to be thin. This tape played on continuous loop.

To spend time with Dad, (who was usually out of a job, or hating the sales job he had) I needed to eat with him, usually cookies and milk an hour after dinner. To win his approval, I had to be entertaining and funny. While he was deciding between vanilla wafers or Oreos, I'd be agonizing to myself. "Dad won't talk to me unless I'm funny. Do I have jokes for tonight? Will he laugh? Do other kids just show up and talk to their parents without a monologue?" The seeds of food insanity and comedy lust were planted at the family dinner table.

If I filmed a movie of my upbringing, it would all take place on one small set. My childhood bedroom, faded ballerinas on the walls, was the size of a prison cell, so small I couldn't have a door and a desk. Because there was no door, I had a small desk and a polyvinyl curtain (colored in simulated wood) at the entranceway. Every time it opened, a crinkling noise erupted, like the sound of tearing gift-wrap. But it was no gift when Mom or Dad entered unannounced, invading my universe. "You don't need privacy—we're family," Dad would say, whenever all 6'1'' of his gruff Fred-

Flintstone self stormed in. No boundaries. He'd barge in to share a joke or invite me to a piece of pie.

This six by ten-foot space was my world, where I wrote and drew and dreamed. The shelves were crammed with books. Along one wall was the desk where I studiously did homework every day after school, like a good girl. On the desk was a lamp I never liked, but Mom won it at a raffle, and she didn't know what to do with it. The lamp lived next to my collection of old coffee cans crammed full of lead pencils, colored pencils, pastel sticks and paint brushes. I was thrilled when Mom let me pick out something for my room: Peter Max sheets and matching curtains. Moon and stars, moon and stars, gold stars and midnight blue sky, in a half-drop repeat. On lonely nights, I'd count how many stars were on the curtains. And there was a black-and-white TV (large box, small screen), a hand-me-down from a neighbor, that only got reception if I whacked it repeatedly, beating it like a tortured dog. The only thing I ever remember it receiving was "Gilligan's Island," a show I thought was too dumb for me. It played in the background as I drew. Immersed in my world of storybooks, drawing pads, and watercolors, I retreated to an inner universe where no one was ever fat or thin or pretty or ugly.

I moved out of my parent's house a year after graduating college. Three months later they celebrated their 25th wedding anniversary with a lavish second honeymoon. On that trip, they had a gigantic fight. Neither one said, "I'm sorry." Then they divorced.

Children usually blame themselves when parents split up. In my case, Dad actually told me, “When you moved out, you took the sunshine with you. So there was no reason for us to stay together.” Though Dad was actually saying I had been what kept them together, I only heard that I was the reason they no longer were.

I took that blame, stored it deep inside me, learning hard lessons. I’d somehow contributed to the breakup of one marriage so I knew what to avoid. I was never going to have a marriage like theirs. I was never going to have a divorce like theirs either.

CHAPTER 8:

THE SENSIBLE SHOE OF HUSBANDS—WITH A KICK

"A wedding ring should cut off the wearer's circulation."—Gladiola Montana

Rupert won the bid for LeAnn's apartment. While he went through the arduous process of getting co-op board approval, I considered his proposal.

I believed wanting to marry someone should be an easy, clear-cut decision, as in, "Would you like fries with that?" But I had doubts about quirky things like, what would we talk about at dinner ten years from now? Work? Did he know my favorite color? Red. Did he want children? Did I want children? As we were both only children, treated like small adults in our parent's lives, I suspected we didn't think of ourselves as actually having been children, let alone creating some of our own. We'd never actually discussed it. After all, I was 25 years old and hadn't exactly had a good role model for marriage, or parenting.

Was I truly getting to know Rupert or was I just enchanted by being treated like a princess? Our daily events were ripped from the reviews in *New York Magazine*. Every restaurant or play that got raves, we were there.

But I wondered—What was his everyday self really like? When did he have time for an everyday self, squiring me around town? Having a vibrant, highly cultural life was important to both of us—that was a potent point of connection. Did we love each other? We mumbled "I love you" during heated, passionate moments, probably too overheated to be thinking clearly, or even thinking at all. We were usually too busy dressing for evening events, racing to make reservations on time, I never asked. Many affluent Manhattanites lived like this. Wanting to fit in with them, I was excited that someone chose to make a life with me, and offered great sex too. Caught up in our rousing whirlwind, not knowing the answers to any of those questions, I was certain the next opera or martini would melt my concerns.

Meanwhile, when Rupert met with the co-op board, he learned they were a "no pets" building. His love of LeAnn's apartment faded. Peaches had loved him and been with him longer than any wife or girlfriend. He wasn't going to abandon her for a snooty co-op. So the search began again, further uptown. Pre-war buildings in the West Eighties had cozy-sized rooms and old-fashioned amenities. But he didn't like "old." He liked new. We looked at luxury high-rises on the East side. He liked very tall buildings, to be high above crowds.

Finally, we saw an apartment with a panoramic view and the rarity of a living room with northern and southern exposures. The lower Manhattan skyline was illuminated while eating dinner in the dining room. From the living room terrace, on a clear day, you could see uptown, past Harlem. The ultra-modern apartment had loft-like spaces.

"This living room is so big, Fred and Ginger could dance here," I said.

His eyes perked up. "Could you see me living here?" he asked again.

"I'd visit you here," I added, not realizing the impact of my flip aside.

"Could you see YOU living here?" he asked, deadly serious. He had a lot of money riding on my response.

Everything about this place seemed rich, magical and worlds away from my life in Brooklyn. I laughed and said, "This apartment is out of a dream."

Rupert waltzed to the terrace, glided the sliding door open, stepped outside and gazed in all directions, noting every sight that would be his new view of the world. He breathed deeply, taking in every sound and building and cloud. Turning back into the apartment, he studied me as if I were one more view he was committing to memory. Striding back in, closing the door, he joyously declared, "It is a dream, I'll take it."

I had no idea what this dream cost or how out of line it proved to be with his current salary. Rupert seemed elated with the thrill of a new, big, bright home. I joked with myself, anticipating his hopes: that if I liked it, I'd be his first furnishing. Also, if he let me decorate it as I liked, then I'd never leave. As darkness fell, we headed to a romantic French restaurant, where we both had too much Bordeaux. After dinner, we walked five blocks arm-in-arm down Madison Avenue looking in designer store windows, laughing, and kissing.

If this man wanted me so badly and this could be my everyday life, why was I feeling tentative and fighting it? We made love all night long; another winning performance by the maestro of the magical cock. After sex, I wanted to give him a standing ovation. When we were in bed together, our life seemed ideal. Later, when Rupert was blissfully snoring, I was painfully awake and alert, taking inventory of my life. After years of emotional and financial struggle, here was someone offering me the opportunity to be free from those worries. Maybe my luck was changing. He seemed to be a devoted companion eager to shield me from life's uncertainties.

Saying yes to Rupert should have felt easier and been less of a dilemma. He struck me as the "sensible shoe" of husbands. In my footwear shopping life, I craved sleek stilettos with sexy carved heels, but always settled for sturdy walking shoes for their durability and endurance. I felt too young for an Eleanor Roosevelt styled shoe or marriage. But getting married screamed of practicality, so I deemed Rupert a sensible choice. Indeed, he was the choice—pragmatically assessing my life's trajectories, the economic gulf between yes and no was staggering. And he adored me. He showered me with Manhattan's finest of everything—Manhattan, the world I loved. Plus, being with Rupert and thinking he was the best guy a girl like me could ever hope for, had roots in my lonesome over-eating and cravings for someone to help me change my life.

Reflecting on my parents' marriage, how their biggest problem was money, I remembered there was enough for daily life with some left over, for one nicety each year, like a vacation or a new kitchen appliance. They'd spend six months fighting about which choice they'd make. I decided as a child that I'd never get into a situation like that. Here with Rupert there was enough money to never have those fights. I thought we'd have a better shot than my parent's 25-year marriage. Now the most important question: did I love him? Building a life together, I knew I'd grow to love him. Hearing him snore, I gazed at his smile, barely visible in the dark. Could I exist happily beside this sound and smile for years, decades, the rest of my life? I looked at the clock. It was almost 4 a.m. I'll think about love tomorrow, I told myself.

Days later, Rupert met with this co-op board. They were fine with Peaches, especially when they knew he was putting 50% down towards the apartment purchase. Everything moved so quickly, like a montage scene in an old movie. Now Rupert owned a huge empty apartment. The evening of the closing we went to dinner at *The Russian Tea Room.*

As our cocktails arrived, I smiled, “New suit? Big meeting today?”

“I have a big meeting tonight,” he announced, lifting his glass for a toast. “Now that I’m a land baron, this is the moment where I formally ask you to marry me.” We clinked glasses and sipped our martinis. When I put my glass down, there was a tiny velvet box on my plate. Yup, the ring. I opened it, revealing a tasteful carat in a simple setting.

My day had been filled with job rejections, a broken heel, a cancelled audition, crowded, stalled trains and attempts to balance a checkbook where the income barely covered the outflow. After years of struggling in my life alone, Rupert offered the antidote to that—a love declaration—complete with jewelry. My small, lonely life needed changing. Yet it felt so dreamlike that I was numb. It seemed possible that jumping out of bed into marriage was my Prince Charming ending.

Rupert put his glass down. I, on the other hand, took a giant gulp, and swallowed hard—fearful and anxious. The thought of a guaranteed endless supply of Rupert’s life-affirming cock registered in my mind as I heard myself say, “Yes, yes, I’ll marry you.”

#

Getting engaged didn’t really sink in. Still in my dreamlike trance, instead of telling anyone, I packed to spend the weekend at Rupert’s pride and joy—his cabin in the woods, nestled in a secluded lakeside community in Stockbridge, Massachusetts. The cabin was half a mile from the classical music mecca, *Tanglewood.* When I heard "cabin," I thought of all the rustic mishaps and horrors of my adolescence at sleep-away camp. Rupert assured me there was indeed indoor plumbing, and now my bunk mate would be a cultured adult. Since I'd agreed to marry him, I was excited to see the real Rupert in his natural habitat.

At this time in my life, I didn't believe that happy things happened to me. Taught as a child by my Russian ancestors (who'd survived pogroms) that the minute you fully embrace having something good in your life it will be snatched away from you, I became a knotted bundle of fear. The ride to the cabin involved 2 ½ hours of Friday rush-hour highway traffic followed by scenic roads filled with breathtaking mountain views, and fall foliage. During the drive, skies darkened, eventually to near black. Even with our bright lights, it was difficult to see the roads and the other cars. Every time I saw illumination from somewhere I couldn't identify, I was certain the night would end in a fatal car crash. I even thought I heard my late grandfather's voice, mit accent too, "Vatch de cars, coming towards you. Don't let them hit you."

I'd hoped conversation or the radio would dispel the voices in my head. Rupert didn't like to talk and drive. He found rock music a distraction. I took a nap. By the time I woke up we were in Stockbridge, the town that illustrator Norman Rockwell painted, and singer James Taylor wrote about in his song "Fire and Rain", referencing a mental institution where a friend killed herself. The town was both postcard perfect and a great place to commit suicide. Maybe they were one and the same.

Finally, we approached a winding tree lined country road. The path was a dirt road, covered in leaves. He stopped the car in what seemed to be the middle of the road.

"We're here," he chimed proudly. First, he opened the door for Peaches. She hopped from the car and found her way to the front door. As we stepped on the deck, the light sensors came on, illuminating the house, a modest "A" frame with gigantic windows. As we entered, I glanced at the wood floors and the wall of floor-to-ceiling bookcases, the tiny kitchen and dining area, all nestled in one room. The place was more functional than cozy, hardly a place I'd feel at home. My face had a blank expression.

"You don't like it, do you?"

"I'm just looking around," I said calmly.

"You don't like it," he pouted. Then he walked out of the house.

This could have been our first fight, if either of us knew how to argue. Instead, as only children, when we couldn't cope, we'd leave the room and hope the agitated feelings would vaporize when we returned. I wasn't alone, because Peaches was with me, deflecting my angst with her need for dinner. I rummaged through one of Rupert's bags, found her food and put it in her bowl. I tried to get comfortable. All the chairs were wooden and straight-backed. The couch was hard and unpleasant as well. Not a cushion to be found anywhere. No warm cozy spots. I felt lost and ill at ease.

Rupert returned, a half hour later, rubbing his eyes. Apparently, he'd been crying. Silently, he took his largest bag to the main room and unzipped it. The contents were more than a week's worth of newspapers. "I hope to read all of these this weekend." Rupert walked towards the living room reclining chair that was clearly only for him, because of the three-foot-high stack of newspapers next to it. He gently placed these new offerings at the top of the pile, turned on the reading lamp, sat in the chair, and picked up the top newspaper.

"What are we doing tonight?" I felt invisible.

"I'm reading," he announced. "Didn't you bring something to read?"

"I did. I thought that was for when we had nothing to do," I mumbled.

"We'll do something tomorrow. I had a hard week. Just let me relax. Tomorrow I'll show you the town. Why don't you take a hot bath or something?"

As I sat in the tub, hoping the warm water would calm me, my mind tuned to James Taylor's *Fire and Rain* again, especially the line, *"I've seen lonely nights that I thought would never end..."* When I got out of the tub and dried myself off, I looked in the cabinet under the sink for moisturizer. Instead, I saw boxes of tampons, wrapped in plastic bags with matching twist ties. There must have been five identical half-empty boxes, all bagged and tied. In the medicine chest were lipstick and make-up. Some woman felt comfortable enough to leave her personal items here. Who was she? I dared not ask on the night of tears and newspapers. I crawled into bed, hoping tomorrow would be better.

The New England air was much cleaner than New York City's polluted offering. I slept deeply and awoke refreshed. Rupert bolted out of bed, eager to go into town for fresh baked goods and the day's newspaper.

"I make this ride every Saturday morning, early and alone," he said. "I'll be back with a delicious breakfast in half an hour. All you need to do is make coffee." I kissed him goodbye and he rolled off to the bakery in town.

As a city girl who didn't drive, I barely knew where I was, or how to get around if it wasn't on foot. So, in this cabin in the woods I felt like a prisoner. Rock 'n' roll would set me free. I found the Beatles' album *A Hard Day's Night*, put it on the turntable, turned the sound as loud as possible, and twisted and shouted my angst away.

I found the coffee pot and opened the freezer in search of coffee. Here I found six half used bags of coffee, each wrapped in a plastic bag with a twist tie. Next I searched for the silverware drawer, but first I encountered the "junk" drawer. Every item in there was wrapped in a baggie with a twist tie. There was even a baggie filled with twist ties that was closed with a twist tie. The smart thing would've been to say "Hey, fiancé, what's with all the sterile little packages tied with twist ties?" Yes, that would've been the smart thing to do. Instead, I made a pot of coffee.

Finally, I discovered the silverware drawer where I found spoons and no twist ties. I needed one more dance with John Lennon before Rupert's return. So I "twisted" and "swam" and did the "mashed potato" in the middle of the living room, fiercely dancing off my anxiety. I heard the glass door slide open and Rupert entered like an enraged dad.

"What's going on here? What are you doing? It's so loud you'd think the Beatles were *in* the house." He raced to turn down the stereo, and reprimand me.

"I made coffee." I smiled, playing the congenial kitchen girl.

He placed the newspapers and bakery bag on the kitchen counter. Rupert was easily pleased by any girlish behavior. So I channeled my inner-teen, melting his anger with a cup of coffee.

"Did you bring me a surprise?" I cooed, eyeing the smallish bakery bag.

"I wasn't sure what you'd like. I know you've eaten bagels before, so I brought you one of those." He placed his hand in the bag and presented me with a plain, tired flavorless bagel. Did he actually think I was a plain bagel girl? Hadn't he learned anything about what I liked? For himself, he had a luscious peach Danish. One of each, nothing more. Did he think I wasn't worthy of choices or the same sweet treats he ate.

"It's only a bagel; don't create an incident," I scolded myself, searching for butter, peanut butter, or cheese to salvage the lifeless doughy mound. Chewing the bagel, I consoled myself, "Be a good houseguest, not a complainer. Next time, tell him what you want. Women who think men are mind readers eat by themselves."

To my surprise, he offered "I'd love to show you the town." Springing up from the chair, his arms wrapped around me for a lingering bear hug. "I'm so glad you're here with me," he whispered into my ear.

Feeling superfluous and desired at the same time, too bewildered to understand the push-pull of his behavior, I leaned into the hug—a banquet for my hungry heart. After the comforting embrace, we got into the car and drove past quaint homes, garage sales, and well-dressed women tending their gardens.

I was the only non-blonde in this zip code. As a Brooklynite, I thought these Aryan women were wondering "Who's this Hymie-town Hebe?"

We pulled into a spacious parking lot. "In the mood for a big auction?" he asked, enthusiastically. We entered a church-sized room that looked like town meetings were held there. "Cindy is the best auctioneer in town; she's really something," he said as we took two hard-backed chairs in the sixth row. Cindy, mid-30s, petite, seemed to have one eye on Rupert and one eye on everyone else.

During the break, I went to the ladies' room. When I returned Cindy and Rupert were talking and drinking coffee. I walked to them and said hello, her demeanor changed.

"This is Arlene," he announced proudly. She turned sour, shot a piercing gaze through him, turned on her heel and walked away. Rupert took my arm saying, "We've had enough of this auction for one day. It's time for cocktails."

We drove along a scenic country road to a turn-of-the-century inn, a place Gatsby would have taken friends for drinks. As we entered through the heavily carved door, everyone greeted Rupert by name. We strolled through the spacious lobby, casually elegant, lined with overstuffed chintz-covered sofas. Rupert opted for the garden with hard, high backed chairs. Our waitress, Gloria, took our drink orders. She looked a lot like Cindy, the auctioneer—both small, dark and cute without being too pretty. Rupert was friendly and jovial with her. But once she saw me, she was icy, just like Cindy. She returned with our frozen daiquiris and slammed them down on the table. When it was time for us to order another drink, she'd switched stations with another waitress. After we'd finished that second drink, Rupert seemed uneasy.

"I thought I wanted to eat here, but I've changed my mind."

We went to a local Mexican restaurant, sat down to paper menus listing a variety of burritos and combo plates. A growing insecurity stirred my cravings. The burrito/enchilada platter was calling my name. Mary, our waitress, came over with all smiles for

Rupert. She, like the two women before her seemed to be his age and height. When she realized I was with him, I was sure she'd spit in our food.

After dinner, which seemed to be spit free, riding back to the house, my mind raced. I was concerned about how all these women behaved. So I casually asked, "How come every woman we see in this town acts like she's had sex with you?" (Um, subtle, right?)

"You don't know what you're talking about. This is a small town; people here are different than in New York. You're a city girl," he said, placating me.

Had my pint-sized Superman fucked every woman in this town who matched his age and height? Had he fucked them stupid, like me? If he had been bad in bed, they wouldn't be mad. Is that why they were so angry now? Because they were clearly angry, directing these sentiments toward me. If he was a lousy lay, then they would've given me looks of sympathy, not anger, right? Whose twist ties were in the plastic bag closed with the twist tie? How could a short nerdy dweeb have the raucous sex life of a rock star? Can you imagine Woody Allen in the sexcapades of Gene Simmons?

The way I process any emotional anxiety is first, to go for the joke, and second, to blame myself. So in this sit-com like moment that seemed too crazy to be believed, I thought I was just reading into things. Was my writer's imagination overactive? Was I afraid of feeling stupid, or wrong?—or right? At that price, how much did I really want to know? I apparently decided the price was too high—I let the matter drop. It felt too crazy to even talk to anyone about it. Nowadays, of course, it would be fodder for a long, heartfelt phone call to a friend—or a shrink.

Instead, I vented on a comedy club stage:

I just got engaged to a man. A real one this time...How do I know? He's a cultural colossal, speaks five languages, is world traveled, and an award-winning news writer, but he looks like Underdog without the cape. I hoped love would grow...like moss on the north side of a pine tree.

My first 25 years were so lonely that whenever I heard the Beatles singing, "She's leaving home after living alone for so many years..." I thought they were singing about me. I said yes because he asked me, because Prince Charming isn't coming, and 'cause this may be the last white horse galloping through my life before I'm thirty.

Maybe men just want playmates they can own. I should have a partner, like a swim buddy, only we file a joint tax return."

But this wasn't comedy. It was therapy. And I wanted to buy the audience a drink for being my shrink.

CHAPTER 9:

FORK OR FINGERS?

"If truth is beauty, how come no one ever has their hair done in a library?"—Lily Tomlin.

For those who have said, "My mother is a piece of work," Mother Santo (as she wanted me to call her) was a meticulously fashioned ice sculpture. Poised like a frigid sparrow, face-framing grey-haired fringe to match, Rupert's mother was clearly not a hugging, cookie-baking mom who'd prepared her offspring to be an intimate partner. But neither was mine. In retrospect, maybe I was marrying a version of my own mother.

At almost five feet tall, dressed in a loden green cashmere skirt set, and Ferragamo flats, she wore no jewelry or nail polish, just a hint of lipstick. It was hard to believe she was 72.

Saturday brunch at her home in Larchmont, New York; as we'd entered the well-appointed, home, I was struck by how everything was clearly expensive when new—a quarter century ago—but not replaced or updated since. The most eye-catching item was a photograph featured prominently near the entrance that tugged at my heartstrings: a black and white portrait of Rupert, aged five, in a suit and tie, with thick, coke-bottle eye glasses, holding a violin. At first glance, you'd think this was a small man, sort of a strange Gainsborough's Blue Boy oppressed by classical music. The face was of a lost, sad child with the same expression as the poor, hungry children of third world countries in the *Save The Children* campaigns. Young Rupert's face screamed, "Please help me. Set me free. My life is starving me."

The minute I saw that portrait, mirroring my own childhood angst, I knew I had to protect and care for him. I believed our lives were sealed together.

Of course, with age and experience comes wisdom. Now I would just see it as two lonely souls brought up in similar circumstances—not exactly a match.

"Mother Santo, that's a lovely color on you," I said.

"Thank you dear. What you're wearing is attractive too."

Looking around, this was a jarring contrast to my childhood home. Our furniture was comfy, easy chairs a kid could climb into and curl up, with couches that would have you reclining almost instantly.

Coziness was elusive here, from the hard, mid-century Danish modern high back chairs, to the well-worn rugs and antique vases housed in the library shelves, all too delicate to be touched and admired—not unlike Mother Santo herself.

For lunch, there were small portions of cucumber finger sandwiches and lemonade: tiny, bland and bitter, also like her.

"I'm using my good china for this special occasion," she said, while pouring lemonade into crystal glasses, her hands shaking slightly, but enough that she spilled on the linen tablecloth. "I serve lemonade because it does not stain when I spill it."

Rupert and I looked at one another, unsure of what to say. "You look well, Mother," he forced, wincing at seeing her struggling with pouring.

"How good can an old woman look?" She countered, now seated, delicately chewing a cucumber sandwich. "I've lived in this house since Rupert was three years old. My husband left me 20 years later. He owed his life to me and he abandoned his wife."

"Mother, not now, we just walked in the door. Arlene doesn't need your history."

"My history? My life alone in this house. See the wingback chair by the picture window? That's where my husband sat reading newspapers every night. I still keep his slippers there and a pipe in the ashtray on the side table. When delivery men visit, they won't think I live alone."

I now saw why Rupert liked me so much. I was the joyous antidote to her.

All windows closed, the chilled air was dank and thick. In the unrelenting silences, I tasted what dead air feels like. How ironic that a radio producer's biggest fear also characterized his relationship with his mother.

Prideful Mother Santo insisted we tour the house. Rupert's eyes darted to mine, hoping I'd decline the offer. But I felt sad for her, and eager to learn more about him, so we walked from room to room as she led the tour. Each room was tiny, dark and had such low ceilings, I thought I'd hit my head. Rupert's bedroom—single bed, cowboy motif, crooked cotton curtains she'd sewn herself—seemed frozen in an Eisenhower time warp.

"Mother, it's like a museum in here. I'm sure some charity might like a bed or the books that no one is using," he offered, gently.

"I like to keep things the way they were in happier times, when you were a boy." She showed me her sewing room and cedar closet, opening doors like the unveiling of a mummy's tomb. Selecting a drawer, she slowly slid it open to reveal a dress wrapped in tissue paper.

"This was the dress I wore to Rupert's prep school graduation," she explained, pulling back the paper, revealing a white collar, yellowing from age.

"Mom, that was decades ago. Why do you still have it? You don't wear it."

"I might have an occasion. Tell me dear, what do you wear when you dress for the theater or the opera? I have a lovely collection of opera gloves you might like."

Rupert's eyes met mine, both of us unsure who should speak and what to say.

"I haven't dressed up that much lately—only one opera this year."

She continued to another drawer, another dress, another ancient story. What I know now that I wished I had known then: Mothers are a key to how a guy will treat his wife. Rupert's key had been hidden like buried treasure. I should have met his mother before we got engaged. A boy and his mother, worlds apart. Clearly, he didn't know how to engage her, nor did he want to. Now he was engaged to me. I should have run away screaming.

We feigned other pending appointments, said goodbyes, offered rigid, hesitant hugs, and made a hasty exit. Rupert was an expert at rushing me around. Whenever there were moments where I should stop and think, he had me hurrying to the next activity, impairing my ability to reflect or consider something odd. Opening my car door, he exclaimed, "You are my savior."

I wondered about the freakish scene I'd just witnessed. "How many of your girlfriends have met your mother?"

"You think I'd bring my girlfriends to meet my mother?" He retorted. "I only bring the women I marry," he added briskly, trying to change the subject.

"So I'm the second? Right?"

He nodded in affirmation and drove away as fast as he could.

#

A week later Rupert took me to my first five-star restaurant. What does a goofy gal who scrimps from paycheck to paycheck wear for a vetting over dinner by the successful friends of her fiancé at a fancy French restaurant? Since I didn't have a corner of my closet devoted to formal dining frocks, I found something timeless (old) and elegant (like my mother would wear) purchased off a sale rack in the last decade and coupled with a New York life lesson: when in doubt, wear black.

Arriving at Le Escargot, we found Rupert's best pals since college, Barbara and Royce, already seated with their respective spouses, Colin and Christina. Eagerly smiling, I wanted everyone to like me, and see me as a jewel on Rupert's arm, like the Rolexes they were all wearing on theirs. The men were dressed in well-tailored suits with au courant lapels, appropriate for their high visibility in the financial world. Both women wore dresses I'd seen in magazines, and were adorned with tasteful gold earrings. Barbara ran a major men's magazine. I'd read about Royce in *Forbes*, described as a rumpled Brooks Brothers garbed Wall Street wunderkind, who'd recently made a million from just one deal, on his way to more millions by year's end.

Royce hugged Rupert warmly, like a long-lost brother. "Roop, great to see you."

"You too, Royce," proclaimed Rupert, proudly putting his arm around me and offering introductions.

"Rupert's told us so much about you, "Barbara offered kindly. "He's quite taken—I can see why." Barbara was trying to put me at ease; still, she was speaking in a tone people usually reserved for slow children or foreigners.

Meanwhile, Royce ordered wine and appetizers including escargot, in French.

Bite sized escargot en croute arrived. "Fork or fingers?" I asked myself. "Fingers, you silly ass?" I chastised myself. "You're not walking down Flatbush Avenue, eating pizza. OK, which fork?" the sensible side of my brain chimed in, to the arrogant ranting inner voice—the one wishing I was on Flatbush Avenue instead of here.

"Rupert's told me you're a stand-up comedian. Have we seen you on television?" Barbara enquired. Then she looked away, and around the room.

Before I could answer, Royce chimed in, pleased with himself. "Our housekeeper tried comedy, at an open mike night. She's back doing our floors."

"I was on TV, but it was a segment for a humorous gift to give on Mother's Day," I shared, meekly.

Unimpressed and disinterested, Royce—whose sister was a heralded humor playwright—veered the conversation back to his interests: politics, congressmen they knew, and college pals with books reviewed in *The New York Times*.

"I had lunch with Alexander Liberman yesterday. He wants to give me my own magazine," Barbara tossed off casually.

While I was realizing that Liberman—practically magazine royalty—was the editorial director at *Condé Nast* (1962-1994) a family of magazines that I'd received rejection letters from, Royce requested a waiter bring him a new wine glass, pronouncing that his was flawed.

Silent, feeling akin to the snails in our pastry, I nursed my unflawed glass, trying not to drink my wine too quickly. When Rupert reached for my hand under the table, a soothing calm washed over me. Salads arrived. Royce sent his back for detailed modification. Once his salad was returned satisfactorily, conversation stopped for at least three minutes. As the king chewed, all was calm. While everyone ate I felt their eyes on me, one person at a time, as if to say, "We'd like to like you. You're much younger and prettier than Rupert's usual type. We're not sure about you yet."

Our hushed group became aware of a noisy trio seated four banquettes away. They'd clearly had too much to drink, as both bottles on their table were tipped face down in their wine chillers. They caught my eye, at first looking familiar—then famous: Truman Capote, with another man. Sitting between them was either Liza Minnelli or a transvestite dressed and coiffed to resemble her from the 1940's styled film, *New York New York.*

Royce, perturbed by their disturbance, groused, "That's the high-end riff raff you get here." That was his take on a literary legend? How annoying. I could see how Royce made CEO's shudder. He never looked at me. His wife, Christina, had a toothy grin, no make-up and man hands. She nodded and spoke briefly—just to agree with him. I decided that behavior was a wisp of a personality. My nickname for her? "Wispy." Rupert later told me that Wispy grew up on a farm, no electricity until her teenage years.

This was not my tribe. Years later, I would discover that any group that made me feel that uncomfortable was not worth my time. But back to our dinner. Nouvelle cuisine was just part of the evening that promoted discomfort. I laughed at the three shavings of carrot, nestled next to fingerling potatoes the size of a baby's fingers. This meal mirrored my table companions—i.e., the challenging team—pretentious, expensive, and ungenerous.

Rupert emerged from his own silence, announcing, "I've invited my dearest friends here tonight to announce that Arlene and I have just gotten engaged."

I heard a fork or two drop to the plate, clinking with shock. Christina's almost empty glass tipped over. A cold wave of Titanic proportions hit our table.

Royce robotically raised his glass. "A toast to Rupert and his new bride!"

"A big surprise for everyone," Barbara added, looking down.

Raised glasses, fake smiles, and icy elegance—I felt like I was sitting at the kids' table at holidays. To top it off, my pantyhose was painfully strangling my waist. But at least this gave me something to focus on instead of my tablemates' reluctance to accept me as one of them.

CHAPTER 10:

WHERE'S THE REST OF HIM?

"The biggest commitment I'd received from a man before now was the promise to share a pizza."—Me

Needing guidance and validation from someone I trusted, I hoped my family's assessment would soothe me. For the first meeting, I downplayed our engagement and left my ring home, thinking I'd share our news at a future date. I wanted them to like him and reinforce his great qualities, and not see him as I did—as *Underdog* without the cape. In *Underdog's* defense, he was my favorite Saturday morning TV cartoon anthropomorphic superhero—always humble, lovable and bumbling. Voiced by nebbish actor Wally Cox, *Underdog*'s physical demeanor and tone resembled Rupert's.

Since my parents lived in Florida, I took my 5'5" fiancé to meet my much closer New York relatives for Sunday dinner at Aunt Judy's house, in Forest Hills, Queens—about as far as you could get from Larchmont.

Judy, my mother's sister, was glamorous and blond. She looked like Marilyn Monroe, if Marilyn had made it to fifty, and was a two-time cancer survivor. She had personality to burn and a cigarette perpetually attached to her lips. I hoped she'd see the charms and flaws of my little *Underdog.*

We were greeted by my cousins Michelle and Louis, both 6' tall, and my uncle Jacob, who is 6' 5". Shell shocked, Rupert shook their hands like a dwarf visiting the valley of the giants.

Then my Aunt Judy breezed in and gave him a hearty hostess handshake. Rupert breathed a sigh of relief—finally, someone his own height. And me, I felt my first pre-wedding glow of pride because Judy clearly liked him.

"You must be parched from your trip. How 'bout a ginger ale?" she asked in her throaty smoker's voice, charming the small pants off my fiancé.

Stealing a sidelong glance at this man I was about to marry, seeing the sheen of sweat on his brow, I realized that I didn't quite know who he was.

"That would be lovely," Rupert smiled, following Judy into the kitchen. Seconds later, he was back to find me, searching the living room with frightened eyes, to join me on the couch. "You didn't tell me everyone was so tall, I would have worn cowboy boots," he whispered. Instead, I used the powers of denial to hear, *"There's no need to fear, Underdog is here!"*

"Dinner is ready," Judy said.

Everyone but Rupert stood immediately. He studied the tall people lifting themselves from the couch, their heads mere inches from the ceiling. I watched as he waited until they were seated, viewing the giants' parade, making sure the only seat available was the one for him.

I tried to stick close to Rupert, primed to promote familial comfort. After the snail incident with his friends, I was glad no big marriage announcements would be shared tonight—just a family dinner—with ping-ponging personalities and home cooking.

Judy burst from the kitchen, carrying a brimming bowl of matzo ball soup in each hand, cigarette dangling from her mouth.

"Ya think you could put the cigarette down for one minute, I don't want ash in my soup," said Jacob.

"You won't get ash in your soup; I've got my thumb in it. That's where the flavor is," she answered, coughing, placing a bowl in front of her brother.

"Please stop smoking, you only have one lung," he pleaded.

"I'm smoking on the other side."

I watched Rupert's spoon gingerly flitting through the bowl.

Michelle noticed too. She eyed him, then me. "How's the soup, Rupert?"

"Flavorful broth," he said.

"Not a speck of ash," Louis laughed. "I noticed your British tailored sports coat. Did you get that in England?"

"No, Bloomingdales," Rupert said.

"A man who shops at my temple," Michelle said, raising her glass to him.

Rupert ate quickly, yet politely, as if eating faster would end his discomfort. Clearly, this was a rough room, tougher than when I met his friends. Everyone here was united by the shorthand of family, minus the constraints of a snooty French restaurant. I could tell by Rupert's posture and sweaty brow that the family scrutiny of the fiancé felt more invasive than a proctologist's probe. Just as this analogy popped into my brain, Rupert turned his head and coughed. Freaky coincidence.

Judy sat down, beamed at me and said, "Rupert, we're delighted to have you here. Arlene doesn't bring men to meet the family too often."

"Who says bringing lambs to the slaughter isn't entertainment?" I injected, chuckling.

"I'm having a great time." He smiled. "Arlene is my favorite *human.*"

Rupert's first comment about our relationship seemed odd, like the little man himself. Everyone put their spoons down and stared at him, then at me. Dead silence. Oh no. I punctured the painful stillness with a soup slurp.

"What other species do you associate with?" Michelle inquired.

"Well, I find serenity in my pets, in cats, dogs, birds…" he said.

"And Arlene?" Louis said. "You find serenity in Arlene?"

"Is that so unusual?" I interjected, trying to change the subject.

"How 'bout those Mets?" Jacob tossed out. "Who's your favorite team, Rupert?"

"I don't care for sports…I'm an opera fan. A different Met."

Another alien statement for this group better versed in baseball than Beethoven. In comedy, this moment is called bombing. My family gave a collective eye roll. I could see Rupert was thinking my relatives appeared to be buffoons without symphony knowledge, as his body language was one giant cringe. Then there was me, klutzily roller-skating between two cultural worlds, trying not to fall on my face.

"Is everyone finished with their soup?" Michelle offered. Spoons clanked in the empty bowls. "Arlene, help me clear." We both grabbed dishes and headed for the kitchen. By the sink, Michelle faced me and grabbed my shoulders. "Where'd you find this guy, under a pile of *National Geographics*? Arlene's my favorite human? Who talks like that? Meet someone from planet earth…maybe at a *Knicks* game?"

"Rupert's very intelligent."

I could tell she thought he was an idiot. "So, what, you rub brains all the time?"

Compelled to defend him, I whispered, "He can screw me stupid."

"Apparently so, but that's not enough. And you know, he's short."

"Compared to you, everyone is short," I fired back, looking up. "Don't look down at me," I said sheepishly. We both laughed.

Judy came in, "Can you serve the next course? I'm dying for a cigarette."

Whenever Judy said that I had to turn away. We almost lost her after the last cancer surgery. Now, I was forging into "till death do we part" territory with *Underdog*—I mean Rupert. "Let me take the first platter, I'm sure Rupert's sweating being by himself." I grabbed a plate heaped with a side of beef. Rushing into the stuffy dining room, I saw Rupert. He *was* sweating and chafing under his collar.

Everyone filled their plates, eating quickly, eager to avoid any more uncomfortable conversation. While chewing, each caught my gaze as if to say, "Please don't bring him back!" or "He's not one of us."

After dinner, Louis and I went to the bedroom to get the coats.

"What do you think of Rupert?" I was eager for his opinion and approval.

"Nice clothes, fine labels." Louis pondered, "He'd make a great first husband."

"First husband?" I was surprised, "Like there'll be others?"

"A starter set, or a training bra. You've had those and moved on." Helping me on with my coat, he carried Rupert's things as if they were the king's finery.

I entered the kitchen to say goodbye to Michelle and Judy. As Michelle hugged me, I smelled her *Chanel* perfumed hair and surveyed her flawless French manicure and breathtaking beauty. Then I leaned into Aunt Judy's thinning frame, basking in her strength and sparkling eyes. In the pecking order of dazzling women here tonight, I saw myself as the odd duckling, swimming at the bottom of the barrel. Though Rupert received negative reviews, when I stood with my family, he and I were a matched set, the perfect choice for my awkward self. With *Underdog* by my side, I'd have no need to fear!

On the ride out of Queens and back toward Manhattan, Rupert's comfort zone, I was bursting with questions.

"So how was your evening?" I asked, carefully.

"Dinner was good."

"And the family?" I pushed forward, ever so gently.

"Tall—very tall. I like Aunt Judy." Rupert's voice was tense.

"What did you think of everyone else?"

"They're colorful," he added, smiling.

"What does that mean? A box of Crayolas is colorful." My voice was now insistent, pressuring. If either of us had second thoughts, this was the moment to discuss them.

"I can see that they love you and want the best for you. Can I listen to my music now? We had a nice meal. There's a long drive ahead of us." Rupert took my hand in a soothing, loving way, raised it to his face and kissed it three times, from knuckle to wrist. With those kisses he bought my silence and contentment.

It was no surprise that Rupert got mixed-to-negative reviews from my family. But behind closed doors, our romantic, sexual, fantasy/trance steamed forward, like a runaway train. We planned a small wedding. Other than Rupert's mother, all of his relatives were gone. He really wanted to elope. Someone with few friends and no family, who wants to elope, is either socially deficient or hiding something, that's my conclusion all these years later.

We met with a rabbi who seemed nice enough. Afterwards, Rupert said he didn't feel good about him.

"Why?" I asked.

"I think he may have married me before."

"How is that possible? How do you not remember your own wedding?"

"I was too drunk at that wedding to really pay attention," he murmured nonchalantly.

This comment was the Titanic of casual statements but, as usual, I tried to shrug it off. His surprise declarations frightened me. He seemed to be a much more interesting person away from me than the guy who showed up for meals and in the bedroom.

Apprehensively forging ahead with the wedding, I was afraid to heed my doubts, thinking they were just insecurities. Meanwhile, my anxiety was the kind anti-perspirants and anti-depressants were invented for. Rupert had steadfast urgency, you'd think he was a pregnant bride. The speeding train of sex and marriage, sex, sex, more sex, and romantic interludes on the way to sex and marriage, raced forward at breathtaking speed. Did I really know the man I was marrying? Or maybe Rupert did fuck me stupid.

"Maybe we should call this off," I blurted tearfully, on the phone one night.

"Planning a wedding is a stressful time," Rupert cooed, calmly. "Get a good night's sleep. You'll feel better in the morning. Everything will be fine."

All of my choices felt scary and unfamiliar. As the first of my friends to marry, I was a pioneer, a lone swimmer in unchartered waters, splashing in an ungraceful dog paddle, panicked of drowning in some high-rise, high-income, fear-based fantasy, and clueless of how to proceed.

No one would give me any planning advice beyond cake and music suggestions. Still trying to perform in clubs as much as possible, all I thought about was the Sunday of my impending wedding day, certain that once I survived it, everything else in life would work itself out. As my world revolved around Rupert, friends became a distant blur too. I had stopped calling any of my girlfriends; I knew I'd see them at the wedding.

Rupert and our imminent life together was my focus and my future. It sure looked a lot better than my present, especially Sunday mornings, the weekly stab-and-twist fest also known as the Sunday morning call from my mother in Florida—any Sunday morning, almost every Sunday morning, and always the same:

The phone rang.

"Hello?" I mumbled.

"Why haven't you called me?" my mother chirped.

"It's seven in the morning, on a Sunday, the day of rest."

"I've been up for hours. I wanted to know what's new with you."

"I was sleeping," I whined.

"I mean, what's new in your life?"

"Nothing much," I mumbled, rubbing my eyes. Could I sleepwalk through this or did I have to pay attention? "We're planning the wedding…I wish it were over already."

"Do you want my opinion?"

"Not really."

"I'm the mother of the bride, you know. You should feel lucky this man wants to marry you. It's not like you have a real career. Now don't screw it up."

"Are you done? That sounded like a conversation closer, ma," I said.

"Don't you think you should give up comedy and find a steady job?"

"Didn't we have this conversation last week, and the week before?" My stomach ached. "Let's talk about you. Give *me* a rest. What's new in your life?"

"I don't want to talk about me." She sounded sad and pained. "Life's the same, day after day. That's why I want to hear good things from you."

"If you want to hear good things, call somebody else—I don't have any."

"Was that supposed to be funny?" she was annoyed now. "Your father told you that you're funny. Big mistake. If you were funny, you'd have a real job writing jokes."

"Are you done ripping me apart? Can I go now?" I snapped back.

"Are you still wearing your hair the way I don't like?"

"Ma, do you think before you speak? You say hurtful things. I'd like you to think before you talk to me. I'm hanging up. You go think. We'll talk another time. I'm hanging up *now*."

It was difficult for me to fashion the words to end our conversations, but I persevered from a place of self-preservation. If I could stand up for myself in other scenarios the way I stopped my mother in her tracks (albeit only temporarily), my life might be entirely different. Putting down the receiver, gasping for air, I rubbed my stomach to unknot the tightness. Mom's way of being motherly and caring was more brutal than the group of kids who beat me up in fifth grade. The jab and twist with her samurai sword of questions would devastate me for days. Then I'd muster a few ounces of self-esteem, only to be sliced and diced during the next call.

"Why don't you just peel off the layers of my skin with your beak?" I'd think. My life was a big disappointment to my mother. "For me, it's a picnic in the park, Ma." Her calls were painful reminders of all the things I'd done wrong or failed at in a life that was unacceptable to her and to me. Marrying Rupert, I was becoming a respectable, espoused, home owning adult.

After her call, I grabbed a new, family size box of *Lucky Charms*, ripped the top off, got back into bed and ate the entire box while watching morning cartoons—the same way I had done as a nine-year-old watching *Underdog*. Only now, I was marrying him.

I wished *Ripley's Believe it or Not* had a contest for emotional eaters. I'd be a contender. But with my luck, I wouldn't be the champ, just another disappointment on another one of Mom's eviscerating Sunday calls.

"Could mom's calls be used as a terroristic weapon? Maybe the Pentagon needed to know my mother. More powerful than a locomotive, more devastating than a nuclear bomb a "disarming" call from my mom. Ring ring! Oh, NO, it's HER! I'm sure a few of those long-distant encounters could bring peace in the Middle East. After two or three calls, the enemy would retreat."

Yes, marriage would make me luckier, I mused to myself. When the next maternal inquisition happened, I'd have Rupert to talk about, and snuggle up to in the aftermath.

Although I hadn't been shopping for a Prince Charming, Rupert appointed himself in the role of caretaker, rescuing me from my tough-on-the-outside, fragile-on-the-inside, single girl existence. Somehow, this made him seem powerful in my eyes—and even taller too.

Rupert presented our life together so attractively, treating me better than other men had in the past, and I went along with it—I was warming to being saved. The combination of persistence and patience has always hooked me, then and now.

Years later, I would learn that if men keep coming back and want to put in the time, it makes me feel special, like they care. Maybe they're not a man-child out for immediate gratification, or someone giving you the two-week-rush so common with creative type men in Los Angeles. Also known as new-toy-syndrome (think about how attentive you were to your favorite gift the week after Christmas) there are guys who shower 10-14 days of non-stop romance/food/fun/passion and as soon as you say to yourself, 'OK, I'm in this, I have a boyfriend, this is great,' that's the moment he vaporizes. Rupert wanted commitment, roots and a joint checking account. His devotion became contagious. I caught the bug, like it was a virus, fueled by his magic dick.

Drifting in my pre-wedding daze, I continued in my lingering need for someone—a non-family member whose opinion I respected—to help me envision my path ahead. Josie was out of town with her guy. So I called my other best friend and first boyfriend, Bob. He knew me better than anyone. Sometimes we wouldn't speak for months and then, shortly after a hello, it felt like no time had passed. I needed that instant connection right now.

Bob and I had been in love when we were teenagers. He found me desirable and beautiful when I was my fattest. We were very happy together, until I lost weight. Then he said, "You've dieted off all of your playgrounds, the little rolls of fat I loved to kiss and caress around your middle and sides. Maybe we should each look elsewhere." He knew everything about me and was always brave enough to speak his mind. He and I had actually been engaged for a whole two weeks at age twenty, but as soon as we made that commitment, we could no longer agree on anything—our harmony morphed into biting arguments. We down scaled the relationship to friendship, a lot like Jerry and Elaine on *Seinfeld.*

Now 24, Bob met me for pizza—our favorite food when we dated. Like me, he would always lead with a joke if there was an ounce of anxiety in the air. That night I brought a ton.

"So you are getting married to someone hardly anyone you know has met, and you think this is a good idea?" he spouted, smirking.

"Well, you could say that. I know it will grow into a great idea with time."

"You're a college graduate, a smart cookie, a *Brooklyn* survivor, and this is the path you choose?"

"He loves me. When I wasn't writing jokes or performing, he kept us busy with dinners, concerts and theater tickets. He's smart—thinks I'm funny. We spend a lot of time in bed…"

"I think I've solved the mystery. No more callers ladies and gentlemen. You're experiencing pelvic devotion."

"Sometimes it feels like worship."

"You think pelvic worship is grounds for marriage? I think that's coffee grounds. Poppycock. Or Rupert's cock. Who would name a child Rupert?"

I'd never enjoyed pizza or this much laughter with Rupert. I had more fun with Bob than Rupert, but Bob's name wasn't on the wedding invitation with mine. Rupert's was. In that moment, Bob seemed like the better choice.

As the elevator door opened on our floor, I dreaded the Bob and Rupert meeting like a third grader's visit to the principal's office. Putting the key in the lock and opening the door, I was met with the sound of *Vivaldi* filling the air. Peaches padded over. Once she saw it was me, she spun on her heels and went back to Rupert, who was sitting on the couch, eating a container of yogurt, and reading a newspaper. Rupert and I hadn't said "I do" yet. But he'd already developed that married, "letting himself go" look that many spouses seem to cultivate. He looked fatter and older than I'd ever seen him. With each spoonful to his mouth, he seemed to gain another chin. I'd be gaining a multi-chin husband. How alluring.

"Hi hon." He glanced and stood to say hello to Bob, ever the gentleman. They shook hands. My past and current loves had now faced each other. Feeling like a stranger in my own home, I grabbed Bob's arm and exited to the terrace. I speedily closed the door behind us, looking in at Rupert. He'd resumed reading, eating, and harvesting chins. At that moment he looked old, and wrong for me.

Turning away, the view of the city lights against the starry sky was spectacular.

"New York, just like I pictured it. Swimming pools, movie stars," Bob said to break the iceberg-of-a-moment.

"I was just going to say that exact thing."

"You're a long way from Kansas, Dorothy," he joked. "You're a long way from Brooklyn, the F train, schlepping groceries from Bohack or Waldbaums, Utica Joe, Coney Island, or any part of the life we knew."

"I'm happy about that. I went from Ocean Parkway to Park Avenue with one giant step."

"And one short man," he added.

"What do you think of Rupert?"

"He's a guy…with a dog… and a newspaper… eating a yogurt. What do you want from the man?"

"What should I do?" I asked, ready to trust his response.

"What do you mean? There's a man in there who loves you. He wants to make a life with you. Give you a home—two homes. You're not in Brooklyn anymore."

"But do I want to go through with this marriage?"

"Marriage is always difficult, even when things are perfect," he said. "You love each other. The invitations have gone out already. There will be a nice party. You have a nice home. I know you know how to make lemons out of lemonade, honey."

Bob had spoken, and he hadn't said, "Don't do it."

At noon that next Friday, Rupert and I got our marriage license in Westchester County. I was confused as to why he insisted we get the license at a court house twenty-four miles from the one where we lived but, when I inquired about the trek he mumbled, "Shorter lines, less of a wait," which sounded sensible, so I got in the car. Besides, we were going to the Berkshires from there, and Westchester County was pretty much on the way. When we arrived and began filling out papers for our marriage license, the woman behind the counter mentioned that, in order to proceed, she needed divorce papers from a previous marriage. Apparently not anticipating this, Rupert froze, then fled to a phone booth. Wiping sweat from his brow as he returned, he resumed filling out the papers, proclaiming, "My attorney will fax that information to you shortly."

That Rupert—he really knew how to put a woman's mind at ease. He paid, we got stamped and validated and headed to the Berkshires for the weekend. It still seemed odd to get our license in Westchester, but I wasn't too concerned.

Only in retrospect was that a blinding red stop sign that I didn't heed. How could I have?

The next landmine was on our wedding day, mere hours before the ceremony, just after I'd finished zipping up my dress. I guess he saw my asking him to hook the eyes at the top of my gown's collar as the moment I was in it for the long haul.

"Honey, there's something you need to know about money, before we embark on our adventure," he said, all soft and earnest.

"Can this wait till after the wedding?"

"I need to show you something." He explained, showing me the mortgage statement and checkbook. We were overextended on everything. "The down payment for the apartment and the wining and dining courtship that you enjoyed so much were paid for by an inheritance now drained dry."

"There's other money—a saving account, CD's, something, right?"

He shook his head no. So much for my thinking this marriage had financial stability. His salary would never cover two mortgages, two homeowner policies, utilities, and car expenses.

Of course now—and even then—I realized that this was the moment to flee—if only I could manage the guilt. But because of a horrible life lesson I'd learned from my cousin Kara, I could never be a runaway bride. She had done that ten years earlier, and was still repaying her parents from her secretary's salary for those 157 rubber chicken dinners. My mind flashed to her wedding day, Kara locked in the bathroom weeping, while her parents stood, banging on the door screaming at her.

"Don't *ever* do this to your parents," my Aunt admonished.

Now, standing here in my wedding dress, my stomach knotted. I would make it work, I'm not a quitter. Maybe I didn't fully understand the finances. But since Rupert never worried about money, I would just follow his lead—the things we tell ourselves when we feel powerless.

What I would tell my younger self today: when people tell you they have "no money," please believe them. Also—*Not* getting married is worth 157 chicken dinners.

But on that day, the revelry proceeded on schedule. We were married at a restaurant in a townhouse in Greenwich Village: Covent Garden. It was September, 1982, the hottest September in thirty-four years. The sleeves of my cotton wedding dress felt wet and sticky against my arms. Its high Elizabethan collar choked me in the heat. As soon as I powdered my nose it seemed to get shinier. So I just gave up and had a sweaty, shiny day—memorialized forever in wedding photos, where I resemble a shiny marionette, dazed and confused. Friends thought I looked like a "Moonie," the 1980s-religious cult whose members were known for their creepy brainless stares. And I was, in a sense, under a bizarre spell—my guru being a strange little man who promised me a lifetime of romance and rapture.

"I'm Karla, the bride's personal waitress, here to make sure your glass is always full," a young woman said." I had five Brandy Alexanders in quick succession. I'd never had five in a row in my entire life and am surprised I didn't keel over.

I haven't had a single one since.

The wedding cake was three tiers of Grand Marnier chocolate cake nestled inside creamy white icing. Flowers on the cake matched the flowers on my dress. When it was time to cut the cake, Karla presented me with a long knife. Instead of holding it in front of me to cut the first slice, I wielded it over my head like a warrior in a battle scene from *Star Wars* and mimed a mock duel with my new husband. All he had in his hand was a cake plate, which he used as a shield to protect himself from his knife-crazed, Brandy Alexander-dazed bride.

Embarrassed, he smiled stiffly as the photographer captured the frame of me acting out what I really wanted to do.

After our wedding night, no honeymoon, because Rupert had just started a new job—one that paid double what his last job did. He needed this hefty increase to pay for the apartment which I now doubted we could afford to furnish or live in.

That evening, a stretch limousine whisked us to the Helmsley Palace where one night's stay of $225 cost the same as an entire month's rent for my Brooklyn apartment. "We shouldn't sleep. Let's stay up all night sliding down the polished gold banisters and ogling all the chandeliers." I proclaimed, stunned he'd spent so much, even on our wedding night. As we sauntered through the gilded lobby, people stared at me—the bride in her virginal white gown; they smiled knowingly. We breezed into our room, and my eyes soaked in every amenity—the plushness of the towels, the depth of the tub and the dazzling views of illuminated skyscrapers from every window.

"So, Mrs. Santo, what would you like to do now?"

Removing my shoes, so we'd be closer in height, I wrapped my arms around him for a long, warm kiss. Next, I rolled on the bed, stood up and started jumping around on the bed, like a seven-year-old, high on adrenalin and Brandy Alexanders.

"This is such a great room," I sang over and over.

"Come down from there—you're being a baby," he ordered. His reprimand stung, like a parent's slap.

Maybe I had too much to drink and was behaving like a child. Getting off the bed, pouting, apologizing, I switched gears with my best vixen voice, "I'm slipping into something more comfortable." Smiling like a cross between a Stepford wife and a babe from a Doris Day movie, I turned around, inviting Rupert to unzip my wedding dress, then disappeared into the mirrored bathroom. Carefully removing my dress, I slid into my new white slinky silk negligee and peignoir that I'd purchased from Saks Fifth Avenue during a 50% off sale, for $250—still more than I'd ever spent for a nightgown. Before leaving the bathroom, I gave myself a quick once over in the mirror, then zoomed in for a close examination of my face. Did I look married? I took a deep breath, exiting to the bedroom anticipating romantic, cinematic, wedding night sex.

Rupert sat on the edge of the bed in white cotton briefs and black socks. He still had his glasses on. This was not his best look. "Let's dim the lights," I suggested.

Sex that night felt nervous, mechanical and quick. His groping was void of sensuality, passion or desire, more like the body pat down performed by security agents in post 911 airports, when the sensors go crazy from an underwire bra. Was he just tired? Was this rote, ritual "marital sex"? It had been a long day...and it was now over. He rolled on his side and snored. I, frighteningly awake, stared at him in the darkness.

The marriage was now consummated. I was Mrs. Santo, wife of the snoring, obsessive, newspaper-reading elf in my bed. Where was the Superman sex machine I'd grown to desire and expect? As he slept, I worried: What have I done? Could I spend the rest of my life with this man? Did anyone else ask themselves these questions on their wedding night?

CHAPTER 11:

ARE YOU LONESOME TONIGHT?

"The trouble with some women is that they get all excited about nothing – and then marry him." —Cher

The day after the wedding, the honeymoon was over. So short, it may have been a honey-mini, with my mini honey.

Rupert carried our bags into the lobby of our building, kissed my cheek and excused himself to go off on errands. Big smiles from the two burgundy uniformed doormen and concierge who saw me leave in my white wedding dress just the night before. Now, dressed in jeans, I schlepped our bags into the elevator, up to the apartment. Didn't I see new brides being carried over the threshold in old movies and TV shows? Like Shirley MacLaine in the 1964 film *What a Way to Go*. Where was my threshold moment? The wedding was like a play we were in. Well, show's over, everyone back to their everyday lives.

Alone in our unfurnished apartment, I felt numb and gloomy, remembering that yesterday's big party was all about me.

"Congratulations! You married well," family members and distant aunts and uncles I hadn't seen in years had exclaimed.

Walking from empty room to empty room, I hoped some furniture nymph might have flown in on our wedding night, magically making the place come alive with vibrant décor and a sense of home. No such luck. There was still only a bed, a giant old bookcase, buckling from the weight of Rupert's books, and a rickety old card table and folding chairs, donated by Aunt Judy's Mah-Jongg girls.

If visitors came I could say, "Welcome to my oxymoron, my unfurnished luxury apartment."

I brought no furniture from my Brooklyn studio, where the décor was early reject: my childhood desk, make-do chairs taken from relatives' basements, and a plaid sofa bed that was so ugly it looked like clown pants draped on couch cushions. I had been glad to leave those items behind, but standing in the cavernous co-op, the comfort of my old apartment was sadly missing. I had sublet my studio to a friend, but knew I'd never go back and live there. Soon I'd be able to write jokes about this, but today I was too busy being sad.

My new-bride self sat in a chair. I hadn't thought I'd be sitting alone, reading a magazine the first day of my married life. My childhood self envisioned this day spent waterskiing or salsa dancing, even though I didn't do either. Skimming through *Architectural Digest*, I looked up and shook my head. Our 40-ft living room glared at me. Trying to lift my spirits, I kidded myself that I was suffering from “hovelitis:” the need to live in cramped quarters—a throwback to my tormented Russian ancestors.

The sun shone in on endless parquet flooring eager for fine furnishings I now realized we couldn’t afford. Restless in my chair, I paced from room to room, unable to find my “spot”—a place to rest and feel comfortable. When Rupert and I moved in together, two months prior, I had left my studio apartment with lots of “spots.” Like a cat’s perch in the sun, I needed a place to feel cozy, to curl up, read a book, or nap in the sunshine. I struggled to find my cozy spot here. Since we were building a life and making a home together, I had expected to feel more settled, like I belonged here. In the emptiness of these unfurnished rooms, I felt a similar emptiness reflected inside of me. Our new home kind of mirrored a temp job, where you’re friendly, you’re getting used to rituals and routines, but you’re not getting too cozy—no investment, no personal items on display. I felt like I was babysitting or house-sitting. Soon the adults would come back, thank me, and send me back to Brooklyn. When would I feel at home here?

I didn’t really believe I lived here. Still, after two months, every time I’d walk into the building along the lengthy walkway, I’d see the lobby staff: a team of three to five uniformed men, scrambling to their stations just to open the door as if they were greeting dignitaries. I’d always glance over my shoulder, looking behind me, to see who was walking in right after, who the fuss was about—

certain it was never just me. Who were they really holding the door for?

Then came the verbal part of what I deemed "The Doorman Dance."

"Hello, how are you? Have a nice day," they'd each chime in, rote yet respectful.

Still overwhelmed by their scurry and scramble, preoccupied by my own inner voices, I'd choke on what to say, resulting in a mumbling stutter sounding something like, "Meeh Meeh gooob, you too." Then feeling stupid, I'd spend my entire ride up the elevator berating myself. Short answer: "Meeh" was uncomfortable having a doorman.

In stark contrast to the fanfare of the lobby, the stillness of the empty apartment got me churning with too many emotions. So, I raced to the fridge for stability. A song began playing in my head, Peggy Lee singing, *Is That All There Is?* I stood, eating a blueberry yogurt over the sink as the song continued, "clowns and elephants and dancing bears…" I laughed, then languishing.

About an hour later on this, our first day of married life, Rupert returned and kissed my forehead, just like my dad would. Errands completed; I hoped he'd bring me flowers. Instead, he brought his shirts from the dry cleaners.

Maybe he was anxious about transitioning from radio to a live TV show. As news editor he oversaw the writers, secretly wishing he could write himself. Maybe that's what he liked about me: my creativity and ability to be funny.

"Tonight's the first night at my new job. I'm taking a nap," he announced.

"May I join you?"

"I really need to sleep."

"How about a cuddle before sleeping?"

"One cuddle, maybe two." Rupert laughed. Minutes later on the bed, he held me close, strong arms, heart beating. I kissed him, mouth open and eager. He returned the smooch, soon to turn away. "Gotta sleep, up all night, new job."

What a difference from just weeks ago when he'd slide his hand down my pants to see if I was wet enough for a quickie. I too rolled on my side, looking out the window at the Upper East Side skyline. Daylight shining, horns honking, ambulances racing, how could anyone sleep during daytime in this city? Rupert had no problem; within minutes he was snoring away.

Just as I began preparing our first dinner together as husband and wife, Rupert woke up. He put Chopin on the stereo and read the newspaper. I served the meal. We ate to music, barely speaking. I tried not to feel bothered by his aloofness, reasoning this was new job anxiety. When our eyes met, he took my hand and smiled reassuringly, then returned to eating. After dinner, I kissed him good night and wished him well as Senior Producer for the new BBS news show *Eventwatch.* The show was live, on the air from 2:00 a.m. until

4:00 a.m., when the only people watching were either nursing mothers, insomniacs or drunks. Not unlike the comics drawing late-night slots, he'd be working from 7:30 p.m. until 4 a.m.

On our second night at home as a married couple, I served a lovely romantic dinner—filet of sole and a giant spinach and mushroom salad—followed by sweet kisses at the door to see my husband off. I was sad to see him go, and horny for the hot lovin' I'd hoped for on our one-night non-honeymoon. Now that we were married, my husband wouldn't be in bed with me until 5 a.m. on weeknights–not an ideal lifestyle scenario for newlyweds.

Night three, I begged him to call in sick. Rupert thought it was cute when I pouted, welling with tears, whispering, "Please don't go, stay with me tonight."

I needed to know that he wanted to stay with me. "I'd love to be with you too, but I can't," he mumbled, then went to work.

As we'd eat, I'd gaze out the dining room window, at the panoramic view of Manhattan, the lights like a jeweled necklace encircling the city. I'd zoom in on windows of the high-rise apartments within view, seeing other couples having cocktails or dinner, just settling in as the evening began. My eyes would come to rest on Rupert, eating his meal, smiling at me. But our early dinner and romantic bonding time was continually cut short by his having to leave for work. This was the fourth night in a row. He did have a new high-powered job, but we were brand new newlyweds. The timing was lousy.

#

At five in the morning on this fourth night Rupert returned, exhausted from work. I heard him tiptoe into the dark bedroom, and slip off his shoes. The rattle of his belt buckle as he removed his pants brought me out of a deep sleep.

"How was the show?" I asked.

"Terrible. Crummy guests, segments too long. Call in's where nobody called. No one sane or smart watches TV at three in the morning."

"That can't be possible. I'm gonna stay up and watch the show!"

"I wouldn't waste your time," he responded dolefully.

I felt sad for Rupert, thinking he was embarrassed by his best efforts. Did he ever feel sad for me when I didn't want him to see me doing comedy? Now that he was working nights, I had no excuses; I could be in clubs more often. Somehow I wasn't feeling motivated. I wanted to get my marriage on track, and then I'd go to clubs more—I'd talk about the fun stuff of being a newlywed, as soon as I could find it.

Meanwhile, every time the radio was on I heard John Cougar Mellencamp's *Jack and Diane*. The song's hook seemed to be speaking directly to me: *"Oh yeah, life goes on, long after the thrill of living is gone..."* I'd heard of women getting depressed after having babies, but not after getting married. No one I'd ever known was unhappy the week after their wedding. So it must have meant something was wrong with me.

As Rupert was ready for bed, I drew back the covers, inviting him into the cozy slumber zone. Hugging me, he kissed my cheek and neck. We drifted off to sleep, entwined together.

When he woke up, I was at work, at a temp job in a law firm. The first week after marriage, I didn't take time off from work either; we needed every penny to feed our exorbitant mortgage. Mortgage rates were a high 14-16% so any situation was rather costly. On the weekend, he was tired and just wanted to read newspapers.

The second and third weeks were a replay of the first: husband goes to work after romantic dinner. Wife sits around all evening like an old shoe.

After the fourth week my temp job ended, so I was home during the day when Rupert woke up. I was excited about that. New job, mismatched schedules, we hadn't had sex since our wedding night. Eager to reignite our hot sex life, I made a point to be home when he woke up in the afternoon. I thought surely this would be our time for intimacy. He woke up at 3:30, padded around the apartment in pajamas, eating a banana. He looked cute. While he read the paper, I kissed his neck. He warmed to me, so I straddled him, still neck nibbling. Now my hands were inside his pajama top, rubbing his chest.

"Are you almost done reading?" I whispered, seductively.

"Almost." Then he tickled me, biting my neck.

"Do me, do me now, do me anywhere, even here on the floor," I pleaded silently, afraid if I said it out loud, he'd say no. I hoped he'd get turned on and follow my lead, but instead he withdrew, "I should take my shower now—maybe help you with dinner."

"Should I shower with you?"

"I'll be quick. Meet you in a few."

Rupert did take a speedy shower. Since it was a sunny day, he suggested we wander around the neighborhood. While walking on Park Avenue, we saw a pretty young woman with a beautiful, almost doll-like baby girl in a stroller.

Looking at the stroller admiringly, I then studied Rupert to discern his reaction. "Pretty baby, huh? You know we never talked about a family. Do you want children?"

"If that's something you wanted…we could talk about it," was his detached response.

"We'd have to do more than talk about it." Would now become a sex conversation? No. Rupert just kept walking. He never asked me if I wanted children, and I didn't offer. It seemed my life was adrift, and I was just floating along, waiting for my married life to get into gear, unsure of how I'd get there.

We hadn't had sex since our wedding night. This stark fact startled and frightened me. As newlyweds, that seemed like a long time, right? Was I being childish, selfish and impatient? Was I a little ungrateful considering that my breadwinner was working so hard? *When would we have sex?* The man I married behaved like an elderly neighbor I barely knew. I didn't want to dry up like a prune before my time, or develop cobwebs on my private parts.

#

Getting nowhere, I sought comfort in my two dearest friends: the refrigerator and Bob. Beginning in the second month of marriage, every night after dinner Rupert would kiss me goodbye. I'd then lock the door and race back into the kitchen and have a sandwich or two. Yes, sandwiches right after dinner. I'd stuff my face until my gut ached, sometimes doubling over with stomach cramps.

Then, when I felt sick enough, I'd call my pal Bob. We liked the same television shows and movies, and we'd talk about what we watched.

One night, when I performed at Pips, a comedy club in Brooklyn, near his house, Bob snuck in, just to see me. After the show he gave me his review:

"I wouldn't say you were good, but I did laugh once or twice and chuckle a bunch. As they say to actors, don't quit your day job."

"You didn't like my set?" I asked.

"I'd see you again. You look good onstage. You'll improve. That comes with time. As soon as you're good, I'd stop coming."

"Why would you stop, once I got better?"

"Then there'd be nothing to pick apart. Besides, you'd need the extra seats for your fans."

Always cheerful when I called, Bob was my only friend.

"Bob, what's up?" I chirped, eager for human contact to spice up my evening of brie, bread, and lonesomeness.

"I just did this trial run for the racetrack, using today's racing form. If we were there tonight, we'd have won $397," he said confidently.

"That's more than a day at any temp job. We should go."

"Wanna go? We can go tomorrow night!"

The following night, Rupert left at this usual time. Soon after, Bob's station wagon pulled up to the circular drive of my apartment building. The doorman buzzed for me. My husband went to work minutes earlier, and now I was driving off with a younger man—I had become the newest, juiciest bit of gossip for the doorman and building staff.

We drove to New Jersey for a night at the track, using Bob's handicapping system. That night I was not a newlywed home alone—I was a player, out on the town. Rock music blared. As we crossed from Manhattan to Jersey, I felt the adrenaline overdrive of someone who'd just robbed a bank.

We entered the Meadowlands racetrack and perused the racing form.

"I don't know much about horses," I said.

"Don't worry, I'll teach you. Tonight, school is in session." Bob advised that we watch the first race, get a sense of the betting odds, the crowds, and the feel of being there, live.

Then we dropped over to the concession stands and ate corn dogs, fries, and hot pretzels with mustard. At every stand, the server made a point of complimenting us on being such a cute, compatible couple, to which I'd reply, "Don't tell my husband that!" or "It's the thrill of being out on parole."

We bet the second race and won $58. Then we shared a cotton candy, bet the third race, and won $124. In the fourth race, a horse lost its footing, upsetting the other horses and the handicapping odds—we lost that one. But now we were both hooked by the thrill of the race, the exhilaration of winning and the delightful way in which the corn dogs gave us indigestion.

Home in time for Rupert's bedtime tuck-in call, all I said was that I saw Bob. The next night Rupert left at seven o'clock. Reliable Bob pulled up at 7:05. I could tell when the doorman held the door for me that he had now created a steamy scenario for us. Little did he know that Bob had no interest in me that way. We drove to Jersey for another winning night.

The third night was a repeat of the first two. This time, at the end of the evening, Bob came upstairs and slept on a fold out bed in the living room—Rupert never even knew he was there. During our nightly call, I told Rupert of my new occupation: professional gambler.

"You're kidding me. Gamblers always lose," he informed me.

"We always win. Tonight, we won $160," I confided, proudly.

"Really, you? I'm surprised! I was a gambler. I had a bookie for years. Most newsmen have bookies. I lost thousands of dollars and my shirt."

"How could you gamble and lose that much?" I was stunned to hear yet another significantly defining declaration being tossed off like an old necktie.

"I was young—I made too much money," he quipped. "Gotta go—they just had an explosion in Bolivia and I have to find archive footage."

After I hung up, I still heard his voice echoing, "I was young—I made too much money." I'd married a man with little regard for money: a rude awakening, just in time for bed. Next morning Bob and I had breakfast at a local greasy spoon. Rupert was still sleeping.

"You'd have a great apartment if it looked like you lived there. What about some furniture?" Bob proposed.

"We don't have any money," I mumbled.

"Try telling that to the doorman and concierge and your doctor and lawyer neighbors. What about credit cards? I thought your husband was a big fan of plastic."

"Maybe we could window shop," I conceded.

"If I'm fixing your life, I feel a sense of obligation to decorate it as well. Let's go." Bob and I flew out of the coffee shop and took the #6 subway downtown. Within minutes we found ourselves in *ABC*

Carpets and Rugs. While I was a wide-eyed stranger in a strange land, Bob had a mission and a plan.

"As a bachelor on a budget, I created a cozy man cave for myself. For you I'm thinking Berber in taupe, something neutral so we can build around it." Seconds later, he was over in a corner looking at a group of rugs before I even processed what he'd said. "I like this one!" he exclaimed. A salesman and I simultaneously arrived at his side.

"Will that be Visa or American Express?" smiled the salesman, not missing a beat. Such speed, such smoothness, these two were naturals at this.

"Oh, it's for her—she's the wife," Bob pointed to me.

"You're not together? You make such a cute couple," the salesman simpered.

Bob and I shared a knowing look. At that moment, I wished I'd married Bob, a man-child with an ever-growing comic book collection, he wouldn't know what to do with a wife if he couldn't seal her in a comic book storage box. So we had decided marriage was a bad idea for us.

"You and I may share more than my husband and I do." I professed, wistfully leaning into our easy rapport, something that always precipitated in him a kind of reticent discomfort.

"We're not married" he reminded me, "but once you feather your nest with Rupert, it will feel more like a home," he reassured me. "Make a commitment to this Berber rug and you'll never regret it.

And if things go sour, you can always carry it out on your back. Fold it well; hey, it fits in the trunk of a cab. It's a few hundred dollars. You said 'I do.' Now say you'll decorate."

"You missed your calling in sales." I smiled in surrender. "Wrap it up, I'll take it." The salesman fondled my charge plate and scurried away.

"Doesn't it feel good to spend money?" Bob spurred me on, rallying my spirits. "Let's get your ass to try out some sofas."

"You think we should?" I hesitated.

"Otherwise the Berber would be lonely. We can't have a lonely Berber!"

"You're right. No lonely Berbers for us! Let's go." We headed for the *Sofa Emporium*. "This sofa is too hard. This sofa is too soft. This sofa is too plaid." I felt like Goldilocks. Then we both spotted a modular sectional, our eyes met and we knew it was meant to be. We strode toward the maroon and grey woven pieces, hearts pounding with excitement.

"This fabric goes with the rug." I reached for the price tag, read it and jumped away like it was on fire. "This thing costs thousands of dollars." I was shocked.

"Calm down. That's for all 16 pieces. You'd only want five. So, it costs a lot less," he affirmed reassuringly. "You want the sofa, the two connecting singles, a corner and that long chaise, the princess divan for you to watch movies."

“The princess divan? I'm liking it,” I smiled, mesmerized. “But how do I know what will fit in the living room?”

“We'll take measurements. Whatever fits, we can come back and buy tomorrow.”

“Measure today. I'll buy tomorrow?”

“Yes Mrs. Santo. I know you can do it,” he asserted.

“Get a tape measure, I'm measuring.” I exclaimed. We went home with the rug and arrived just as Rupert was having his 4 p.m. morning coffee.

“Hi guys, what's new?” asked Rupert, trying to be Bob's pal.

“You're the proud parent of a new Berber rug,” Bob exclaimed fervently like a game show host, as he laid it on the living room floor for Rupert to see.

“I love it. It’s great,” Rupert replied, taking it in.

Bob and I locked eyes, knowing this was the moment to sell Rupert on the idea of an expensive modular unit, and that Bob was the designated salesman.

“We saw the perfect seating unit for this room.” Bob started.

“Why didn't you get it?” asked Rupert, eager for an instantly furnished home.

“First, we need to see if it fits. We're going to measure. Don't you want to know how much it costs?” I added, anticipating an objection.

“If you like it and think it's worth the price, then get it. You're good with money.” Rupert beamed. At that moment, I remembered why he had charmed me. He'd taught me how to play harder and worry less about money.

Bob and I measured, the new pieces would fit perfectly. I called the store and placed the order. Then the three of us sat down to dinner. Thanks to Bob, lively conversation and laughter filled our dining room.

Rupert went to work. Bob and I loaded the dishwasher and went off to the track.

We drove past one or two couples walking down the street holding hands. My new pastimes: gambling, decorating, and contemplating if my husband and I would *ever* have sex again.

CHAPTER 12:
CAN'T MATE IN CAPTIVITY

Foreploy: Any misrepresentation of yourself for the purpose of getting laid.—Unknown

Buying furniture didn't take my mind off the fact that Rupert and I hadn't had sex since our wedding night. After three months, our living room sitting area now had sumptuous cushions—cozy and comfortable. Fantasizing about what sex would be like with my husband, in this room, on our new furniture, I craved him all the time. I naively thought his avoidance had something to do with me, that my overeating had made me fatter and undesirable.

But as I would come to learn, it had nothing at all to do with me. Speaking of fatter, since Rupert started his new job working nights—and eating brownies at his desk every evening—he'd gained 30 pounds. I had always found chubby men cute, so Rupert was still attractive to me. The extra weight made him seem larger and stronger.

But, I could be naked, or in sexy underwear, or ready with the nearest woman to join us—it didn't matter. Rupert's attention was always elsewhere.

My Dad visited for dinner shortly after our three-month anniversary, took a look at the buttons puckering on the front of Rupert's shirt and whispered to me, "He looks healthy. I see you're a good wife in at least one room of the house."

With that wisecrack, I felt like everyone knew, even my dad, that we hadn't had sex since our first night of marriage. I was brimming with embarrassment and shame. Who could I tell? What would I tell them? So on a nightclub stage I said:

"I feel so insecure, that when people in Europe are whispering, I think they're talking about me. Just like an animal in the zoo, my husband can't mate in captivity."

My efforts at seduction felt worse than bombing onstage: Cooking gourmet dinners and wearing sexy little outfits—nothing. Playing his favorite Beethoven concertos with candlelight at bedtime—more nothing. Offering fresh baked croissants for Saturday breakfast while wearing French underwear and stilettos—*absofunkinglutely* nothing. Everything I attempted to be more alluring, resulted in the opposite effect, a distancing and fleeing.

I was reminded of the first joke I'd sold in my career: *"I have a new way to sexually satisfy my wife. I let her sleep."* Now, the joke was on me.

The sensuous love master with the dick to die for that I'd thought would be my ever-present pal, had become a memory to me. The sad truth I couldn't face enough to flee at the time: Rupert without sex was a dull guy.

One Saturday night, after a relaxing day, an Italian dinner, and an enjoyable movie: *Come Back to the Five and Dime Jimmy Dean, Jimmy Dean*, I saw bedtime as my "cock-opportunity." As frustrating as this marathon dance of disappointment was, at the time I believed that if I wasn't with Rupert, I'd probably be alone. Other than Bob, there weren't long-term relationships to reflect on for comparison. So I labored at trying to make our marriage work—hoping sooner or later harmony and sexuality would fall into place—maybe tomorrow or next week. What I thought was going to nourish me ended up as something to stay away from, like an addiction.

Meanwhile, that night, rolling around a few times, back and forth, ending with me on top of him, we both seemed breathless with anticipation. I unbuttoned his pajama top and proceeded to kiss his neck and chest. Rupert moaned with delight. I continued, buoyed by his positive reaction, my mouth kissed and nibbled down his chest, until I got to the waistband of his pajamas. I took a breath, then moved my hand into his pajamas, certain a hard cock would greet me. Sure, there was a penis there. But it was soft, almost frightened, like a cowering puppy. I tried to rouse it with my hand. Then, as I lowered my mouth to deal with the challenge, Rupert grabbed my shoulder, pulling me up.

"Let's just have kisses."

While we kissed, my mind raced with what to say. I knew I needed to be kind and sweet, but I was pissed and frustrated. "Are you feeling okay?"

"It's been a stressful week."

"But what about our newlywed life?"

"I love our life; I love my wife."

"But what about our sex life?"

"We have a loving life together. This apartment, my new job, many things are stressful. If you had a big demanding job, you'd feel more stressed too…you wouldn't be thinking about sex so much. Instead of temping, you might want to get a real job, an adult job, and be a responsible woman. Go to sleep." Pulling the covers up around himself, Rupert turned away from me.

Still stinging were the words "adult job" and "responsible woman." Even my parents never made me feel that small. No sleep for me. No sex for me. The one time I spoke up for myself, I was cut down and dismissed, like a poorly performing servant. I didn't see at the time that he didn't answer my questions. Instead, he turned things on me so I'd back down. My self-esteem felt crushed—too puny and ashamed to even reach out to friends, who might have given me guidance in dealing with the situation.

In hindsight, I see that I allowed myself to be manipulated and silenced.

I now devoted all my energies into getting a job. After about two weeks, I found a full-time job as a copywriter at the *Leon Auerbach Advertising Agency*. The only woman in the creative department, my office was the closest cubicle to the men's room. For the first time in my life, I reveled in male attention. They'd stop at my desk to talk, all day long—handsome, single men complimented me on my new red boots or noticed when I changed my hairstyle. Now that I was married, men flirted with me, sometimes two at a time.

Sexually invisible at home and the popular babe at work, I saw this as a cruel joke. I had flirtation, temptation, and options. But I chose to stay faithful to my husband, sure that he was doing the same, just adjusting to marriage.

There's an old joke where the husband says to the wife, *"Honey, you never tell me when you're having an orgasm."*

The wife says, "You're never around."

CHAPTER 13:

MY OTHER LOVER

"The more inches you give a man, the more he becomes a ruler."— Unknown

Between feeling unwanted by my husband and flirting with co-workers, I longed to leave the house in the evenings to stride a comedy stage. Performing in clubs was my great love elixir. Whenever I felt morose and depressed in my cold, lonely four-month marriage, I found refuge in the warmth of an audience. I knew where I could get a fix of validation. Like someone addicted to 12 step meetings, I knew when all the clubs had open mike nights. Tuesday, Wednesday and Thursday nights, when my husband was at work, and so was I. This was the one good part of Rupert working nights. I saw it as a sign that I was truly meant to be a comic. His change in schedule was my opportunity.

"So I married this guy, I guess because he was the first one who asked me. The biggest commitment I'd received from a man before now was the promise to share a pizza," I'd lead with my new standard. Sometimes Tuesday night audiences were so sparse, when

they were quiet, it felt like talking to an oil painting. But tonight, being center stage, bathed in the limelight of the laughter and the glow of bright lights, I felt lit up on the stage, better than being in a sad, dark place, watching TV on my couch. I was glad to be out of the house. Rupert was happy for me too; pleased I was out honing my craft and not waiting home for him. A killer set, lots of laughs and applause on a weekday show would garner a weekend booking of three more spots: Friday night, the early Saturday and the late Saturday, all for a whopping $150 and all the liquor I could drink. No wonder the best comedians are drunks. My big payoff was the laughter. A killer set was better than an orgasm…and many more people were grateful.

I began staying in the city some weekends to perform, while Rupert went to the country house. “You don’t need the 150 dollars,” he petitioned. “Spend the weekend entertaining me. Just make me laugh. I’m your most loving audience.”

His statement cut to the heart of my pain. I wanted to be a good wife and win his love, appreciation, and sexual desire. If I stopped performing, would he fuck me again?

Of course, it didn’t matter what I was doing, but I was willing to trick myself with anything, thinking that’s what it took to get our life on some “normal” track. That was my expectation. I wanted to believe that if I stayed with him on evenings and weekends that our sex life would return. Torn between holding onto my identity and healing my relationship, I gave in and stopped performing.

Somewhere, in giving in for the sake of my marriage, I gave up a vital part of myself. I lost Arlene the comedienne to become Rupert's lonely wife.

He enjoyed seeing me performing on television, and as a madcap cut up around the house—I'd be different characters, or have a dialogue with the furniture—as if we lived in *Pee Wee's Playhouse*. Rupert never saw me in a night club. Although he liked the brazenness of me performing in clubs, his straight-laced European upbringing fostered an old-world snootiness about females in nightclubs: they were wicked women with low morals. In hindsight that seems right up his alley—like prostitutes with jokes.

Ironically, the woman Rupert liked dating because she bravely told jokes in night clubs was now squashed and dormant like a half dead bug on a windshield, increasing my feelings of displacement and depression.

Onstage, I was outspoken, engaging a room full of people. Now, my steady diet of being off stage, home became my emotional jail space where I felt voiceless, caught up in some cartoon version of being a good wife. In biology molting is the manner in which an animal routinely casts off a part of its body (often, but not always, an outer layer or covering), either at certain times of the year, or specific points in its life cycle. Was I molting with married life, like spiders, mites or ticks? I knew I was ticked off and didn't know what to do about it.

I tried to spend more weekends away with Rupert, even though watching him read for hours on end made me feel old, bored and superfluous. I developed elaborate fantasies of how to rouse him to stop reading and study me.

One evening, I went into the bathroom, took a shower, and walked into the living room wearing nothing but eyeglasses and high heels. I hoped he'd snap out of his newspaper daze and discover me. He did look up and take notice. Without even a smile, he said, "What are you doing? It's cold in here." He stood up and raced to get the woolen throw from the couch, bringing it towards me.

I hoped he'd drape it on the floor in front of the fireplace, for the two of us to lay down on, basking in the glow, warmed by the flame, igniting into passion. That must have been my Walter Mitty moment.

Instead, Rupert draped the throw around my shoulders, kissed my forehead, hugging me briefly before sternly stating, "Go put something on."

Fantasy deflated. He was never emotionally or physically abusive, this kept me from being totally discouraged. Optimism flowed through my veins.

Since Rupert didn't enjoy buying groceries, to win his lust and affection, we visited supermarkets together. Making the shopping experience enjoyable and event worthy, whenever I'd take something from the frozen food cases, I'd give it a voice, and have it sing and dance its way into our shopping cart. Rupert's favorite was the *Eggo* toaster waffles.

"I'm Mr. Waffle, coming to your house for breakfast," I'd sing, dancing the box into our cart, like it was a Barbie doll from my childhood.

Then I'd stroke his hand. He'd move away, "You're so funny and sweet," he'd say. I knew "sweet" wouldn't get me laid. Continually defeated, in my spare time, I overate and kept to myself. I'd lost my joy, but masking it with jokes, felt less painful. Angry, frustrated for losing my voice, I'd sold myself to someone who seductively murmured, "Live with me, I promise you a better life than living alone." Who knew that once I unpacked he'd retreat? And who knew I couldn't bring him back?

Even Bob, my racetrack accomplice, was fading from my life. One night, he called, "Hey babe, should I spring you from jail for a night at the racetrack?"

"I'm kind of busy…" I said.

"Doing what?"

"Being married…" my voice trailed off, uncertain.

"When did that become a full-time job? I don't remember your husband working on your marriage at all."

"You never liked him, did you?" I said sourly.

"Well, not for you."

"Why didn't you ever tell me?" I shot back.

"I didn't want to hurt you," he said, gently.

At that moment, I felt wounded. It was as if my friend betrayed my trust with caring and kindness. Dragging the phone to the kitchen, the receiver between my right ear and shoulder, with my left hand, I yanked the fridge door open, peering inside, scanning the leftovers. I shoved a wedge of brie, the size of a baby's fist into my mouth – while I chewed it, I mumbled, "You didn't want to hurt me, so instead you've let me make a life choice that's been grim and ugly."

"Not ugly, dear," he snapped back. "Your home is decorated fabulously. Ugly is a state of mind. You're the pageant winner in your state."

"Now you think I'm ugly?" I accused.

"It's your word. How many nights did I cheer you on in comedy clubs? I was your biggest fan. Where have you performed lately?"

"I haven't been performing." (Stand-up *OR* other sexual positions, I thought to myself.) "That's what's making me grim."

"Should I force you into the outside world? I want you to be happy."

"Maybe, sometime soon," I said, on the verge of tears. Hanging up, I continued with my other best friend, my frost-free *Frigidaire*. Three pieces of cold pepperoni pizza wrapped in foil were calling my name. I took the tin foil teepee that housed the pizza out of the fridge and placed it on the counter. Opening the foil, like a curtain parting, I said, out loud, "Now presenting, the singing and dancing pepperonis," grabbing a slice and holding it high, as I danced it into the air. "And now, ladies and gentlemen, Arlene Schindler Santo, procrastinating bulimic extraordinaire will consume this slice in its entirety!" I took a bite out of the pizza and out of my loneliness. "And the crowd cheered…come back next week and watch me consume vast quantities of meatballs from around the world. Enjoy the rest of the show."

#

The first real marriage marker, the six-month wedding anniversary, is a cozy, romantic time for most newlyweds—most normal newlyweds. I fantasized about their celebrations: going out to dinner, sex toys, jewelry or costumes. Then there was us, the Santos—no sex since our wedding night. The groom was oblivious. The bride felt like a tear stained sow. What to do? I took a survey in *Cosmopolitan* magazine. To answer this question: *What do you wear to sleep in:*

Pajamas

Teddy

Nothing

My response of pajamas netted a zero score for that question. Teddy was worth 3. Nothing was the 5-point winner. A sexual loser even on paper, I wasn't sexy enough. Now, soured on quizzes too, I was reminded of a friend's joke, *"I felt so clueless in the bedroom, if given a choice between oral and anal sex, I chose written."*

I decided the answer was cooking a big dinner and wearing French lingerie. If I was sexier, say, act like a prostitute, maybe I'd win him over. I saw the scene perfectly in my head, straight out of a French film. I'd walk into the dining room holding an impressive platter of food worthy of the pages of *Gourmet,* while wearing an exotic bra and matching panties worthy of *Playboy*. Picture Marie Antoinette striding in with a glorious feast. Can't miss, right? Any healthy man would have all of his senses standing at attention.

After finding the most enticing Merry Widow out of all the bustiers, lingerie and corselets at *Bloomingdales*, I raced home for anniversary primping, feeling hopeful. I had an equation: marinate and inebriate to fornicate. For dinner I followed a French recipe, marinating, then cooking meat in a Cabernet sauce. Self-marination was a hot bath followed by an extra generous coat of body oil. I'd be soft, silky and irresistible.

For inebriation I prepared a pitcher of margaritas, chilled glasses, sliced fresh limes. So pleased with my infallible plan, I called the concierge in our front lobby. "Please let me know when Mr. Santo has arrived."

Table set, candles lit. As for me, dressed in a black lace merry widow that cinched my waist to barely breathable, pushing my breasts up for jiggly cleavage. Lace panties, black stockings, black high heels, dressed to be the evening's desirable dessert. My last beauty effort was red lipstick, first on my mouth, drawn twice, then blotted for color that would not rub off. Next, I reached down to each breast with the lipstick and gently colored each nipple and areola, to seem darker, and flushed with excitement. I looked in the mirror, pleased with myself, and feeling pretty, a rarity these days.

The doorman buzzed, “He’s here.”

I threw a black silk robe on to skim my shoulders and frame the picture. Plus, it hid upper thigh cellulite as I walked away. The robe sashayed behind me, like a bridal gown train. Pouring the frothy margarita into a chilled glass, I then walked towards the front door. I opened it, just a crack, giddily anticipating his arrival. First, the elevator ding, as the doors opened. Next, the sound of his footsteps on the carpeting, quickening, closer. His breathing echoed in the vestibule, mere inches away. Full of hope, tits high and perky, tonight was my night!

I was only 26 and tonight I was going to feel like it!

Opening the door to greet him, my heart raced. “Good evening dear,” I uttered breathlessly in the sexiest voice I could muster, feeling irresistible, sexy and with cock sure certainty I was on my way to ecstasy.

“What are you doing?” Rupert blurted, annoyed and angry, like a headmaster at a snooty school who had just found boys smoking in the lavatory.

“I’m offering you a cool margarita at the end of your hard day, to celebrate our six-month anniversary.” Still trying to uphold my breathy, sexy self, I may have sounded like a transvestite.

"What are you wearing?" Upset, recoiling in fear, he now started to cry.

"What's wrong?" His tears confused me. I refused to feel devastated and defeated. "I wanted to make you happy."

"It's disgusting. It frightens me." His crying increased. He took the lapels of my robe and held them close to one another, covering me as we walked into the apartment, slamming the door behind us. "Take those bad girl things off. You're a sweet girl. Put on something sweet and flannel, so we can have dinner." He wiped his tears, sped to the bathroom and locked the door.

Rupert's reaction floored me. Crying like a frightened boy? Brimming with feelings of rejection and stupidity, I was unable to understand why my marriage was grueling and detached. The hot cock of courtship was now a cold distant husband. Obsessing about what I could do for more intimate outcomes, day after day, I repeatedly felt kicked in the teeth.

Defeated, changing into flannel pajamas, I focused on how the soft silky new lingerie felt against my skin, better than how crushed my heart was. Now numb, a robot in my own life, I was itching to crawl out of this cave of dashed expectations for which I blamed myself. The good dutiful wife served dinner. We ate in silence. I sat at the table angrily overeating, wishing instead that someone had removed my new fancy panties with their teeth and devoured me right there on the table. Operation Marinate, Inebriate, Fornicate, became: My-I Fucked-up—a failure. I felt too stupid and diminished to speak;

embarrassed I'd failed at seduction—yet again. Besides, how can you confront a crying man? After dinner, I went into the bathroom, brushed my teeth, masturbated, and then crawled into bed and slept. Happy anniversary.

CHAPTER 14:

ANNIE SPRINKLE HAD THE FLU—HAPPY BIRTHDAY TO YOU

"For flavor, instant sex will never supersede the stuff you have to peel and cook."—Quentin Crisp

On a snowy February day in 1983, I got a call at my copywriting desk from a friend of Bob's, Richard, who said, "How would you like to make a hundred dollars on your lunch hour?"

Since it was just days before Aunt Judy's birthday, I was excited at the prospect of fast, easy cash. Planning a party for her, a hundred bucks would buy a lot of cannoli.

"What do I have to do?"

"Just use your voice...you know, 'that' voice—your breathy, flirty, answering-the-phone voice. Read some copy, and we'll cut you a check."

"This seems too easy—what do you really need?"

"Here's the full deal," he explained. "We're recording some 60-second spots advertising for phone sex. We need a hot sexy voice.

We were using porn actress Annie Sprinkle, but she's got a cold and can't come in. So I thought of you."

"Well thanks, I think," I added. "So you need a woman's sexy voice and you'll pay a hundred dollars."

"Yup, that's the deal."

"Can I bring a friend?"

"Sure, the more the merrier. Could you be here by noon?"

"I'll call you back in five minutes." I ended the call and speedily dialed my cousin Michelle, who worked four blocks from my office. If we could both make a hundred dollars on our lunch hour, then there'd be enough money for shrimp cocktails and champagne. My mission was clear.

Michelle and I met in the lobby of *High Society* magazine's publishing offices. We took the elevator up to the third floor and were directed to Richard's office. He walked us to a small recording studio down the hall, gave us scripts to read as we sat at a round table, with a bowl of ice cubes.

"What are the ice cubes for?"

"You'll see," he responded, ready to start the recording process. "We have a time crunch. We need to sweeten, edit and be on air by 3 p.m. today." Richard was very serious and no-nonsense about his work in the porn industry.

I read the script over. Then I read it aloud. Richard directed me on inflections and enthusiasm. I had to sound like a woman on the verge of an orgasm. I read it again. Michelle tried not to laugh or look at me. Laverne and Shirley go to smut world.

“You say, ‘oh baby,’ then you put a cube in your mouth, slurp, and make it sound like you're sucking a cock,” Richard said informatively, as if explaining how to assemble Swedish furniture. Following his directions, I tried not to snicker.

“Michelle, you try it now,” he instructed her to read and use the cubes. She sounded great. Richard smiled and began to blush. Her mock cock sucking warmed his heart. Richard paced the room, filled with new ideas, “Arlene, you read this part. Michelle, you read this.” We did. He recorded it and then played it back. We all listened. He liked it but wanted to refine it.

“Okay now, you two are twins. You're part of a threesome and then cut to this part in the script, then you moan, Arlene, and you suck cubes, Michelle, then you both breathe heavy.” Michelle and I did it just that way, two more times. Richard got the track he needed. He looked pleased. Then he said, “Since I used the two of you on the one recording, I can only cut a check for one fee. Should I cut two fifty dollar checks or one you can split later?”

“One check is fine. We're planning a birthday party. The money goes for food.”

“Okay. I'll make it out to cash but, Michelle, I'll need your phone number, in case I need you for another recording.” Richard left the room to cut a check.

Michelle and I just looked at each other. "What a hoot," she said. "Lucy and Ethel as sex sirens. After we leave here, I have a turkey sandwich and end-of-month billing. What a life."

Richard returned, check in hand. "Now, if you want to hear your vocal artistry, call 976-SUCK after three this afternoon. I hope you have a great party."

Michelle gave him her phone number. We walked back to our jobs, smiling, knowing we'd been voice vixens for the love of our Aunt Judy.

Back at the office I ate a quick sandwich at my desk. My fellow copywriter Paul was passing by my office. "Hey Paul," I called to him. "Guess what I did on my lunch hour? I had a madcap adventure." I told him about being a voice vixen, the cubes, and the moaning. "So after three today, call 976-SUCK." He smiled, walking to his desk. "Let me know what you think after you hear it."

At ten past three, I called the number and heard myself and Michelle, our cubes and moans. The voices sounded a little deeper, but overall it was good. Then I called Paul. "Did you call? Did you hear it? Come over and talk to me."

"I called three times and loved it. I can't stand up." Later, Paul came to my office. As a smile grazed his face, red flushed his cheeks. It was apparent to me that I was no longer a goofy co-worker to him. I was a sexy, interesting woman he wanted to know better. As soon as his eyes met mine he looked away and glanced at his hands, put his palms together and interlaced the fingers, slowly, sensuously, as if they were not fingers, but instead, a man and woman's arms and legs. I watched his hands' sensuous movements, my heart beat faster. "You know, I've always found you to be full of surprises. I've never met your husband, but I don't think he gets you."

Whoa. This was pretty unexpected, especially since Paul was young, tall and handsome, definitely not a sex-starved office nerd.

"My husband can be too adult and serious sometimes, but he tries." I changed the subject. "I have too much work to be having this conversation now."

"Lunch tomorrow?" Paul inquired. "My treat, to celebrate the new smut star." I tingled with surprise at how good it felt to experience a man's attention.

Later that night after dinner with Rupert, I dialed 976-SUCK, and as soon as it stopped ringing, I handed the phone to him saying, "It's for you." He listened intently; his eyebrows tightening and then relaxing. When the call was done, he handed the phone back to me as if it were a dirty diaper for me to wash.

"What did you think?" I asked, eager for his opinion, thinking he'd be amused.

It was awful. Why did you make me listen to that?" he groused.

"What made it awful?" I wanted descriptive and constructive criticism.

"It didn't feel real. It wasn't live."

"How do you know what's live or not?"

"I work in radio."

I now had to reveal why I was so interested in his opinion. "You didn't like it?" I waited for his eyes to meet mine. "It was me."

"What? What do you mean that was you? It didn't sound like you. What are you doing moaning and sucking on the phone? That's disgusting. How could YOU be so disgusting? Who knows about this? Why did you do this?"

"To make money for Aunt Judy's birthday party." Bewildered by Rupert's response, on the verge of confronting him, but fearful of his already angered state, I reluctantly retreated. It was obvious I couldn't talk about sex with my husband—ours, anyone else's, or even a phone fantasy. So I took comfort in the opportunity to excite thousands of strangers.

"Well, don't let it happen again. Is there any ice cream in the fridge?" he wandered off, disinterested.

Rupert seemed to have a discerning sensibility about phone sex, what sounded real or live. This was a new world to me. What did he know about phone sex?

#

As my husband's stomach grew, so did his ability to keep secrets from me. His other, secret self struck me as more interesting than the quiet, somber, sexless guy he brought home to snore next to me. I was determined to meet that other side.

I noticed suspicious withdrawals in the statements from our joint checking account. He took $100 from the cash machine for three consecutive days. When I asked how he spent three hundred dollars in three days, he snapped at me.

"I took cabs and ate lunch. Why are you probing me? I earned this money," he yelled loudly, wanting to make me feel wrong for asking. He succeeded. Asking him anything related to sex or money made me feel like I was punching myself in the face. I didn't ask him again. Instead, I asked my friends.

I noticed mysterious items on our monthly charge bills. One month there were three charges for $38 for "Creations and Things." I looked in the phonebook and saw a store on the other side of town by that name. When I called, I got a recording that just said leave a message. I called my friend Josie, because she lived around the corner from their address, and was an expert on jewelry and relationships.

"Josie, this may sound weird, but I'm having a problem with Rupert."

"What's up?"

"You know I liked him because the sex was great. Now that we're married, I'm a sexless idiot. I think he may be having sex…without me."

"You think he's cheating? What's going on? How can I help?"

"Well, I found three charges on his credit card, each for thirty-eight dollars, from a place called *Creations and Things.* It sounds like a jewelry store. I haven't received any jewelry. I think it's around the corner from you on 78th Street. Could you please visit the store for me?"

"Sure, I'll look into it," said Josie, reassuringly.

"If I haven't received any jewelry, do you think he's seducing someone and having an affair?" I asked, not prepared for an answer.

"He's not that suave. Let me check into it and I'll call you later."

Josie phoned that evening. First, there was no store at that address. Secondly, she'd asked her accountant about this suspicious charge. He knew the company well. Many of his clients had the same "store" on their bills. It was a phone sex company whose charges itemized on credit card statements as "gifts" so the expenses were not only discreet, but also tax deductible.

I was devastated and confused that in almost the eighth month of marriage, my newlywed husband—the sex stud of our courtship—was avoiding me, but had the time, energy and inclination for phone sex—three times. I didn't know if I wanted to throw up or gorge myself.

That night, I asked Rupert what the "Creations and Things" charges were. He said, "A jewelry store, for my friend Peter. He doesn't have a credit card but needed to send gifts to his girlfriend."

I called Josie, and told her, adding, "I know Peter just filed for bankruptcy and has no credit cards…"

"Rupert is slick. Did you tell him you know there's no store there?"

"I was too flabbergasted. He's got an answer for everything."

"How do you stand it?" Josie inquired.

"Sometimes I want to tie him up and throw dishes at him. I'm stunned; I don't even know what to do. It feels like a giant mystery. Once I solve it, things will fall into place." I felt certain.

"You really think that?"

"Why would someone insist on getting married and then ignore you?"

Josie spoke calmly and slowly, "This isn't a mystery novel. It's your life. The longer you try to fix something that's broken, the longer it will take to repair you."

"Is that your fortune cookie for today?"

"You joke when you're hurt. Let's look at this. Tell me his good qualities."

I had to think about it. "Um, he's…I want to say warm and sweet, but that's kinda faded. He teaches me about music. We're building a life together. We have dreams."

"Dreams die," she said faintly, as if it was as painful to say as to hear.

"This soon?" I volleyed back, in disbelief.

"What about love? Do you love him?" she asked, tenderly.

"I grew to love him." I reflected, warmly. "Especially after we got married. I brought a lot of hope to this marriage.

"What can I do to help you?"

"Tell me I'm not crazy, and I'm not a leper," I implored.

"Oh, sweetheart, of course you're not. Big hugs. Let's get together next week."

#

A few weeks later, I called her back "Hey Josie, it's your favorite asshole friend."

"Who? The list is so long," she giggled into the phone.

"You were right. I was in denial. Let me show my appreciation, take you to a movie." Pacing back and forth in my kitchen, I needed to get out of the house.

"Thanks for the offer, but there's no time for a movie. My boyfriend and I are going on a last-minute vacation in two days. How about coffee later today?"

That evening, Josie and I sat at a small table in the corner of Café Reggio in Greenwich Village, our hands warmed by steaming bowls of cappuccino.

"Where are you going on your vacation?" I asked, keen to learn what people in healthy relationships did on their time away together.

"The Bahamas. Just three days off, while he's touring. His band's at the hotel. I'm taking a bathing suit, suntan lotion, and diaphragm jelly."

"Still having lots of sex?"

"Yup."

"I remember sex," I mumbled, trying not to be too bitter.

"What does that mean?"

"You know. New job, life changes."

"So you're only having sex like once a week?"

"If only," I tossed off, gripping my cup to help contain my emotions.

"Every ten days? Every other weekend? Help me here." Josie sat tall, then leaned into me, intent on answers.

"No sex. Not since our wedding night," I mumbled, too embarrassed by my truth.

"You never told me this before. You only said you thought he was cheating."

"I was too embarrassed to tell you. It felt too weird. I thought if we could prove that he was sleeping with someone else it would explain his behavior."

"How is this possible? Did you marry a gay man?"

I suddenly felt small, kept my head down, really afraid to hear my own answers. "No, he's doing stuff, just not with me." Shame hardened my shoulders. My cup near empty, I clutched the water glass, for a sip. If only I could wash away what I'd said.

"This is alright with you?"

Still speaking softly, full of disgrace and stupidity. "No."

"How did this happen?" Josie threw her hands in the air. She was loud, animated and upset. "How did you let this happen?"

The more she emoted, the smaller and quieter I became. "You're the first person I've told. It just…time passed…then more time passed. I feel like my virginity grew back."

"That's not funny. Your husband is weird."

"Many women have it much worse. Do we need chocolate cake?"

We sipped coffee until the triple layer slice of chocolatey goodness arrived. The waitress brought two forks, but I did most of the eating: fork to plate to mouth over and over again, like locomotion. Josie grabbed the fork out of my hand and threw it on the floor.

"Stop, enough! You're angry upset and not doing anything about it. A chocolate-cake-a-thon is not a sexual substitute; it's a cry for help. Have you tried talking to your husband?"

My head was still down, embarrassed from face stuffing. "Yes. When I try to confront him, I'm told what's wrong with me. So I eat, and hope the next day will be better."

"That's no way to live," Josie fired back.

"Lots of women do it."

"Fat women. Is that your goal? You're too young for this."

"A good friend would be happy I got married." As soon as I said that I became more uncomfortable, wriggling back and forth in my chair.

"A good friend is more upset for you than you are." Josie exhaled, playing with the sugar cubes as if they were dice.

"I'm upset. My family wasn't very emotive. We didn't scream, we just overate."

"I don't get angry; I just eat a cake? What are you doing about this situation?"

"I'm doing things," I murmured, eyes welling up with tears.

"What things? The man needs a baseball bat to the side of his head. If it were me in a sexless relationship, I'd leave."

"You're not married. I made a commitment. I'm not ready to give up. I can fix this," I asserted, more hopeful with each statement.

"Do you love him?" she pressed.

"I thought he'd be a good husband. I'm learning to..."

"Maybe you should unlearn it." She countered, her eyes burrowing into me.

"How could you say that to me? He's my husband." I recoiled.

"I don't care that he's your husband. I care about you."

I twisted to relieve my tense neck, "I want to hold onto my marriage and work at it."

"If you need time to yourself, stay at my place while I'm away."

"Thanks, but we need more time together, not apart."

"Maybe a marriage counselor?"

"Nope. Not me, not yet. I'm not ready for therapy, trying to fix things myself. When I make a gigantic mess of it, then I'll seek help. Sipping in silence for a minute, compelled to defend my position, "Rupert loves me, hugs and kisses me, tells and shows me every day…just not with his dick."

"Deal killer for me!"

"Some women live in hovels, or abusive relationships. My cousin's husband hit her, until she miscarried. I'm better off than her. Tell me more about your vacation." I needed a breather from berating.

"Beach, cocktails, hotel sex…cozy time away. Maybe that's what you two need."

"He says he's tired all the time. We never had a real honeymoon. Maybe if we were away from work for more than a weekend we'd have hotel sex too."

"I hope so for your sake. Get this resolved. Stay away from cake. You need to get laid." She lifted her cup to toast me. "May we both have hotel sex…that's warm and wonderful. No, make that hot and fantastic."

CHAPTER 15:
HONEYMOON FROM HELL

"Getting married is a lot like getting into a tub of hot water. After you get used to it, it ain't so hot."—Minnie Pearl

Nine months into our marriage, my husband said, "Honey, I think it's time to take our honeymoon. I've been working so hard we haven't had a chance to be together, relax, and cuddle."

Did he say cuddle? That sounded like hope to me. Yearning for a lot more than cuddling, I took his interest in going on vacation as desire for me. Desperately wanting to get our marriage back on track, I believed 'Let's go on a honeymoon,' meant he was interested in rekindling too. Call me crazy, but that's usually what the words mean. My older, wiser self cringes at how trusting I was.

Before we got married, he'd promised me April in Paris. Now, this faraway dream was actually going to become a reality? It was too good to be true. Rupert's excitement over this trip thrilled me. So, still drinking my cocktail of hope, trust, and dreams, I let him make all the plans. Plans that burst my bubble before I could get truly excited—like insisting that even though we went to a lakeside community in

Massachusetts each weekend, our time away should not be in Paris, but at a lakeside community in Maine. "Are you freaking kidding me?" I would say to him now, or to any man who dared dangle something in front of me that I had been dreaming of only to yank it away.

It was many years and much therapy later, when I learned that men like him are like dictators meting out the worst punishments in mild mannered tones.

To make matters worse, he was adamant that the road trip include modest hotels that accommodated pets.

Hoping we'd be a duo, I felt upstaged by Peaches, the precocious pooch. "If Peaches and I were in a boat and the boat turned over, who would you save first?"

"I can't answer that."

I was appalled, "Why not? She isn't in the room!"

How did I get here again? Oh right, I was swept off my feet into—what?—a better life? This was another time when I saw the blinking red light and kept going, not valuing myself enough to jump off the cliff into a healthier place.

I faced the trip with hope and dread. Hope because we'd finally be together again. Dread because I already knew that on a vacation with lots of free time and few distractions, what little our relationship had left would disintegrate. I'd have to face the fact that I'd made a lifetime commitment to someone I barely liked.

I packed my bathing suit, casual clothes, some sexy lingerie and hopes for a romantic honeymoon. The day-long car trip began on one of the hottest days of the year. Four hours into the ride, the air conditioning died. We stopped every hour for Peaches to cool off and have a water break. Rupert's focus was clearly his dog. I was just the stranger along for the ride. Feeling like a talk show host with a monosyllabic guest, I tried to engage Rupert in conversation. Loneliness throbbed in me like a life-threatening tumor.

During the first eight hours of the ride, Rupert and I said ten words to each other. On the honeymoon from hell in a hot, locked car with a silent stranger, still trying to think positively, I remembered what every humorist from Mark Twain to Fran Leibowitz has said: tragedy plus time equals comedy. Soon this would be a funny story I'd share with my friends or tell onstage. So I told myself that I wasn't just having a bad experience; I was gathering new material.

A few hours later, we finally arrived at our destination on the coast of Maine. Energized, getting out of the hot car, I was glad to be somewhere, anywhere new and different, and to share the experience of a place my husband clearly loved. Parking a block from the restaurant, near the pier, he got out of the car and marveled at the clear sky, cerulean blue water, and peaceful, breathtaking views.

When I got out and looked around, I thought someone had played the cruelest joke on me. After twelve hours of driving, I was horrified to see that this patch of the coast of Maine looked just like the pier in Sheepshead Bay, Brooklyn, a place I visited every weekend of my childhood with my parents, ten minutes from our house. I felt as though he'd driven around the block a thousand times for the past twelve hours.

My eyes welled up with tears of disappointment. Rupert saw them as tears of joy and kissed my cheek.

"It's beautiful here, isn't it? Glad I could share it with you." He clumsily hugged me, taking my hand as we walked. The sun was setting, one of those picturesque sunsets, the kind that become souvenir postcards. Rupert suggested a walk along the water, then dinner before checking into our hotel. Pleased by his romantic plan, I anticipated a hearty meal to soothe my anxiety. Finally, after not speaking for hours, he was relaxing. Maybe he'd just been waiting to leave the city, maybe it would all be different now. There was a tree near the side of the restaurant. "See that beautiful tree. Let me take a picture of my pretty wife in front of it." He took the camera out of his pocket; I posed.

After picture snapping, my arms around his neck, I pecked his lips. "Thank you for taking me on an adventure. I'm glad to be on vacation with you." What a pleaser I was trying to be.

Rupert rhapsodized about the lobsters at a particular place, assuring me we'd have an excellent meal. Once we entered I noticed there were only six elderly patrons in the cavernous restaurant. The carpeting and walls looked like they'd seen better days—same with the diners. I saw one white-haired woman, shuffling with her walker from the restroom back to her table. The dining hall smelled like an assisted living facility. I'd gotten the sense that this place had peaked a decade ago; now everything about it was barely hanging on.

Our server, Angie, was so old I wanted to say to her, "Sit down, and let me get it." But she gleefully told us the seafood specials of the day, all of which seemed to be either cod or scrod, fried or smothered in cream sauce.

After hearing the choices, I looked at Rupert thinking, "Say the secret word, get us the great lobsters you've babbled about for hundreds of miles."

He turned to the waitress, "We were interested in lobster."

"Yes" I said. Finally, he'd rallied to the moment.

"I think we're out of lobster. It's such a tourist thing, ya know? Let me check." Angie waddled off, her sensible shoes squeaking on the worn carpet, no doubt her arthritis was flaring up with each step.

"It's a lobster restaurant; they can't be out of it," he protested, incredulous.

I saw this moment as a divine sign, dripping in symbolism—if only I could grasp all of it and burn it into my psyche as a painful life lesson. This may have been the first dinner of my honeymoon but it was really a surreal cinematic moment. I was in an Ingmar Bergman film, and I was the only one who wasn't speaking Swedish.

"We're out of lobster," Angie said, jolting me back.

"This is a lobster restaurant, you can't be out of it; there's got to be some back there— please check with the chef and manager,"

Rupert insisted, ever the newsman. Looking at me, he smiled a nervous smile, squeezing my hand. “I’ll get you your lobster, no matter what.”

“Is there another place down the street? There’s lots of restaurants here.”

“No we’ll eat here, it will be fine,” he said firmly. End of discussion.

“Why did we have to eat here?” I said to myself, knowing he was weirdly intent on it. Why would he want to?

Angie returned, almost exhausted from her journey to the back of the restaurant. “My apologies, sir,” she said accommodatingly. “We do have lobster, one lobster—it’s one of the smaller ones but I can serve it up with an extra side dish or free dessert. We have wonderful Nesselrode pie.”

Rupert seemed pleased and in control. “My wife will have the lobster. I’ll have the scrod with mushroom cream sauce,” he said, confidently. Taking both my hands, he gazed into my eyes. “You’re so pretty—I’m glad I married you.” Was this my prelude to seduction? Then he added, “You look a little tired, I’ll make sure you get to sleep early.”

“Thanks, daddy,” I thought to myself. Another sexless night. At least I’d be having a great dinner.

Rupert clearly enjoyed his entrée, which looked like a big glob of condensed soup on a cafeteria plate. I found this peculiar as he’d always had a discerning gourmet palette, especially when ordering in

French at French restaurants. For Rupert, a snobby Manhattanite and four-star restaurant connoisseur, how and why did this place measure up? I bet they didn't even have one star. If they did, it was probably covered in leftover gravy.

My bright red lobster tasted dry as if it had been overcooked or heated and reheated or had experienced some dreadful life even more tortured than mine in the last 5 minutes.

"Taste my lobster—it tastes bad," I said, trying not to sound like an ungrateful child. I fed him a forkful. He chewed and thought a second.

"It tastes fine to me," he said assuredly.

"May I taste yours?" I tasted his, a flavorless glop with a mushroom that looked like a fingernail. I wanted to spit. And I wanted to stand up and shout, "Okay. Where's the *Candid Camera*?!" Instead, I quietly ate only my vegetables, trying not to feel sour about being unable to eat the fish in a seafood restaurant on a pier in Maine. Rupert was only 36, older than me, but this felt like Sunday dinner with Grandpa—maybe because all the food was gray and easy to gum. Two more bites of lifeless vegetables, I wanted to slap my cheery self in the face. This was a nightmare, right? It had to be.

I told myself, "You survived the drive. Things can only get better. Remember, this is your honeymoon—a time for romance and enjoyment. Look for the good things; you'll find them." Ever young and hopeful, couldn't things get better?

Not likely—I was on the honeymoon from hell.

Where was the man about town who'd procured better seats than Aaron Copeland? I was out of the Ingmar Bergman film. I was now in *Rebecca* or *Gaslight,* it seemed my husband was doing things to make me think I was insane.

So distraught by our dinner, going to sleep early seemed like a good idea—shorten the long, crummy day. Tomorrow would be better; it had to be. As I put my head on the pillow, my demons whispered to me, "Has anyone ever committed suicide on their honeymoon?"

The next morning, I awoke to Rupert looking at me lovingly. Smiling, he stroked the hair out of my eyes and kissed my face, following with a lingering lip lock. Running his hand down the side of my body, I heard him moan. Kissing him, I rolled on top of him, heart pounding, anticipating. As soon as I'd positioned myself so that my pelvis was touching his, he withdrew from the kiss.

"We should go to breakfast now!"

"Let's take a few minutes," I cajoled, kissing his neck.

"Now, let's go now, before they stop serving," he insisted, gently pushing me off of him. "Start getting ready," he raced into the bathroom.

While he was in the bathroom, I grabbed the phone.

"Josie, I'm calling from the cootie-head honeymoon suite. It's still terrible like back home. I feel like a leper," I blurted, verging on tears. "I can't talk to him. So I called you. I'm whispering while he's in the shower."

"Oh my God, Arlene, I can't believe going away didn't help. I hoped you'd have hot hotel sex like we talked about."

"Me too." Pacing the room, clutching the phone, "I'm still hoping… it's going to happen."

Josie took a breath and then calmly offered, "It hasn't yet. You're really upset. Let's figure out what you're going to do."

"I'm planning on getting him drunk tonight."

"That's your best idea? Please get out of there. Just get a bus and come home. Stay with me if you want. Leave this bad situation."

"This is my honeymoon. Nobody quits their honeymoon."

"Arlene, I love you and want the best for you. Call me when you get back home. We'll figure it all out, okay? Don't worry."

As soon as I heard the shower water stop I hung up, dried my eyes, and threw on shorts and a shirt. Rupert exited the bathroom, towel draped around his waist, still desirable. I wondered how he felt about me. Other women would have a major confrontation, right now. And Josie—forget it. Why couldn't I?

The more he avoided sex, the more I avoided talking about why he avoided sex. As time wore on, and my pulsating blender of emotions whirled faster, I had become more afraid of knowing why. Plus, I was fearful of creating a fight that would have no end and no place to retreat to. I felt utterly trapped in the middle of Bumfuck, Maine. Being a city girl from New York, and not knowing how to drive, bit me in the ass yet again. I'd never wanted to drive more in my life than right then. Clearly things had to be coming to a head, but if I'd picked a fight, or even alluded to the obvious, there would be no neutral corners to run to. Trains, planes—none were near here. Besides that, who ditches their own honeymoon?

I was consumed, exhausted—paralyzed by fear, guilt, anger, and confusion. I hadn't known myself all that well going into this marriage, and I felt further away from myself now than I'd ever been. I was lost. I had no clue how to find my way out of this. And so, against all logic, and though I knew that I knew better, I defaulted into self-delusion, believing the unbelievable—clinging to the belief that by spending this time together we could fix everything, begin fresh, like everyone else did on their honeymoons, clinging to the worn out belief that, if I could just hang in, I'd get my marriage to resemble other people's normalcy.

I perceived myself as being without choice. It could have been one of my jokes, but it was my life. There had to be sunny side to my doom. I was certain of it.

"What are we doing today?" I asked.

"We'll walk along the water, and see the shops in town. By then it will be lunchtime. Maybe some light reading and a nap before dinner."

"When's shuffleboard?" I thought. My entire body was tense as a prize fighter's clenched fist. I paused for a deep exhale, hoping anger and frustration would melt away. Clearly not the honeymoon I'd envisioned at any point in my life, I decided I'd find enjoyment in little things. They were getting tinier every minute. Breathing deeply, I hoped each breath would cleanse me of my unattainable wants.

But he didn't tune into me, or want to. I had to face the fact that I was on my honeymoon with a senior citizen.

That afternoon we went into town, just a few blocks of shops selling quaint knickknacks and nautical memorabilia. Maybe I'd buy a souvenir for my dad. When we got to the first store I said to Rupert, "Let's go in."

"Why?"

"To see what they have," I explained.

"Nah, I don't want to."

"Come in with me. We'll be quick. Let's just see what they have."

"I'll wait outside for you."

Forging ahead, I entered the store, looked around quickly, and left within a minute or two. When I went outside, Rupert was leaning on a parked car, looking forlorn, then relieved to see me so soon.

"You okay?" I asked. "Let's keep moving," I took his hand, determined to make this a pleasant experience for at least one of us. We passed a store or two. Then we came upon a place that had soaps and perfume. "Come in with me. Maybe they'll have bubble bath. You like bubbles. We can take a bath together."

"No, you go in, I'll wait outside," he insisted.

"Why? Come in with me…they don't have dragons in there!" I pleaded.

"You go. I'll wait outside. I'm not into shopping."

There was nothing we wanted to do together. He didn't have that "go along to get along" compromise gene that helped other marriages endure. Instead of the unity and harmony I'd hoped would take seed, this trip was driving us further apart by the minute.

Later, walking along the water, I took Rupert's hand. "What are you thinking?"

"I'm just enjoying the beach."

Always trying to turn a sentence into a conversation, it felt like climbing a mountain. "What do you like about the beach?"

"The clouds, breeze and sand." He let go of my hand, and walked faster.

Panicking that I couldn't connect, "Anything else?" Boiling over with more effort than on a nightclub stage, with a bad audience, I thought of my desires as a dry, sandy beach where the waves would never wash over the sand.

Rupert stopped. "What are you looking for? What do you need?"

After such a long time, could I ever speak the words, 'Why haven't we had sex since our wedding night?' Plus, I'd held my hurts and inquiries in for so long, no answer could ever be enough. If I ever let it bubble up inside me and come out, my whole self would explode, a volcanic eruption. I said nothing. A series of choices that had seemed to make the most sense over the last several months had led me further and further from my own center—my core—where my voice dwelled, forgotten, utterly abandoned.

Rupert hugged me tightly and robotically, and said, "I want to sit on the beach and read newspapers. I'd love for you to join me."

The torture was complete.

I opted to nap in our room after crying myself to sleep. About an hour later I was awoken by Rupert's kisses. Dressing for dinner, I envisioned umbrella drinks, lots of umbrella drinks, ready for enough alcohol before, during, and after our meal to dull my pain and put my husband in the mood to touch me.

Dinner was at a place about ten minutes away. As soon as we'd arrived, he said, "See that bench? Let me take a picture of my pretty wife sitting on it."

Still edgy. "Your pretty wife? Can you call me by my name?"

"I was trying to be complimentary, honey."

"Honey is not my name either," I frowned.

Laughing, "Yes, Mrs. Santo."

"Call me Arlene." I posed, his camera clicked.

I had higher hopes for this restaurant than our lobster fiasco. When Rupert asked the maître-d about our reservation, they couldn't find it. I urged him to tip the guy. The uniformed man grabbed two menus, walked us towards the most picturesque part of the restaurant, then stopped short of the scenic tables because they were occupied. Rupert looked disappointed. I was relieved that this place seemed alive and from this century. We drank wine, both relaxed and laughing. So I took another stab at conversation.

"You know, I'll never forget the first time I met your mother."

"Why do you dredge up such bad memories?" He was upset.

"It was a good day for me."

"How is that possible? We saw her."

"That's the day I saw your portrait, in a suit and tie, holding a violin. Your "Save the children" sadness stole my heart. We'd both lost our childhoods to classical music, practicing our instruments at seven years old instead of playing with other kids. Seeing your childhood self, I knew we should be married."

Visibly surprised, he raised his glass, giggling. "That sounds happy. I toast my lovely, lively bride with my last few sips of wine."

Little did he know how I felt right then: If I stayed to help that sad boy, I might very likely be lost forever.

Just as I thought our meal was finished, and a check would arrive, instead, a waiter brought another dish, announcing, "Your chocolate soufflé."

I blurted immediately, "We didn't order that."

"Are you going to shoo him away, because you didn't order it? It took me three phone calls to arrange this. I wanted a sweet, perfect end to this meal, to please you."

My heart was full; the moment was perfect. I put my hand over my mouth to fight my tears, remembering the last soufflé on one of the best days of our relationship. Was that a lifetime ago? I picked up my spoon, dove in, offering Rupert the first bite. Smiling, he sighed with joy. If we ate slowly, how long could we savor this happiness?

After dinner, Rupert took more pictures of me near the water. Walking back to our room arm in arm, we entered kissing passionately. First, he pressed me up against the wall, then stumbling towards the bed—deep, fierce kisses. He undressed me. I undressed him. Passion percolated. In anticipation, as he removed the bedspread to pull back the blankets and reveal the cool crisp sheets, I bolted to the bathroom for a quick pee. When I returned two minutes later he was fast asleep and snoring. I tried to wake him, but he was out cold.

Working so hard and getting so little, I felt sad, mad, and boiling over with contained rage. "Fuck me," I mumbled, defeated, for leaving the room and missing my husband's heated 30 seconds of desire.

He may have stuffed me with chocolate, but that didn't quench my desires. Staring at him, snoring, I hoped he might stir, roll over and be conscious enough for slumber sex. Still out cold, studying him, feet poking out from under the sheets, I never noticed he had such long pinky toe nails, and a wreath of hair around his ankles, like hairy ankle bracelets. I walked to the other side of the bed, pulled the blankets back and slid under the sheets. After tucking myself in, I glanced at him—he was peaceful, oblivious to my pain. "Love me, please," I whispered.

As I lay on the bed next to him, I had a vision of myself. I saw a gutsy, fearless me leave my body, get out of the bed, walk over to Rupert's side, shake him, wake him, and slap him hard. Then she packed with the flurry of a tornado, bolted from the room, slamming the door. I exhaled. I knew I couldn't carry out any part of that decisive, self-satisfying fantasy. Continually mystified by his behavior, I hadn't sufficiently regarded the stark reality that, in trying to avoid rocking my marriage bed, I'd become this flat, passive, powerless creature. I didn't want to be with her—or him.

More than a crummy, lonely vacation, this was my belated honeymoon. I had to see it through, right?

Haunted by another recent honeymoon, three years earlier, I replayed how my parents' marriage had blown apart on their twenty-fifth anniversary/second honeymoon. Their venomous anger had shot out rat-a-tat-tatting with jarring cruelty, spraying bullet holes, shards shattering everywhere. The recounted bitter slaps of their hateful screams, "You bastard, I gave up everything for you and now I have nothing," still rung in my ears as if I had been there.

Terrified of ending my marriage the way Mom's truth killed hers, a single naked fact pierced my sensibilities—what she had said then and what I believed right now, were one and the same. The abruptness with which her harsh words had ended my parents' quarter of a century together left me shell-shocked. And the undeniable reality was that I now felt equally explosive. As if I were a hand grenade engraved "Queen of Bad Choices," I dreaded anything so much as the slightest misstep—one wrong move, one strong statement and my fury would be unleashed. My life would implode; I'd be broke, back in my Brooklyn studio, jobless, with a failed marriage…blown to a million pieces and alone.

More devastatingly, I'd be giving up—on the illusion, promise, and dreams of marriage, just like Mom. Letting go and getting out was about more than just the tangible stuff like money or property, which of course I had none of. No, I think what most women mean when they say they were left with nothing is that they had put aside their personal dreams and potential, who they wanted to be as an individual, for a marriage in which they invested their hope and their belief in promise of a better life. Then they saw all of those things wither and die—along with the promise of marriage, in which they had invested all that was left of themselves—all of it, gone—that's the gut twisting pain. They gambled on loving someone, and crapped out at the roulette wheel. All of their chips were taken away. They'd lost everything.

There was a piece of my heart that I had saved for marriage—the trusting, optimistic, budding flower—that never fully bloomed, that dried up and fell away once my marriage became too grim to be bearable. Over the years I have mourned its loss, knowing full well it won't grow back. In hindsight was I repeating a pattern? Rupert was so unavailable emotionally, maybe I was used to that from growing up with Mom. Perhaps her aloofness mirrored his initial charms and endearing qualities. Instead of seeing our patterns (or our parents), we just keep repeating them. Of course, I couldn't see that then. I only saw my fears.

If I ended it and walked away, I'd be alone with me, myself and I, hardly a dinner party. At the time, I didn't realize the opportunities this might present.

I remembered an afternoon sitting with Mom after her divorce, and her telling me, "I dream about your father three nights a week."

"What happens in the dreams?"

"He puts his arms around me and says he misses me."

This was one of the saddest things I'd ever heard. "Do you miss him?"

"I thought I'd have a new life, be happier. I traded in one kind of unhappiness for another. Let's change the subject. Got any coffee?"

I'd already had the unhappy and alone life. I didn't want to revisit it, smell it, or think about it. Fear burned through my veins like spilling hot coffee on the inside of my skin. Shuddering from my own immobility, it most certainly was me who had gagged, bound and imprisoned myself. Yet, realizing this, I didn't know how to undo the damage.

The honeymoon from hell, nothing more or less than a metaphor for what life had become, could not end fast enough. The following days were dull and uneventful, like an old oil painting in an aging dentist's office. A few more days of dashed expectations, mediocre meals and spectacular sunsets, we got back in the car and headed home.

All I really had to remember from the trip was a roll of corny photos that I'd developed the day after we returned home. Most of the pictures were of me in front of places or things. There were two photos of Rupert in front of boats. No photographs of us together.

CHAPTER 16:

THE BOY WITH BLUE EYES

"Inner beauty won't get you laid."—the magnet on my refrigerator

As soon as we were back in the city, I was back to work. Feeling unwanted at home, work was quite the opposite situation. Still the solo woman in creative, my cubicle next to the men's room, I was bombarded with male attention. Although I'd been at the ad agency three months, I still remembered the first time I had met Paul Patterson. He dragged his confidence around like a hunter with a bear skin he seemed to own. His piercingly light blue eyes shot through me like a cannonball imploding deep inside. Looking into his eyes in that moment of our first meeting, I saw the movie trailer for our entire relationship—we'd become friends, then best of friends, then intimate confidantes, then it would turn sour, then ugly.

I shook his hand anyway.

We started out as equal copywriters, in spite of my having three years more agency experience. I was the only woman in the creative department who wasn't in a secretarial or bookkeeping capacity.

Younger, taller and breathtakingly handsome, Paul's curly dark hair and beard framed his twinkling eyes. No one could say no to those eyes. Shortly after we began working there, he asked for a new title and raise and got them both. He became senior copywriter and my superior. I teased him that he was now "on top of me."

He flashed me a smile and a low, lingering laugh.

I never thought he paid attention to me until my time as a phone sex voice vixen. After that day, a month prior to my honeymoon, we ate lunch together almost every day. Nights when Rupert worked late and I was winding down before bed, Paul called, lingering on the phone for hours, the two of us sharing our deepest secrets, pillow talk in the dark. This was the intimate relationship I longed for, the one I'd wanted with Rupert. When I thought about it, I realized I was having my own form of phone sex; only mine involved real emotions and desires with a person I knew.

One snowy weekend when Rupert went to the Berkshires without me, Paul had a birthday party at his place. There were 40 people between work, his old job and college who stopped by to celebrate. During the party I talked, danced and drank. Time flew. I chose not to notice that the last guests had said their goodbyes.

By 2:30 a.m. Paul and I were alone. I offered to help clean up. We took stray glasses and plates to the kitchen. At one point we bumped into each other. First there was a nervous laugh, then a heated glance that melted into a clumsy yet passionate kiss, both overwhelmed by the night, the booze and the moment against the backdrop of our daily lunches and nightly phone calls—it had been coming to this. Strong, decisive, and desiringly, he carried me to a gigantic armchair and propped me on his lap without losing a second of lip lock. So parched for the heat of this moment, my heart and body melted into it. Simultaneously, my mind—my censor—fiercely interrupted, "Hey, what's going on? You're married, and this isn't your husband!" Feeling breathless with passion and desire, I pulled my lips away from Paul's to gasp for air. Placing my palm on his chest, I thought his powerfully palpitating heart would burst out and slam into my hand as if it were a fly ball hurling into a fielder's mitt.

"Is it hot in here or is it me?" I smirked at the cliché.

"It's us." He claimed his moment, kissing me again, harder, holding me tighter, groping with desire to rip deep inside me. His body felt so strong, hot and muscular. The instant was electric, until I short-circuited.

"Don't you think we should stop?" I questioned, half-heartedly.

"Or move to the bedroom," he breathed into my ear. "I've never done anything like this with a married woman before." He rubbed the wedding band on my finger, as if he could erase it.

For me, the mature, married woman, it was my moment to take charge. "It's late. I should go. Walk me out to catch a cab."

He stopped kissing me as if doused by a bucket of cold water, angry the flame was extinguished. I stood, straightening my clothes. The elevator ride was an eternity of silence. We walked into the clammy night air. It was raining, hard. We stood under the building's green awning. All cabs were occupied. The harder the rain, the fewer cabs we saw. We spent a half hour watching the traffic. Finally, a cab arrived. As Paul held the door for me, our eyes met. We were both rain drenched. How would I face this man on Monday morning? How would I face my husband on Sunday night?

#

When I was at work, I tried not to think about my marriage. But I couldn't stop thinking about sex: how to have it (with my husband?), who to have it with—Paul? Paul was desirable, within my grasp—and he desired me.

"Here's the Rolex headlines for that display ad." Every time I brought a sheet of copy to his desk for review, the heat between us could have ignited the page. Our eyes met in heated agreement, then glancing away, regaining composure. Lunchtimes arrived, and neither one checked in with the other. Our daily habit faded without a word.

Paul asked for another promotion at work. They gave it to him. Since our bosses needed extra money to pay him, they axed me. The man who was an irritant in my crumbling marriage had also inadvertently screwed up my work life. Yet, I still found him irresistible. So, though distraught at the prospect of being unemployed, I was relieved to be out of the ad agency and away from my daily temptation. I turned my attention to tackling the prospect of looking for a new job as a copywriter, and to do this I needed to assemble a portfolio of writing samples hidden away in unmarked boxes, and scattered in closets all over the house.

I took them out one by one and lined them up, over the weekend when Rupert was away, I opened them all up, using a giant kitchen knife to break through the crisscrossed bands of tape. I poured myself a grand goblet of Cabernet to help ease the hours of search and discovery.

Slitting the top of each box, pulling the flaps open, some of the contents weren't familiar. These were books and papers belonging to Rupert. Hmmm...This was search and discovery—I wondered what kinds of things he kept in his boxes? Glass of wine in hand, my curiosity sought satisfaction—maybe I'd learn more about him.

I dug deep into the first box, finding several pairs of old eyeglasses, dusty and oily along the sides of the frames, cigarette holders and pipes still smelling from tobacco, and a small velvet box that held cufflinks. Evidence suggested these had belonged to Rupert's late father. I thought keeping the glasses was a little creepy but overall, saving these mementos was understandable.

Beneath these items was a group of legal folders held together by a rubber band. Inside were copies of letters—the correspondence of the two lawyers who handled the divorce of Rupert's parents. I read the letters, riveted by bitter accusations from both sides. His mother's attorney said Mr. Santo was, "A cold, unfeeling man; ungrateful to have a wife and child." Mr. Santo's attorney said, "For more than 20 years his wife berated him daily, reminding him that he owed his very life to her and her father." It seemed that at the beginning of World War II the Santos were able to flee Hitler-occupied Europe because Mrs. Santo's father was the leading rabbi in their town. He'd used influence and cash to get immigration papers for the newlyweds, who would have otherwise gone to concentration camps and died with everyone else. Blown away by this revelation, I sat on the floor and took a hard swallow of my wine.

Rupert grew up in a house where parents bickered about life and death issues. His mother said to his father every day, "You owe your life to me." How could love flourish in that home? I felt sad for Rupert's boyhood. I carefully put everything back into the box and resealed it, glad to be putting those bitter memories away.

I was aware that I was violating his privacy, picking at his personal effects like a desperate mouse. The polite me knew I should just search my own belongings. But a pent up, blazing need for discovery coursed through my veins. Who was Rupert? Why did a cold, distant man save all of these emotionally wounding mementos? I dug my hands even deeper into the next box, finding more letters—from Rupert's first wife's divorce lawyer.

Fascinated by the disclosures, it seems he had promised her Paris too, but never delivered. Their reason for divorce was "constructive abandonment." I thought this meant that one partner had to leave the other before violence would overtake them. I went to the living room and looked up "constructive abandonment" in the dictionary. It meant failure to have sex. So his ex-wife also had no Parisian honeymoon and no sex.

Back in the box, I found another folder of letters, handwritten on BBS stationery. These were from his secretary, the one who was taken away in a strait jacket. She wrote of Rupert's unfulfilled promises to spend the night with her after hours of torrid lovemaking. One line was especially disturbing: "If you won't stop living in Doreen's apartment and move in with me, I may try to kill myself or both of us."

Torn between closing the boxes and ripping the cardboard apart with my bare hands, I continued; raging to learn more about the promiscuous pack rat I'd married. I found love letters from seemingly geeky women in high school and college: pages and pages from different girls, pouring out their hearts, all enthralled to the point of addiction to my Rupert.

So there it was—he had fucked everybody stupid—too stupid to see they'd been fucked over. At least I wasn't alone. There was an entire club, a harem of awkward girls. Had he fucked every woman who wore eyeglasses?

Next, I pulled out a glossy green leather album, sticky and sweet smelling. "Good," I thought, "a photo album!" I'd get to see some of his friends and their dates. Opening the album, I thought at first it was pictures of college graduation. Groups of 22-year olds were smiling. I noticed Rupert's friend Barbara was in a few of the photos. We'd just had dinner with her last week. The girls in the pictures wore miniskirts, and the boys had on bell-bottoms David Cassidy would've been proud to wear. Then the last photo sent a shivering stab to my heart: it was a man's hand and a woman's hand. They were both wearing wedding bands. The hands were entwined in front of a wedding cake. A wedding cake?! This was a wedding album! This was a wedding album for a wedding I'd never heard anything about. Some papers fell out, letters from the bride. She wrote "Dear Rupert, I am delighted we are marrying. I'm looking forward to our trip to Paris." Who was *this* woman? Who was Rupert?!

"I can't believe this!" I blurted out loud. "Fuck! Fuck!" I stood up and jumped around the room, hoping the bouncing would prevent my racing heart from leaping out of my chest. Feeling dizzy, I crouched back on the floor. I was on fire to reread these letters, to assemble a timeline from the dates and postmarks on the envelopes. The woman he told me was his first wife, Audrey, was really the second wife. The first wife, Cynthia, was someone he'd mentioned as "just a girlfriend." Nobody ever went to Paris. Divorced, nobody lived happily ever after!

As if I hadn't seen enough, I found another album, this one of honeymoon photos from *their* trip to Maine. The pictures were mainly of her, wife number one, plain and schoolmarm looking, without a spot of make-up. They would have seemed like normal, ordinary photos to anyone but me. To me, they were exact replicas of the same photos we had taken on our recent mockery of a honeymoon.

She was poised in front of the exact tree at the same restaurant as I was. Every photo was painfully familiar to mine; even the one where she coyly looked over her shoulder with a swizzle stick in her mouth. Had he actually posed me for pictures to echo the trip with his first wife? How rude and insulting. And how creepy.

Rupert had created a déjà vu honeymoon. I wondered if he could even tell the difference between one woman and another. Perhaps we were just one long continuation of the same concerto, with Rupert as conductor, the ongoing opus melodious only to him.

Oh shit, oh no! Each revelation was more jarring than the last, I trembled, feeling beaten, pummeled with crushing blows from the inside out, ill-equipped to fight back. I cried, one of those terrible, heartbroken cries that turned to a shoulder shuddering weep. Tears and otherworldly wailing, my pain had unleashed itself, heralding its arrival with the moans of a caged animal. As someone who rarely felt her feelings, it was as if my body cashed in a 25-year savings bond of pain and emotions, all due that very minute.

Exhausted and overwrought, I needed to compose myself. After the weekend, the stranger in these boxes would be sharing a bed with me. Frightened by how truly damaged my husband was, this knowledge had changed my ability to trust. Yet if he knew what I'd done, his berating of me would be unbearable. Shocked by the history, mysteries and evidence, I gulped down the wine.

It was now after midnight. I had to reach out to someone. Josie was probably entertaining her boyfriend. She'd be annoyed. Calling

Bob, there would be a wise-cracking "I told you so," leaving me feeling angry and stupid. So, like an idiot, I called my mother in Florida.

"Ma, you're not going to believe this," I blurted, not even saying hello or apologizing for waking her up. "I'm not the second wife. I'm the third…I think."

"What are you talking about?" she asked, half asleep.

"I found a wedding album from a marriage I'd known nothing about, his first marriage. The woman he told me was his first wife was really his second."

"Oh shit." She was awake now. "I can't believe you found a crappy husband too. I thought you'd do better than me. We both find the worst men."

How had she turned this around to her? Clearly I made a bad call…again. "Mom, I'm gonna go. Everything's a mess here." I hung up the phone, smashed my wine glass against the wall and crawled into bed.

The next morning, I put everything back in the closet. I cleaned up the broken glass. Now all I had to do was find answers for my broken life. I called Rupert's friend Barbara, hoping she'd tell me about the wedding. I dialed, then hung up. Would she be honest with me? Did I dare ask her these painful questions? I dialed again. After lots of rings, I wanted to hang up, but she finally answered.

"Hello, Barbara. I'm sorry to bother you, but it's a bit of an emergency. I noticed you were in a photo album of Rupert's from right after college. Was that Rupert's first wedding? He told me he had only been married once before."

"Oh dear, I'm so sorry," I could feel her sympathy through the phone. "Yes, he was married twice before. Make him tell you everything."

"How do I begin?" I felt helpless.

"Sit him down and ask him. Talk to your husband," she said soothingly.

I decided that when he returned that night I'd invite him to lunch the following day. In a public place, I'd confront him. What could possibly happen?

I was tense at lunch, determined not to waver from my agenda.

"How's your salad?" I asked. He nodded. "How many times have you been married before?" I asked in the same tone.

"What do you mean?" He put his fork down.

"How many times have you been married before? It's a simple question that has a numerical answer," I responded coolly.

"Why do you need to know?" he insisted.

"Because you're my husband." I tried to remain calm.

"How many times do you think I've been married?"

"Obviously, more than you've told me," I added, a bitter lilt to my voice.

"Well, that's ridiculous. Where'd you get your information?"

"Barbara told me."

He was furious, "Now you're harassing my friends? How dare you."

"How dare you lie to me!" I felt a bolt of strength race through me.

"I didn't think it was important," he calmed and backpedaled.

"A marriage is an important chapter in your life. You're a newsman. Who edits your life?" I volleyed back.

"I didn't think it was important. Like an abortion," he said, calmly.

"An abortion is important to tell someone about. I've never had one."

"Well, now that we've played 20 questions, I have a meeting to go to," he placed a twenty-dollar bill on the table and stood up. "Have a nice day."

Before I could say another word, he was gone. I felt numb. As for me, alone in the restaurant, I finished my salad. Then I finished *Rupert's* salad. *I don't get angry; I just inhale a table full of food.* With each bite, I pondered my future, vowing to leave him as soon as I had enough money. How could I live with a sick evil stranger until then?

I may not have known what to do, but I quickly learned what to look for. My newsman revered research and facts. I was determined to find enough incriminating info that he'd have to be honest with me.

A few weeks later, Rupert took a new job as Entertainment Editor at the *New York Daily News*, working 9-5. Soon, he worked late and wouldn't call, showing up three hours late, wilted and tired. Other times, he'd call, saying he had to stay overtime. On those nights, he came home at the end of a 12-hour workday smelling freshly showered.

Whenever he'd arrive home, I'd race to hug him, and gently rub my nose along the side of his neck. He thought I was being the loving wife. But I'd become a suspicious wife. No longer the naive newlywed, a trained scent detective, if he reeked of sweat and stale cigarettes, I knew he'd really worked overtime, side by side with his coworkers.

Yes, people could still smoke in their offices, at their desks. After all, it was 1983; people had ashtrays on their desks and cocktails on their lunch hours. Creatives and especially newsmen lunched at bars, the three-martini lunch or two beers was standard. Popular near where we both worked was a restaurant chain, Beefsteak Charlie's, offering an all-you-can-eat salad bar as well as unlimited beer, wine, or sangria. So, if he smelled freshly washed and deodorized, instead of like an earthy newsman, I knew he'd had a hard day and a hard-on with someone else.

I really had to say something. When he'd hurriedly call from the office, I'd clumsily ask about news stories he was working on. He'd ignore me. When I tried to confront him and ask if he was really still at work all this time, he'd berate me.

"If you had more interests in your own life, you wouldn't have to run around like a hawk watching me. Get a life and stop harassing me," he'd demand.

Shaken speechless, if we were just dating, I'd end it. Taking my marriage vows seriously, that "for better or worse" clause twisted in my guts. I told myself this was newlywed adjustment. Dog paddling in a sea of uncertainty, afraid of drowning in naivety, I hoped it was true.

I spent too much time alone, which no doubt fueled my fixations. The relationship with Josie, my supportive pal, was feeling the strain. "Our time together is never about you, or fun or comedy. Rupert is the topic: complaining, confusion, sadness. I need to drink after seeing you rather than with you. He's got problems, and you're getting sick obsessing about him."

She was right, but I didn't want to see it. I begged Josie to be patient. Soon I'd become my old self, the friend she enjoyed. Even Bob was tired of my complaints.

No longer trusting Rupert about anything, I thought I'd feel better if I stayed a step *ahead* of him. So each month, when charge bills arrived in the mail, I steamed them open, made note of the "mysterious" charges and then glued them shut. I had high hopes that whatever he was doing had stopped. I was usually wrong, and bitterly disappointed. Mad and ashamed by my own behavior, I placed the perfectly resealed envelopes in the pile with the other bills. I stuffed my emotions down with bubble gum, chewing hard to offset the rages eating away at me, followed by blowing and bursting giant bubbles.

Hundreds of dollars, practically the equivalent of my salary, was going towards mysterious charges that were somehow sexually related. None of this looked like the expenditures of cheating: charges to jewelry stores, restaurants I'd never been to, expenses for a girlfriend or a hotel room. Instead, the bills included lumber and plumbing supply companies and car repairs for cities nowhere near our home.

As new deceits surfaced each day, I'd developed an overwhelming self-hatred. Every time I'd sneak, snoop or try to catch him at his game, I learned new things that I didn't really understand which only made me loathe myself more.

One afternoon I turned on the television, to lose myself in a talk show. Phil Donahue was on, the white-haired, paternal caretaker of the self-evolving woman. The theme of this day's show was "sexual addiction"—something I'd never heard of before. The panel included experts and married couples. They shared incidents and experiences; many were identical to my own. By the end of the show, I realized my husband wasn't screwing around. He was sick; he had a *disease*—a disease that made him plough through too many dollars for sex with strangers, unable to rouse interest in sex with me.

This was one of those times when television could reach out and change a life. I felt so comforted that my problem had a name and that there were experts and books that were addressing it. I was no longer alone, crying in my bedroom.

Shocked by this revelation; I called Josie and told her about it. She said, "Confront Rupert. Give him an ultimatum."

My husband adored high drama in opera, but not at home. I knew confrontation was not the answer, not now. All I needed to do was become an expert on my husband's illness. So my new obsession became his sexual addiction. Fueled with caffeinated lunacy, I made it my mission to learn everything possible about sexual addiction. I studied as if my life depended upon it. Before I was married, I went to the gym, I saw my friends, and I saw movies. I had goals. I worked at building a career as a comedian.

Now my spare time was spent unraveling my spouse's demons. His spare time was spent healing his self-loathing with fucking. Each of us was swirling in a hellish whirlpool. In learning about his illness, I saw that this pattern of behavior began in his childhood, thrived in his twenties and thirties and continued for many years before he'd even met me. This knowledge helped me. But I still cried myself to sleep each night knowing his double life was tearing our marriage apart.

Why didn't I leave? Mom's past, and my fears of a lonely future, without hope that I'd be happier later on, all kept me frozen in my discomfort. When my friends called the house while Rupert was home they'd ask, "Are you alright? Your voice sounds like you have a gun held to your head."

One night Rupert called from work and said he and another writer were working on a special edition issue. He'd be home around midnight; could I please give Peaches her evening walk. Special edition, my ass. I knew he was going out to feed his addiction. So I went out to feed mine.

I hated going to nightclubs alone, but that evening it burned too much to stay home. I called Josie to meet me later that night. After more than a month away from comedy stages, I ached to touch a microphone and see an audience. My house echoed with emptiness, as I lined my lips in toasty coral with a fine sable brush, filled them in with color, and then gloss. Things sound much funnier coming from bright, pretty lips. My hair was styled in a Veronica Lake do, highlights glowed a coppery red. I grabbed my grey trench coat from the closet, tossed it on and tied the belt. I slammed the front door locked and floated on the plush mocha carpeting to the elevator. I smelled brisket and broiled potatoes wafting from an apartment on my way down the hallway, making my mouth water. Jabbing the elevator button with my finger, I was on the prowl. I hoped the elevator would be empty, as I hated neighborly small talk. The doors opened 20 floors later. I slunk past the doorman.

"Good evening, Mrs. Santo." (But I knew he meant "Out again tonight without your husband, Mrs. Santo? Sure you're really married to Mr. Santo?")

Putting my collar up, hands in my pockets, I walked from 85th and Park Avenue to 3rdAvenue, for the downtown bus to 31st Street, strolling past limousines and uniformed doormen walking tiny poodles, while old hippies padded down the street with scruffy mutts. After the half hour ride, the bus stopped on the same block as the club; I got off, straightened my hair, and checked my teeth for stray lip gloss.

Good Times was a dark, smoky, underworld of a comedy club, where dishes clattered, and conversations ping-ponged over the performers. The dim lighting and faceless strangers made me feel even lonelier. I shook hands with the MC, then the bartender. He offered to take my coat and give me my "usual."

Clutching the stem of my white wine, I gulped, and looked around the room. I walked to the stage and grabbed the microphone.

Forty people in the audience, savvy New Yorkers in their 20's and 30's, I only saw the faces of the six people at the table up front, Wall Street types of mixed races. They smiled as if cheering me on. I wanted to win, for them. The one person I could see clearly was me, in the full-length mirror on the back wall. Looking good…and thin…tonight. I hope I'm funny.

"My husband's a newsman, for the New York Daily News. So whenever you use the newspaper for your dog's poop-scooping, know you have my bread and butter in your hands…Ya know, my husband is so neat, he hangs up his pants during sex. He's kinky and immature. He wears rubber underwear…with Smurfs on them. He's so into anonymous sex, he thinks sex with a partner is a group experience."

One Indian woman at the front table laughed, but everyone else just stared at me. My ten-minute set was agony. I sighed deeply, like the few seconds before a dentist's drill. My heart pounded, forehead damp, mouth dry. I mumbled "Thank you, enjoy the rest of the show," as I fumbled the microphone back into its stand. I crept away from the stage, head down, wishing the floor would swallow me up.

Josie, my support system was sitting at a back table. She raced to my side as soon as I left the stage. I gulped the rest of my wine, put the empty glass on the bar, and retrieved my coat, barely making eye contact with the bartender. Josie and I left the club walking briskly in the midnight silence.

"Glad you're back onstage. I know it makes you happy." I heard her say.

"Bombing is not happy." I exhaled, still feeling stressed.

"A microphone in your hand is a high for you."

"Why did I bomb instead of getting a standing ovation?"

"Cause all of your jokes are about that asshole you can't confront. Stop obsessing. Come back from the dark side and write jokes about people in the real world. Then you'll be funny."

"I'd rather be killing than bombing," I insisted.

"It all seems so angry and destructive if you win or lose."

"Yup," I snapped back, still walking at a brisk pace, mad at myself.

"Like divorce," she fired back.

I stopped walking and stood frozen, as if the "D" word splashed me with a bucket of ice water, immobilizing me. Josie and I had piercing eye contact.

"It was very kind of you to come out tonight. Thank you. I'm not thinking about divorce. I just got married."

"People make mistakes. You married with insufficient information. Now you know more." Ouch, that stung. My feet pounded the pavement. The faster I walked, the more she talked. I knew it was all constructive, but painful to hear. "You thought those jokes were funny? Only to you. A nightclub stage is not a place for your therapy sessions. You want someone to talk to, pay a shrink. Your husband pays for people to open your door, clean your house, park your car, blow him…you can pay a therapist to talk to you."

"I know you're right. I'm just on overload tonight." It hurt to smile.

"I love you. I only want the best for you. When you're happier, you'll feel funnier and be funnier too." With that, Josie hailed a cab. I wanted to walk further, so I kissed her goodnight, closed the cab door and sent her on her way.

I walked a block or two. "Aaaaaah," I screamed at the black sky, verging on tears.

Then I remembered. "I can go meet my friend Pizza!" Pizza was spicy and cheesy and always happy to see me. Each slice, with its big pointy triangle-shaped tongue, kissed me hello like a horny teenage boy. That first steamy bite was rapture. I may have died onstage, but I came to life with the thought of hot pizza, fresh from the oven, engulfing my mouth. Did I dare cater to my midnight whim? Hell, Rupert catered to his whims with paid pussy. All I wanted was hot pizza. Just one slice would not do it, however. Decadent bitch, I bought an entire pie, carried the large flat box with both hands, gracefully, as if presenting a tiara to a queen. Finally, home, in my kitchen, I opened the lid and let the hypnotic aroma of hot dough and oregano waft towards my nose. Yum. I closed the box.

I went into the bedroom and took off all of my clothes. I walked back into the kitchen, grabbed the box with one hand, paper towels in the other, (in case I spilled food anywhere) and a diet coke can nestled in my arm. I glided to the living room, exhilarated with anticipation. Sitting cross-legged on our beige Berber rug, facing the pie, I popped the top of the soda can. Diving into that first slice, like ripping the blankets away from a hot lover, revealing their naked passion. I gorged on the next slice, moaning to myself as ecstasy overtook my taste buds. I inhaled slice three, nibbled through four and five, while I gazed out at the Manhattan skyline, hoping it would speak to me, imparting wisdom.

After six cheesy, dripping slices, when my gut ached, I knew I was fed up and full. I'd swallowed all of my emotions and chewed all of my crust. I grabbed an afghan from the side of the couch and curled up on the floor, caressing my empty soda can, like a Bowery bum after a bottle of whiskey.

#

I found a job shortly thereafter writing catalogs and brochures for the *Girl Scouts of the U.S.A.* After two weeks, I knew the difference between a badge and a patch. A low pressure, low visibility job with few challenges, I had lots of time for personal phone calls and other diversions. Most days I spoke to seductive Paul from the ad agency on the phone. Usually, that was the highlight of my day.

Now, when the weekends came, Rupert didn't mind Massachusetts alone. We welcomed our time apart. For me, weekends in the city, dressed in a trench coat and jeans, the New York City Greta Garbo like uniform of invisibility. I was going to the movies or museums, usually alone. But I was doing things I enjoyed, instead of being arm candy for a guy who read newspapers all day long and only wanted me for an hour or two of restaurant interaction when dining with his snobby classical music friends. A new job, coupled with more autonomy made my life seem manageable.

One Friday night, when I was home alone, Paul called me, breathy and full of daring double entendres. I was needy for flirtatious male companionship.

"Come on over," he pleaded over the phone.

"No, it's late."

"Late for what?" he smirked. "Now you're a girl scout, a goody goody."

"What does that mean?"

"You wouldn't dare come over here and try to seduce me!" he challenged.

"Are you saying you want to be seduced? Is that a dare?"

"I know you've been banking all of your sexual energy. It's time for a transaction…some deposits and withdrawals. You know I give good interest."

Cabbing to Paul's place, I showed up in sexy knee-high boots and a trench coat. For whimsical effect, I wore only a bra and panties underneath, in official Girl Scout green. My mission was to feel admired, feel sexy, feel something…

Thrilled that I'd arrived, dressed like a fantasy, Paul whipped off my coat. He undressed like a man whose clothes were on fire, then jumped on me like a superhero, ready to save me—groping and wrestling with passionate urgency. Heavy breathing, the heat, his and mine, moist skin, deep kisses, as if we had a minute to live. Touching, groping, skin to skin, immediate and electric. Then, like a blaze doused by a giant fire hose, he came in my hand, leaving me wet and disappointed as he exited into the bathroom, embarrassed.

What just happened? I questioned myself, as if I'd dozed in a movie theater and snoozed through an explosion. Did this count as lust, sex or stupidity? Curled up on my side, I heaved a long sigh. What did I do wrong? Here? Again? Am I some kind of ironic superhero who makes men's dicks shrivel and shrink? My adulterous sexploit turned out to be a frustrating joke, just like my marital relations. Would a convent take a Jewish girl?

CHAPTER 17:

THE SINGING DETECTIVE

"Being with a jerky guy is like having a piece of food caught in your teeth. Everyone notices it before you do. —Livia Squires

Finding more deceit every day, like phone sex bills and other charges, ate away at my insides. Instead of addressing the issues, I snapped at my husband about other, small, insignificant things. I'd gripe in loud tones about chicken bones hanging out of the garbage pail or newspapers strewn around the living room. This seemed easier and kinder than screaming, "What are you doing with your dick? Why aren't you doing it with me?"

I realize looking back, my behavior made me seem crazier than him. Why was I so afraid to be unkind to Rupert? This is what the Rupertification of Arlene looked like. I was playing my role in our co-dependency addiction gavotte.

As our life disintegrated, I grew to hate myself. Yet I couldn't just walk out, like my life was a movie theater where the film just didn't captivate me. This was my marriage; I gave it everything I had. I didn't want to be seen as a failure as a wife, to others, or to myself.

Of course now, I realize I overstayed after that very first month.

This was the era before Google and cyber-sleuthing, or any other kind of computer searching that has since become commonplace. A friend who worked on Wall Street told me she knew a private investigator who could help me learn the things I just didn't have the ingenuity to find out, like what Rupert was really up to, where all the money was disappearing to, as well as what and where were all of Rupert's assets—this marriage wasn't working.

One day, I told my supervisor at Girl Scouts that I had a dental appointment, then left work early to meet with the private investigator. I'd never known anyone who'd done anything like this, except in movies. I felt like Mary Astor in a Sam Spade film or Faye Dunaway in *Chinatown*. Keeping with that motif, I wore my trench coat and dark red lipstick, thinking I should be wearing a hat, with a black-netted veil that covered my face.

As I sat on the crosstown bus I looked at the other passengers, wondering if any of them could even imagine that I was en route to visit a detective to track down the wily ways of my wormy, wandering husband.

When I got off the bus, I walked down a less than busy street to an older brick building. Inside there were long dark hallways just like in the film noir in my mind. I found a smoky glass door, pressed the buzzer and entered. There I was greeted by a buxom, blonde receptionist with a warm, friendly smile, cracking gum.

My life had now become a B movie.

"You're here for Jimmy? He's expecting you." she walked me into his office, sashaying her curvaceous hips like a film noir dame. Jimmy stood up as I entered the room. He was tall, with a big warm handshake, reminding me of the neighborhood guys where I grew up—tough with bullies and sweet with women. Jimmy was a police detective turned private dick. He had the people skills of a psychologist, the supportive smile of a kindergarten teacher, and a kind, baby face—just the guy I'd always wanted as my big brother. Jimmy explained to me the process of a "matrimonial," how his operatives did searches, followed guys and everything.

I told him Rupert was leading a double life and money was disappearing. I added that I was thinking of divorce and wanted to know my options and assets.

"You seem like a nice woman," he began. "I have to tell you, I don't like doing this kind of investigation because whenever you go looking for a skeleton in a closet, you're bound to find a live body." That kind of talk sold me on Jimmy. He asked me about my husband's hobbies and habits, his evenings, and weekends. I mentioned the extra ex-wife and the mysterious charge bills. Jimmy was impressed that I brought copies of those bills.

He told me that the standard routine for a matrimonial was to begin with a $250 retainer and then see how much tracking and following the client needed. He reluctantly took my check, stating, "You're too nice to be in this mess. You know you want to leave. I hope I can find some secret accounts you can go after. Let's nail the bastard."

Visiting Jimmy a week later, I entered his office to the sounds of Dave Clark Five singing *Glad All Over*. He was singing along and playing imaginary drums—adorable.

Jimmy shared his report: $60,000 had disappeared from our joint assets that he couldn't trace, no explanation, no receipts. When we married, I thought I was the second wife. After the night of the surprising boxes, I learned I was the third wife. But what Jimmy helped me realize was that I was actually wife three-and-a-half. The half was a four-year cohabitation. My husband had outright lied repeatedly, and with detailed back stories. If I'd known at the time Rupert proposed that I was going to be wife number three, especially to a guy in his mid-thirties, I never would've married him. I mean, are you going to give a college scholarship to a D student?

"There's more. That apartment you said he owns on West 87th Street that he said he'd sublet to his ex-girlfriend?"

"He told me it's on the market for half a million dollars. He tells me details about people wanting to buy it. Every few weeks the buyers change their minds or the deal falls through."

"I'm sorry, he doesn't own it."

"It was her apartment all along?" I thought out loud.

"Neither. It belongs to her aunt. If you leave, that's not an asset."

Jimmy told me that the recurring monthly charges on our credit card bills were all for phone sex. These were things I already knew, but it was comforting to have my suspicions confirmed. Then Jimmy dropped a bombshell. There were also 88 different charges for welding supplies and home repairs, which were from companies that sold—well—welding supplies and home repair stuff. But they didn't sell Rupert welding supplies and home repair stuff—Jimmy had found out that these companies were actually shell companies for a house of prostitution located in Vernon, Connecticut. Mastercharge, Visa, American Express AND Morgan Stanley private assets account all showed charges for "Renovation Supplies" which were legal, tax deductible, and were billing for more brothels in Connecticut.

Prostitutes—really? At first I thought it might have been just hand jobs; something kind of functional and impersonal, surely not intimate. It never occurred to me that Rupert was paying for full-on sex. Okay, now I was stunned, and on several levels. First, my husband was making regular visits to prostitutes—88 times, to be exact. Second, he was driving out of state to have sex when I was right there, and I didn't charge. Third, he was using our damned credit cards to pay them. Fourth, they were billed as home repairs so they were freaking tax deductible.

After giving me his report, Jimmy was too disturbed to look at me. Shaking his head, he took a sip of coffee before making eye contact. Finally, I had someone to look me in the eye and say that my husband was paying for sex with prostitutes. I felt disconcerted yet relieved knowing where the money and Rupert was disappearing to. Shielding and protecting me, unlike my family members were able to, Jimmy was very kind—why hadn't I married someone like Jimmy??

"You're good at your job, Jimmy," I said, taking a breath.

"I didn't do that much. I made a few calls, a few minutes of police work."

"Do you need anyone on a part time basis?" I fantasized.

"Your only job is to care for yourself. You have all the facts now, everything you need to know to decide if you want to leave. I hope you use the information wisely. You deserve better than this schmuck."

"Did you hear him, Arlene?" I said to myself, in my mother's pointed tones. "Now you know what's going on. It's time to act. Even Jimmy said it."

"Thank you for all you've done," I said out loud, to him.

"I wish you well. Oh, and because you're a good kid, and I didn't have to do that much, here's your check back." He stood and pulled my original check out of his pocket, putting it in my hand saying, "Take care of yourself and good luck."

#

Jimmy's report freaked me out. When? Why? Committing with marriage, yet withholding intimacy, that's someone with an icy core of cruelty. I was sick to my stomach. If I didn't factor in here, then why did he marry me? What now? I'd found incriminating information I thought would give me the last word. Hard facts could not be shouted down or disputed. Facts are a newsman's Holy Grail. I'd be right. I'd win.

But what was the prize? Seething with determination, afraid of acting irrationally, I wanted to let my new realizations sink in a bit.

That's what I told myself then, but looking back I was immobilized by the harsh truth. My marital problems were beyond the scope of anything I'd ever anticipated. A good imagination, coupled with lots of book reading, gay friends, and years in art college had left me thinking that, at 27, I knew the world.

Turns out, I had no idea.

To take my mind off of obsessing about my husband, I did practical errands. Cleaning and moving piles of junk, and collecting clothes to bring to the cleaners. The pile included Rupert's Ralph Lauren tweed jacket. So handsome on our early dates, it gave him the elegant allure of a confident professor. Now it was sorrowful, crumpled and balled up, at the bottom of a heap of pants. I cleaned out his pockets and found a phone number on a piece of paper, with no name on it. The number ended in 6969, but I didn't think much about it. After dinner, reading the *Village Voice*, I glanced through the back pages, which featured sex services. A phone number jumped out at me. It ended in 6969. The same number I'd found in Rupert's pants! I called Bob and begged him to call it for me. He did.

Bob said the number was a house of prostitution, a few blocks away from where Rupert worked. They quoted rates by the half hour and hour. They even had lunch time specials. How economical for the budget-conscious newlywed. He could spend his lunch hour having a *half and half*! At our local deli, that was half a pastrami sandwich and a cup of soup. Here, it was a blowjob and a screw. Appalled, it was painfully clear to me that instead of a three-martini business lunch like his peers, my husband spent a sum equal to my salary visiting prostitutes. He'd have a three-hooker lunch a few times a week, plus weekend marathons. When did he have time to do his job? He was having sex all the time. No wonder he was tired.

If I didn't do something, his addiction would bankrupt us. While I brown-bagged it and window-shopped without buying to save money, Rupert was popping over to the cash machine, withdrawing hundreds, strolling to the *Belle du Jour* neighborhood, having a blowjob, then picking up some Chinese food to eat at his desk. The ritual sounded efficient, methodical, and emotionless, just like my husband.

Deep in denial, I remembered when I first became aware of Rupert's frequent phone sex. Since it didn't involve touching another person, somehow I justified it as a childish outlet for the stresses of a new job. Perplexed when there were other charges for sexual favors, I wanted to believe they were for lap dances, nude twerking, hand jobs—a multitude of impersonal sexual services. Humiliated and heartbroken, I continued to rationalize. I just couldn't wrap my brain around the bizarre reality of it all. But once I learned about repeated episodes of intercourse and weekend fuckathons, this all changed. My new obsessive thought was Rupert touching a stranger, skin to skin, moaning, and exchanging fluids, a torturous movie repeatedly racing through my brain, which was now bubbling in endless anguish. There are things that you hear or learn or know. Then there's the moment when you take them in and truly comprehend their impact. This was my moment.

Until that day, I'd naively hoped something magical could breathe life into my joke of a marriage. Jimmy's report was the coffin lid slamming that hope shut.

I was finally ready to return Josie's calls; I hoped she understood that I needed to retreat before facing the truths I wasn't ready to see.

"Hello, I've been avoiding you, because I wasn't ready to face what you had to say." I told her everything Jimmy had told me.

She said, "You really have to confront him."

"I did that. I failed miserably, and he made me feel guilty! He berated me whenever I tried to speak up and assert an ounce of power. His pudgy finger of blame needled me…'If you had a more interesting life, you wouldn't be such a nag.'"

"If you weren't there, you couldn't be needled. Think about that before you speak. I've seen you deal with hecklers in nightclubs."

"I never took wedding vows with a heckler."

"Think of the worst heckler, sitting on a toilet, naked. You can do this! Give him an ultimatum, you have *documentation* now!"

"I could never tell him I'd gone to a private investigator."

"Why do you care? You've done research. Complete it. Wrap it with a big shiny bow."

Confrontation was never something I'd initiated with anyone. I'd rather eat a cake. The only way to confront Rupert was to speak his language and approach him in a kind, friendly way, not unlike confronting a grizzly bear in the woods: no sudden moves, and speak softly.

I spent so much time trying to get into his head, he must have gotten an ear ache.

I rehearsed my approach to be calm and gentle, like a kindergarten teacher. Wearing something soft and cottony and red, the color of warmth and the heart, I'd gently go for the gut. Speaking of gut, I'd noticed from the charge bills that I'd steamed open that day, then glued closed and put back in the pile of mail, that his weekends away were marathons for all of his indulgences. You'd think he was using a stolen credit card, the way hundreds of dollars were spent, all on the same day: charges for phone sex and prostitutes, and usually three hundred dollars or so for music and videos, as well as charges for Baskin Robbins in excess of fifteen dollars each. He was having sex without me and eating my favorite ice cream cakes! Now he was screwing around with food, my domain. That was the final straw.

Did I think Rupert would say, "You win, you're smarter than I thought—so I'll fuck you now." Would that happen?

After lots of deep breathing, with kindergarten teacher calm and honor student preparedness, I thought I was ready for "Operation

Confrontation." After being married ten months and armed with my new knowledge, I tried to engage in a heartfelt discussion towards the end of our evening meal, which I could hardly eat.

"Honey," I said, lovingly and calmly, "I know that on weekends alone you buy yourself ice cream cakes and eat them all by yourself." I envisioned him looking at me, wide eyed and childlike, shameful and horrified to be found out.

"Yes, but you weren't there," he justified, confidently.

"So I'm punished and denied because I wasn't with you?"

"I was lonely, so I ate an ice cream cake," he said, firmly.

"How would you feel if I ate an ice cream cake without you?" I asked, moving closer to the meat of the matter.

"I'd be sad. I'd feel left out," he pouted.

"Think of the bad feelings you'd have if I had a cake without you, by myself. That's how I feel when you go out of town and have sex without me," I confided, relieved to have made my point. Rupert stared, speechless. Then my outrage got the best of me, barking. "I know you go to prostitutes. Why do you do this when you have a loving wife?"

"That's an explosive charge." I finally had his back against the wall. Surely he'd come clean now. "What makes you think that?" he demanded, putting me on the defensive, worse than the anticipated scenarios I'd feared.

"I checked all the charges that appeared as phone sex with an accountant and the other unusual charges too. He confirmed they were *all* for prostitutes."

"So now you're sharing our dirty laundry with other people?"

"Stop denying it. Why do you do it?"

"It's not about sex. It's a calming, impersonal release, like playing tennis."

"Tennis? You've never played tennis in your life. Fucking strangers is like playing tennis? You've got some racket! Get a load of the balls on you!" My reined in comedienne never knew when to show her face or hide.

"It's not about intimacy. I've never stopped loving you," He looked into my eyes for the closest moment we'd shared in months. Then the phone rang, breaking the moment like a shattered window. We both stared at it, immobilized.

"Pick it up!" he ordered, loudly, distressed.

At that moment, I hated all phones. Reluctantly, I answered. It was Paul. "I can't talk now," I promptly hung up.

"Who was it?" demanded Rupert. When I told him it was Paul, his anger raged. "You accuse me of sex with strangers, but you're the adulterous one in this marriage. You have intimacies, emotional intimacies with other people."

Rebellious, I raised my voice. "But I'm not having sex with them. I'm not having sex with anyone." We were both boiling over with emotion.

He composed himself and coolly stated, "In Europe millions of men go to prostitutes. I don't see what the problem is."

"We're not in Europe. Here, millions of men don't go to prostitutes. I want one of them." Yelling in the situation about the situation, rage raced through me, demonic, like I was in one of those teen werewolf films—if I kept screaming, my body would sprout mounds of hair, long spiky teeth and I'd be grotesque beyond my imagination.

"I don't know why you can't accept me as I am—I love you." He stormed out of the room and out of the apartment, with Peaches on a leash. Banging that door had the sting of a full body slam.

I'd finally shouted my truth, months after it needed to be said. As someone who'd rarely felt her feelings before this moment, a five-alarm bonfire was blazing in my bones. Finding a new place to live was no longer a passing thought—it was my number one necessity. With Rupert's slamming of the door, the planning and packing for my exodus began.

As the slam stopped echoing through the walls, I called Josie, my life preserver. "Hello, I think I'm ready now…" My voice trailed off, drained.

"Arlene, are you okay?" Josie's tone was cautious.

"I can't believe I'm lonelier married than single," I whispered.

"Still? It's that bad?"

Yes. He's a brick wall with eyeglasses and pants. Talking to you makes me feel like I'm not crazy."

"You're not crazy. Just remember what keeps you sane and happy."

"What? What does? I've been too crazed to remember." My heart flip-flopped, knowing that when our talk ended, I'd be alone with my own thoughts.

"Comedy."

"Comedy?" I parroted back, not quite consoled or understanding.

"Remember how good it feels to be onstage, holding a microphone."

"You think a microphone is a dick substitute?

"Do you want me to be honest or kind? I don't think this is about sex."

"No sex for months is not my problem?"

"That's a problem, but the bigger issue is identity. You thought having a husband was going to solve your problems."

"No I didn't, it just got me out of Brooklyn, that's all."

"You let Rupert consume you. You consumed him. Sex is a metaphor. Fill that empty hole and you will never have to learn who you are. When he's not there, paying attention to you, consuming you, who are you?"

"So his addiction is sex, and my addiction is him? Or do I have consumption?"

"Stop being a wise ass. I hate to say this, but you're an addict too. Instead of snorting cocaine, you're trying to mainline him. Only you can solve this. Think about it."

"Are you saying distance is the best medicine?"

"Many people separate. Sometimes things change. If you don't try it, you'll just be agonizing and overeating. It's time to stop hiding in your marriage and go find yourself. Feeling empowered, but still needing some cheerleading, I called my friend Bob and told him I had resolved to leave.

Bob instructed, "No annulment, Arlene. Get a divorce. An annulment is like it never happened. This man has hurt you. Make him remember and make him pay."

"That's kind of cold."

"Hasn't he been an iceberg to you?" he asserted. "Make him hurt too. The only way to hurt rich people is in their wallet. Make him pay."

CHAPTER 18:

BLOOMINGDALE'S REVENGE

"Men get married 'cause they can't hold their farts in any longer. Women get divorced 'cause they can't take the crap."—Me

"Given the fact of your short marriage, which you entered with no assets, all you're likely to get out of this deal are the clothes on your back. I suggest you go out and get a really nice outfit," said Allen Berger, the divorce attorney.

"Even though he was adulterous?"

"You're younger and pretty. You'd be considered a gold-digger."

"So your advice is…go shopping?" I questioned, incredulous.

"Shop and save a little bit from each of your paychecks for a new place to live. Try to bank enough for your security deposit, first and last month's rent—get those ready. Then you can pack with freedom, leave and make a new life."

"What about presenting all the charge bills for prostitutes in court?"

"If the judge or any of his friends go to prostitutes, they'll only laugh at you. To many men. it's no big deal," he asserted.

He was right. At that time, in 1983, the AIDS epidemic was beginning to be frequent front-page news, mainly impacting the gay community. No one really knew how they contracted it, or that anyone could die from it. So for straight men who paid for sex with credit cards, it was busy-ness as usual.

"Where are the men who don't go to prostitutes—when will I meet them?"

"That I can't tell you. In the meantime, go to Bloomingdales, five blocks from here. No one shops as fiercely as a woman scorned. The store banks on that—lots of affluent, angry women who aren't getting what they want from their husbands in this town. They'll probably be in the dressing room next to you."

So I dashed to Bloomingdales. I'd always breezed past the "Young Collectors" department, because the designers were too rich for my blood. But that day my blood was boiling hot. I made a beeline for an Armani jacket and pants, designed with architectural perfection. I looked at the price tag. The suit cost over a thousand dollars. There was actually a comma in the price. I grabbed the hangers and slinked into the dressing room, glancing over my shoulder as if someone would know I'd never tried on such an expensive outfit, afraid I'd be stopped in my tracks and ordered to go downtown to Macy's sale rack.

Gently removing the suit from its hanger, I zipped the pants, buttoned the jacket and looked in the mirror. I now knew the meaning of "like butter." The suit was magnificent. I looked beautiful in it. Glancing at the price tag again I took a deep gulp. Then I thought of all the charges I'd found for phone sex, prostitution and other crap. I did a little math and added together what each act of sexual deception cost on a weekly and monthly basis. Buying this suit would only make a small dent in evening that score. Suddenly the suit's shocking dollar amount didn't seem that exorbitant. If I'd spread the purchase price over a few charge cards like I'd seen Rupert do, the cost of my Armani would look like a pennies-a-day investment. I looked in the mirror again. My reasoning was as seductive as this suit. I may soon be out of a marriage, out of a luxury apartment, but I'd be out in Armani.

#

As the morning sun screeched brightly through the window, I faced the bathroom mirror to brush my teeth, taking in my wild eyed, crazed gaze, with dark circles and red blotches on my face and neck. I no longer wanted to leave my husband—I now had to leave him to save myself.

Five paychecks and two and a half months after seeing an attorney, there was enough money in my new secret bank account for a new apartment. Still, I had to plan slowly and carefully. Only make calculated moves in the event Rupert would react bitterly to rejection. I'd heard horror stories about snubbed spouses changing locks, canceling credit cards and bank accounts, tormenting tales of mean, violent behavior.

An apartment with a roommate was the most appropriate scenario, both financially and emotionally. I still wanted to live in Manhattan, yet was too shell-shocked to be alone. If there was a roommate, the voices in my head would be drowned out by a living, breathing person who would, hopefully, feel like less of a stranger than Rupert. Whenever I'd brush my teeth, I'd look in the mirror and say to myself, "Soon I'll be free! New life, new hopes."

First, I had to find an apartment. Since 1983 was before the internet and cell phones, this meant scouring newspaper ads, making calls and visiting buildings around the city; all challenging to do while working a full-time job and keeping my actions a secret from my husband. Then again, Rupert was the royal master of secrecy, leading his double life. Taught by an expert, secrecy became my new middle name.

It was easy for me to say I went to happy hour for drinks with a friend when I was really checking out prospective apartments around town. As for Rupert, he was either at work, or called to say he was working late, which meant he was leaving the office for yet another fuckathon. So I guess we were ignoring each other.

After living in a luxury doorman building on Park Avenue, finding a room I could afford on my Girl Scout, non-profit salary, in a safe, attractive place was going to take a magical feat that would astound Houdini, himself.

I fervently looked at ads, circled them, called and visited. In the event I liked the apartment, the final step depended on whether the lease-holding roommate liked me. Quite a few nights I'd told Rupert I was having dinner with friends after work. Instead, I was scouting new escape sites, uptown and down.

It was quite a journey; one apartment I saw was a nine-room, pre-war palace, with a woman who described herself as "older." When I arrived, it was a cat-infested cavern with 23 felines plus their excrement in every corner of all the dimly lit rooms. When I told the woman I was a writer, she told me she'd entertained another writer friend years ago, in this very room.

"Maybe you've heard of him. He wrote a few books. Scott Fitzgerald."

"Fitzgerald was here?" I wondered where he'd found a clean place to sit.

"Right on that very couch," she pointed.

I moved closer to the couch, only noticing the multiple cat stains. How I wished I'd had a flask of Scott's gin just then.

Oh! Then there was the woman who had six colors of spiky hair. She lived in a fifth-floor walk-up above a strip club. In her bathroom, the sink, toilet, and tub each needed to be finessed and jiggled a certain way to make them work at all. Live music from the club made the walls shake. Yeah, I passed.

Next, I met Cilla—tall, thin, with curly black hair, sort of a Goth Shirley Temple. She had a huge minimalist loft space, downtown, a block from the subway. The apartment was a dream. Then Cilla opened with, "My ideal roommate would feed my snakes when I stay at my boyfriend's house. I have a steady supply of live white rats delivered every day. It's one of my few indulgences." She giggled. "I'm not here that much. Could you do the feeding for me?" Ummmmm, I don't think so.

I bolted back to the subway. Finally, one day after having looked for what seemed like forever, I found a quaintly decorated first-floor apartment in a brownstone building just off Central Park, near 96th Street. The woman was divorced and remarried. So she knew the machinations of ending a marriage and how to create a new one as well. She was away on weekends with her four sons, upstate. It was the perfect scenario for me.

Counting the days until I could leave my past and move into my future, my heart and mind had packed and left a while ago. Every time I looked at Rupert, something tugged at my heart—I wished we'd had a different outcome. And yet, I had to close my heart to my husband to keep whatever remnant of sanity I had left. I hoped that once I packed and left and vowed not to look back, my life would move forward.

It was now late November. The new apartment wasn't available until January. Sure, I could stay with family, on their couch, as a stop-gap until I found something more permanent, but too worn out and distraught to keep hopping and running, I wanted to make one move and settle down.

And, as much as I wanted out of my marriage, I didn't want to be alone for the holidays. Thanksgiving was a few days away. Friends left town, visiting parents or siblings. Last year my dad had spent Thanksgiving with us. I invited him again this year, so I'd have a loving family member nearby. Also, I wanted Rupert to think that everything between us was "normal."

Thanksgiving Day found Rupert and I getting ready for the holiday dinner. I'd just put the turkey in the oven; he'd set the table.

We had a few hours to kill, and something came over me. I thought since I'd given up and didn't care about our sex life anymore, now was a good time to spite him. I wanted a balls-to-the-wall sexual moment to prove to myself that I was over him. So, insisting we watch pornography together on our six-foot screen, I turned on the television, found the porn cable channel, and invited my husband to lay down next to me on our wide couch.

Rupert was hesitant at first, but seeing giant naked bodies writhing in ecstasy with heavy breathing in the middle of the afternoon got him going. We watched as most of the girls in the film gave oral sex to guys they'd just met. Women had sex with anyone they bumped into, hardly speaking. Shortly after hello, each woman ended up blowing some guy, taking that whole thing into her mouth. My husband enjoyed watching that—so much so that, after five minutes, the front of his pants tented upwards.

Every facet of this moment was absurd to me. I wanted to play, be phony like a hooker. I kissed his neck, put my arm around him, then maneuvered my hand to his belt buckle, coyly undoing his trousers, and slipping my hand down into his underwear. The second I touched his hardness, I heard his breath increase. He was heating up, and I was ready too!

Or was I? Oh no! This moment fully cemented my feeling completely over him. Stroking his throbbing cock, I became detached, like a sex worker—the women he was frequenting. Like them, I behaved as if I was hot for him. "Oh baby, yes baby," I whispered, resentfully curious to understand and experience detached intimacy. Instead, I pictured Rupert being naked with strangers, his body next to someone else, skin to skin, someone who wasn't me. Rupert put his cock into women who didn't even tell him their real names. Disgusted at the thought of his behavior, I still kept stroking him—his hardness and breathing increasing, keeping rhythm and momentum with the larger than life body parts on our giant television. Physically, I had him right where I wanted him.

"I never knew you could be like this," he said, pleasantly surprised.

In that moment I knew that I didn't want to and would never again have sex with Rupert. I felt a sigh of relief, thankful for my conclusion. "Happy Thanksgiving," I whispered to myself.

As I readied to withdraw my hand from his pants, the doorbell rang.

Feeling empowered and victorious leaving him wanting more—the way our entire marriage had left me wanting—I shouted toward the front door, "Daddy, I'm coming."

"What about me?" my husband murmured, adamant.

"I'm done," I said, moving my hand away from him. "Finish the job yourself. Remember to wash your hands. You have a turkey to carve."

CHAPTER 19:

THE BIG CHILL

"Give a man a free hand, and he'll run it all over you." —Mae West

My escape plan solidified between Christmas and New Year's, the season to be with loved ones and family. In truth, Rupert was my family. I just wished he was a totally different person. Meanwhile, I fantasized about my new life.

In spite of everything, I was frightened of being single again. I kept telling myself, "I'll just stay for one more holiday party, and then I'll leave..." With fervent anticipation, I squeezed myself into one more party dress.

On New Year's Eve, a silent Rupert and I headed to a black-tie celebration at the luxurious brownstone of a couple I'd grown to admire, Rupert's friends, Barbara and Colin. Both magazine editors, together since college, they'd recently celebrated 15 years of happy marriage.

Fabulous food and every writer worth talking to from *The New York Times, The New Yorker, New York Magazine* and *Esquire* were there, all seemingly fascinated by one another like a secret cult. I thought they snubbed Rupert because he worked for *The Daily News,* newspaper of the subway rider. And, of course, no one was interested in the musings of a mere Girl Scout catalog writer. So I befriended the kitchen staff and had first pick from every hors d'oeuvres tray, pleased I could always find my way to food.

Champagne flowed freely, and music poured out into the air. Our hosts had turned the living room into their dance floor, playing Motown songs from the soundtrack of *The Big Chill.* They danced together; first the fast songs, then the slower ones. I was enthralled by their eye contact, smiles, hands wrapping around waists, their twirling and laughing, fascinated as their bodies moved together, hand meeting hand effortlessly, fluidly, knowing the touch was imminent and welcomed. I sat mesmerized watching how each step and gesture showed how much they loved, trusted and knew each other—deep intimacy on glowing display. Whatever it was they had, I'd never ever had so much as an ounce of it with my husband. Seeing their joyful dance further confirmed my decision to end my marriage. I glanced over at Rupert, sitting slumped into the arm of the couch, resembling a sad St. Bernard. No one talked to him either. He watched them dance too, ignoring me.

When the Four Tops sang, "*I can't help myself, I love you and nobody else...*" I forced a smile to mask my emptiness. Midnight arrived. Rupert and I kissed perfunctorily. I looked him in the eye and smiled. Then I looked away, thinking of my escape, hoping this new year, 1984, would be so much better than the last, and that the "Big

Chill" of my marriage would soon thaw into a warm, albeit unknown, future.

#

I called my parents the following Sunday night, beginning with my mother. She and Rupert were a lot alike. He'd know she'd be a soft touch. "If Rupert calls you tomorrow, you don't know where I am, you don't know anything."

"Where will you be?" asked Mom.

"I'm leaving Rupert tomorrow, lunchtime. I'm leaving him a note, letting him know that I've gone. He'll get a letter from my attorney."

"Are you sure you know what you're doing?"

"No, ma, I just woke up and decided to walk out on my marriage…it was either that or get bangs."

"What will you do now, who else would marry you?" She knew how to strum my insecurities like Segovia.

I promptly hung up on her and called my father. "Daddy, I have something to tell you. I'm leaving Rupert tomorrow. You know we've been having problems."

"Yes. You've told me about the phone sex and lying."

"There's been too much bullshit to stay."

"Lots of women in your social world put up with a lot of shit. I guess you couldn't pay the price to live on Park Avenue."

"Daddy, I'm in my twenties. There's gotta be something better than this."

"You're smart, I know you figured this out in advance," Dad said, supportively.

"I'll call you tomorrow night and give you more info. If he calls, you know nothing. Can you do that for me?"

"Whatever you need, dear."

Next morning Rupert and I both woke up together for work. Before he could get out of bed, I reached for him and held him close, as if to take a sense memory snapshot of how he felt, certain I'd never be in this position again. I'd always enjoyed waking up and holding him, moments before we'd rise and face the world. This was a daily joyous memory—a fleeting instant I knew I'd miss. So I lingered, kissing his neck, hugging him tighter than usual.

"I want you to know that I love you and I love waking up with you," I whispered.

"Okay," he responded, clueless. "Me too."

He got out of bed and stumbled into his bathroom. In my bathroom, I showered and put my toiletries into a shopping bag. Carefully placing the bag under the sink, I dressed for work.

As we left the apartment together, the elevator ride seemed endless as I grazed his hand with mine. I admired his suit, inhaled his cologne and caught a farewell whiff of his freshly washed hair. How could I want to touch him in the morning and leave him in the afternoon? When we got to the front of the building, I turned and hugged him again. Knowing it would be the last of its kind, it was a clumsy, clutching hug.

“I want you to know that I love when you make me coffee in the morning.”

“Have a good day, dear.” It was clear his mind was already racing in work mode. He gave me a peck on the lips and we went in opposite directions.

Tempted to look back, I bit my lip, walking down the subway steps. When I arrived at work, I went into my supervisor’s office and reminded her I was only there for a half day. Then I went to the coffee room with my co-worker Stella.

“How was your weekend?” Stella asked.

“I should win an Academy Award for my performance this weekend,” I said, dramatically. “Today’s the day.”

“You’re leaving today?” she asked in amazement.

“Bonnie thinks I have a dental appointment. I’m going home, taking what I need, and catching a cab to my new life.”

“You make it sound so simple,” she mused.

“Like removing a wisdom tooth through your ass.”

“If anybody can do it, you can.” She touched my shoulder, “Good luck.”

Around 11:45 that morning, I stared at the clock, watching the minute hand until it clicked to noon. Operation “leave your husband” was now in action. I took my purse out of my desk, said goodbye to Stella and left the building.

When I got to my apartment building, the doorman smiled at me. We were both surprised to find me there at that mid-day moment.

I felt paranoid, like I was robbing a bank, only I was looting my own closet.

Walking into the apartment, I felt a metronome ticking off time…click click click, hurry up! The air felt thicker. I was never more uncomfortable in my own home than that very moment. Racing to the kitchen, I grabbed two giant shopping bags, filled them with underwear, work clothes and a few pairs of shoes. I knew I'd be coming back later in the week, so I grabbed enough to last a few days. Walking into my bathroom, I reached under the sink and grabbed the bag of toiletries I'd packed that morning.

Heavy hearted, I made my way past our bed, looking at it, trying to remember good times there. I couldn't. On Rupert's side of the bed, I picked up his pillow and held it to my face, taking in the last bit of his essence. It hurt to swallow, and a tear came to my eye. I wiped it away, put the pillow down and speedily completed my packing.

I took shopping bags rather than luggage for two reasons. I did not want to call attention to myself as the doorman, concierge and others saw me leaving mid-day. And secondly, the closet where I was moving was so small, I wouldn't have anywhere to store suitcases. Stay light, be flexible, and keep moving.

I'd written a note to Rupert earlier, at my desk, about how I loved him, but I couldn't live with him anymore. I didn't fully understand all of my mad/sad/angry emotions, but I knew I needed to remain sweet to avoid repercussions. I slipped the note out of my purse and placed it with the day's mail so I was sure he'd find it and read it. My attorney had advised, "Don't antagonize him. Leave the olive branch of peace and reconciliation."

I grabbed my getaway loot, got on the elevator, and walked through the luxurious lobby of our Park Avenue abode. Living on Park Avenue didn't seem desirable anymore. Our neighbors were cold and snobby. Never really happy there, I strode through the double glass doors to the street and enjoyed a deep cleansing exhale. Grabbing a cab, I loaded my bags, sat comfortably and slammed the door.

"Take me to the West Side," I announced to the cabbie. On our way through Central Park, I rolled down the window, exhilarated by the breeze caressing my face. In that moment, I was confident; sure I was on the right course.

The taxi arrived in front of a brownstone that would be my new home. I flung the cab door open and placed my shopping bags on the curb. Eagerly, I walked to the front door, turned the knob and entered. I found my key and went to the first apartment in the lobby. I entered to find all the lights on and music blasting.

"Hello?" I shouted, confused and uncertain.

"Oh hello, baby!" said Lola, the beautiful Jamaican cleaning lady. "You must be the new roommate. Tara told me you'd be coming today. I put fresh sheets on your bed."

I went into the bedroom, dropped my bags down and went to Nola, who was kneeling, cleaning the tub.

"Hello, I'm Arlene," I said, eager to please.

Lola looked up at me, "I know you. You were a comedian at *Good Times*. I've seen you perform there. I've worked there too, singing Billie Holiday songs."

"Yes, I think I've seen you too!" I was excited. I saw this moment as a good sign, and a reminder that, now unencumbered by Rupert, I could resume my comedy career.

Walking into the bedroom, kicking off my shoes, I plopped on my new bed. The song I heard from Lola's radio was Cindy Lauper singing "Girls Just Want to Have Fun," My mind clicked to the phrase, *"Take a beautiful girl and hide her away from the rest of the world. But girls just want to have fun."* Hearing this song at that moment was another sign that my new life would be better.

#

The next morning, I woke up in a plush, quilted, queen-sized bed, with oversized pillows and crisp matching sheets, all by myself. I had set the alarm for 15 minutes earlier than when I lived with Rupert, because now, living on the West Side, my commute would be longer, taking two trains. Fifteen minutes less sleep was a small price to pay to be free of the little man. Cheerfully striding to the subway, I took in the sky, white with snowflakes. It made me smile.

Arriving at the lobby of the Girl Scout offices, the security guard stopped me.

"I have a package for you," he stated, handing me a small shopping bag. Inside were my snow boots, warm gloves and a note from Rupert. "I understand your feelings. Please don't leave me. Stay warm; don't slip in the snow."

Now he chose to be caring and thoughtful? I went up to my desk and the smiling secretary, Norella.

"Good morning, Arlene," she said, "Rupert called six times this morning."

"I just got here. He called six times?" It never occurred to me that I'd be his new obsession. I hadn't known him to do anything six times. I was distressed as my mind raced to all the things he might do or say. "Did he leave messages?" I asked, dreading the thought of speaking with him.

"He said, please call and he loves you."

"Norella, I left him yesterday. I don't want to speak with him. I'm sorry, but I'm forwarding my calls to your phone." At that time, Girl Scouts did not have an automated phone system or voice mail.

"Rupert loves you," she smiled, unaware of the life I'd been living and ever the church-going optimist.

"Please just tell him I'm not here, or I'm in a meeting—anything but here."

Sitting at my desk, I knew I couldn't concentrate. Norella's phone rang.

"Girl Scouts, Norella speaking," I heard her answer. "I'm sorry, Rupert, she's off the floor. I will." Norella popped her head into my office. Before she could speak, I offered, "I know, I know—he called."

A half hour later, the same thing happened and a half hour after that, too. By noon every time the phone rang, I jumped. The shrill tone seemed to shout: "*I need to talk to you, talk to me, I won't ever let you leave me!*" I felt frightened, as if he was lurking, just inches away, to pounce on me. On my lunch hour, I bought Norella a plant and a Whitman sampler. I hated involving her, but dreaded talking to Rupert even more. Later that day I called my parents.

"Did Rupert call you?" I asked Mom.

"Of course he did. He's a very sick individual."

"What did he say?" I was curious.

"He cried," she said, sadly.

"Is that adult behavior?"

"He's got problems," Mom defended him. I guess classical music nerds stick together. "Do you have food and blankets?"

"I'm going through a separation. I'm not in a war zone."

I then spoke to Dad, certain he'd be my champion. "He asked where you were. I told him he ruined your life."

"You did?" I was surprised and pleased.

"He's a sick bastard," Dad took my side. "It's good you are away from him." I gave Dad my new phone number.

That night in my new apartment, I got into bed shortly after arriving home from work. How did I feel sleeping in this queen sized bed alone? Simultaneously happy and sad, my mind wandered to what Rupert might be doing at that very minute. I pictured him having sex with another woman. I grabbed a pillow, held it close to my face and screamed into it. Taking a deep breath, I punched and fluffed the pillow while turning it over. Then, caressing the pillow close to my body as if I were spooning Rupert, I fell asleep.

The next morning, well rested, I dressed for work and caught my trains just as they were pulling in. Day two of freedom was off to an excellent start. When I entered the Girl Scout building, the security guard stopped me again, apprising me, "there's someone here to see you." He pointed behind me, against the wall, near the elevator banks. I turned and saw Rupert. His usual crisp clothing looked disheveled, as if he'd slept in this outfit.

"Hello Arlene," he started.

"Hi Rupert," I raced. "I've got to get upstairs."

He grabbed my arm, "You've got to come back home."

"I can't have this discussion here."

He wouldn't let go. All of my co-workers were crossing the lobby, entering the elevators. My dirty laundry was now flung for all to see.

"I need you. I love you," his eyes filled with tears like a child having a tantrum. I put my hand on top of his to release his grip. He held tighter and got louder, "I will not let you go!" Trying to break his grip, my handbag fell to the floor, making a "splat" noise.

The security guard came to my side, "Ma'am, is this man bothering you?"

"He won't let me get into the elevator," I offered, desperate for an out.

The guard addressed Rupert, "Sir, I'll have to ask you to leave."

Glancing over again to the people in the elevators, witnessing the scene, I noticed my boss, Bonnie, just inside the door. She glared at me, horrified and angry, shaking her head in disgust, apparently embarrassed that someone who worked for her would have a personal argument in a public place for all of our coworkers to see. I looked away from her and back to the guard. He grabbed Rupert by the arm, escorting him to the front door. Rupert was gone. Now I had to face my boss. Sure enough, before I could get to my desk, Bonnie asked to see me in her office. Quickly, I erased the mortified look from my face.

"What is going on here?" she demanded. "You're making a spectacle."

"That was my husband," I explained. "I left him two days ago."

"Keep him out of here," she ordered.

"I…I, yes, Bonnie," I mumbled. As I walked into my office, I heard Norella's phone ring.

"Girl Scouts, Norella speaking," she offered cheerfully. "Hello Rupert." I walked to her and gestured "No" wildly like an insane person playing charades. I was on the verge of tears.

Stella strode into my office, "What's going on?" she implored, anxiously. "Everyone's talking about this man in the lobby and a struggle you had with him."

"That was Rupert," I blurted, diving into Stella's arms for a motherly hug. My crying escalated. Sobbing and shaking, I leaned into Stella, who stroked my head, like a parent comforting a frightened baby.

"Everything will be okay. Just keep Bonnie out of it. She gets jealous when she's not the center of attention for any reason." Stella warned, as I eased my grip on her.

I sat down at my desk in an effort to get calm. Soon, I could breathe without shaking. The phone rang. I was afraid it was Rupert. Instead, I was called to a meeting to discuss the new Girl Scout catalog—nothing like talk of Girl Scout uniforms, tents, and canteens to take my mind off my misery.

When I got back to my office, there was a stack of pink message slips on my desk—Rupert had called five times in one hour. The messages read:

"I have to speak with you."

"Please see me."

"Don't leave me this way."

"I want you and miss you."

"Please call me, I can't spend another day without you."

My leaving Rupert had created an obsession that was bordering on stalking. It *was* stalking. I became petrified every time the phone rang that there'd be a crazed, whiny, begging man-child on the other end. I was frightened, and angry—now that one of his possessions had jumped its shelf, it seemed, he'd use any means necessary to get it back.

It was both scary and ironic that all the time I had spent working at my marriage and trying to garner Rupert's affection, I would have achieved greater attention from him if I'd left.

Like a child, he wanted what he couldn't have.

I would just be embarrassed in the work place a thousand different ways by his outbursts. Terrified of his next move or intrusion, I knew I had to rein him in, before my job was put in serious jeopardy by his actions. I told Norella that the next time Rupert called I'd speak to him. This gladdened her. She thought he'd worn me down and a romantic reconciliation was next. No such luck.

When Rupert called, I calmly said, "Hello."

"Hello, I'm happy to speak to you," he cooed as if trying to date me.

"What do you want?"

"I need to see you. I have to give you something."

"What do you have to give me?" I asked, suspiciously.

"I'll show you when I see you. Meet me for lunch, and if, after I give you this, you don't think I've changed, then I won't bother you."

Intrigued, I felt a step closer to ending Rupert's hysteria. He wouldn't act out in a public place, during a crowded lunch hour. "Alright," I sighed. "I'll meet you at the deli on Second Avenue, at noon, a booth near the front.

"You won't be sorry." He said "bye," and hung up.

I already regretted my decision. On Monday at this same time, I was carving a new life for myself. Today was a definite step backward and I wasn't calling the shots.

I arrived at 12:05. Rupert was already there, with the careful politeness of a boy in the principal's office. He stood up from his seat as if to hug me, like a warm, loving husband, but the look in my eyes said, "Don't even think about touching me."

"So what do you have to give me?" I asked, impatiently.

"Look at the menu first. Eat something. You're looking thinner."

I said briskly. "What do you have for me?"

"Well, I know you've been unhappy with some things I've been doing."

"That's an understatement," I glowered.

"If I were unable to do those things, then I wouldn't do them, you'd be happier and maybe…"

"What'll it be?" barked the waitress. We ordered. She left.

"What things?" I demanded.

"You know, on the phone, in those places…." He mumbled.

"Sex? Fucking around? Phone sex?" My anger and voice were rising.

"Shh, keep your voice down," he urged.

"You can't say it. You can't do it with me. What is it you think will make me happy?"

"If I give you my credit cards and you cut them up, then I can't behave badly." Rupert wanted me to move from the role of sexless wife to controlling mother. Cutting up his cards would be a punishment, not unlike a spanking. This scenario would tie me into his chastisement.

Opening a wallet, he pulled out six credit cards, throwing them on the table like they were dirty tissues. "Take them. I can't control myself," he cried.

"I don't want them," I shuddered. "It's not my job to control you."

"I can't look at them," he blurted, tearfully pushing back his chair, throwing a 20 dollar bill on the table and rushing from the restaurant. I sat there, shaking my head. My soup and his sandwich arrived seconds later. I asked the waitress to wrap them up, then I left the restaurant too, taking both lunches back to eat at my desk, disappointed and disgusted by Rupert, yet again.

Relieved when the workday ended, I walked out of the Girl Scout building and looked both ways before entering the subway. On the packed train, the overcrowding of strangers felt comforting—certainly more pleasant than being close to Rupert's tortured soul. Reaching my home station, I raced out the doors and up the stairs to the street, longing to hide myself away in my new fortress of solitude. Inches away from my front door, I reached for the knob and turned it. As I leaned inside, a hand grabbed my arm, pushing me out of the street and into the hallway. Thinking it was a mugger, I was terrified, heart pounding through my chest. It was Rupert! “What, what—why are you here?” I screamed.

“I can’t spend another night without you,” he demanded.

“Go away—get out of here,” I shot back.

A neighbor opened their door, “What’s that noise, what’s going on?”

“He was just leaving,” I bellowed. “Get me fired from work, kicked out of my home…that’s love!” I yelled. “Get out of here, now!” I pushed him out the front door then raced to get inside my apartment, locking and double locking the door behind me.

Inside, I shed my work clothes, pulled on a flannel nightgown, wrapped up in a big blanket and curled up into a ball on the couch, shaking and crying in the dark. After an hour, I heard a key in the door. It was my roommate Tara coming home from work. She looked shocked to see her new housemate shuddering in a shadow filled corner, like a dying rat under the stove.

“Hey, what’s all this darkness about?” she asked, as she switched on a table lamp, then two. Holding a bouquet of flowers she’d bought to freshen her night table, she presented them to me instead. “Here—you need these more than I do. Flowers are a great pick-me-up. Let’s go to dinner tonight…to celebrate your arrival. Come on, put on some pants, a sweater, some lipstick. You need some hot and sour soup.”

CHAPTER 20:

UPTOWN GIRL

"Marriage is like a bank account. You put it in, you take it out, you lose interest." —Professor Irwin Corey

When Tara found me in that unlit apartment, cowering on the couch she persisted in prying me out of my depression. For that, I will be eternally grateful.

If an issue of *Cosmopolitan* magazine came to life and became a person, it would have been my new roommate, Tara Bergen. She was a decorator, a chef, and an assertiveness trainer. She brought the fun of Mary Poppins, the spontaneity of Auntie Mame, the sexpertness of Helen Gurley Brown and the dining and decorating finesse of Martha Stewart, all wrapped in a cute, preppy package. Sort of a size 18 Ali McGraw, post *Love Story*.

That night, she cajoled me to get dressed and leave the house with her. We walked three blocks to a Chinese restaurant that offered a free carafe of wine with dinner. As we ate, my spirits lifted as Tara shared stories about her life.

"I see my second husband, Richard, on weekends. He's the father of my two youngest boys. My first husband, Tony, father of my two oldest sons, was a great guy until he slammed the piano lid down on my hands, crushing six fingers and ruining any potential I had as a pianist." She ate a few bites.

"I didn't know you were a pianist."

'Before I moved to our apartment, I was a chef on a local TV station in Albany. I love cooking and entertaining, but I can't seem to get motivated to cook for less than ten people."

Glad to be the new roommate in her wide-eyed, engaging movie, while Tara rattled off her larger than life stories, I wondered if she was lying. But I felt so entertained, delighted to focus on someone other than myself, I didn't care.

"If you'd have moved in two weeks ago, you'd have met this guy I'm having an affair with. I knew him when I lived in Boston. We sleep together every few months." Tara was bursting to blab further details. The more she talked, the less I had to. "Maybe you've heard of him," she gushed. "Ted Kennedy."

"You slept with Ted Kennedy?" I gulped my wine.

She giggled. "He comes to the apartment. We roll around all afternoon."

"Really?" I stopped eating, my mouth agape.

"Yeah, his limo driver waits outside, while we fool around."

"How often does this happen?" I had to do some fact checking. Come on.

"Sometimes every few weeks, or every few months, whenever he's in New York," she confided. "More string beans?"

"How did you meet Ted?"

"Canvassing," she tossed off. "It was years ago; I don't think I had kids or even a husband then."

"But he was married."

"Sure, his wife Joan. Those stoic Kennedy wives, their rambunctious husbands. Ted in his youth reminded me of my first husband—all fiery and full of promise."

"You know, I've only had one husband…."

"Just one? You're young." Tara focused on me now. "What was the big turn on with him?"

"The soothing sound of his radio announcer voice made me feel smart, and hopeful. He had so much journalism experience; I saw him as a mentor, with wisdom for the writing world I wanted to belong to."

"Sounds great, sort of Scott and Zelda-ish." Tara sipped more wine. "Didn't Scott kind of drive Zelda crazy?" she added.

"That's the theory." I continued.

"So why'd you marry him?"

"Speaking of Ted Kennedy, when my husband and I first started dating, your pal Ted wanted him as potential press secretary for his presidential campaign. At the same time, I'd appeared on television doing comedy and was called a star of tomorrow. Thinking we'd either be in the White House or on TV, we each fell in love with the other's potential, not the real person."

"That's exciting," Tara offered.

"Plus, he seduced me with romantic dreams and all the trappings of living in the city. An intoxicating cocktail—I was drunk on the hope of a successful writer's life."

"Sounds like you've figured it out," Tara replied.

"Nah, I'm a mess."

"You've moved to the right place. Never a dull moment living with me. Dinner next week, I'll tell you about my TV show, and cooking dinner for 25 people with my leg in a cast."

Tara's stories were the highlight of my week. On Friday, she visited her family, gone until Monday. I was alone in the apartment for the first weekend after leaving Rupert. Josie and Bob distanced themselves from me, afraid I'd whine about what went wrong with the person they knew I shouldn't have married in the first place. They didn't want to dine with depression and neediness, seeing spending time with me in my current state as the equivalent of being asked to catch pneumonia. Me, with no plans, and no companions, was a sure-fire recipe for self-destruction and despair.

Friday night I ate my way through the middle shelf of the refrigerator, inhaling leftover Chinese food, half a pot of cold spaghetti, a brown banana and half a bottle of Chardonnay. After eating all that, I still felt empty inside. So I drank a big snifter of brandy, hoping I'd feel warmly cocooned from the inside, then numb.

I should have been happy to linger in a bubble bath, but instead it left me feeling sad and depleted. Calling a few friends, I heard only their answering machines. I didn't leave any messages. With no live voice I could crawl into for comfort, I felt lonely and vulnerable. So I drunk dialed Rupert. He usually sounded delighted to take my calls. While the phone rang, the voices in my head had a scream-fest: What am I doing? Bad idea! I'm not stopping! His perky phone "hello" always made me feel exceptional.

"Hi, it's me," I offered, when he answered. When we were together, he weekended in the country. Now that we were apart, it seemed he was staying in the city.

"I was just thinking about you—that I wished I was with you, holding you," he said. Rupert knew how to entice me with his radio newsman velvety voice.

Half drunk and wanting to be seduced, "Really? You wish you were with me?" With nothing to lose, I put my feet up on the couch and took a deep, slow, audible breath. "What are you wearing?" I'd learned that this sentence was a prelude to phone sex. He'd heard it before, many times, and liked it. I could hear his deep, knowing breath. I sensed he was turned on, but hesitant. "You know…" I was breathy, trying to engage him. "I'm wearing red panties," I offered, to see if he would take the bait.

"I'm wearing my underwear too," he sounded delighted, yet frightened.

"Are you lying down?" I asked, inquiring seductively.

"Yes," he said.

"How do you feel?"

"Good," his breathing increased. I felt his excitement, sensing the sounds of his sexual energy. This was who Rupert was with strangers, but not with me. I felt like I'd opened a magic treasure chest, filled with useful knowledge, and messy demons. Now that we were apart, I shared a sexual moment with my husband—the illicit unleashing of his desires.

"Are you touching yourself?"

"Mmm," he moaned, "Are you?"

"Yes, baby," I said, breathing hard.

"Mmm, good," he sighed.

"Are you getting harder and hotter?" I said breathlessly, now touching myself too, taking in the phone sex experience.

"I'm harder, I'm going to explode."

"Me too," I sighed, on the verge of letting go, rubbing myself until I climaxed too. We moaned in unison, more magical than any moment of marital intimacy we'd ever shared.

At first, my body tingled, elated by the orgasm. Then I remembered this was what he'd done with anyone and everyone but me. I'd heartbreakingly collected the charge slips to prove it. When Rupert climaxed on the phone, it wasn't a sensuous moan. He sounded like a deaf mute trying to get someone's attention. Sickened and disgusted, feeling so dirty—I wanted to shower from the inside out. Swimming in shame, I cried.

"I…I have to go," I whispered, hanging up. I curled into a morose heap and wept until I fell asleep.

#

Now that we'd had phone sex, I felt closer to and further apart from Rupert at the same time. Wanting him to change into an honest, open, loving man, I knew my behavior was sick and senseless. Meanwhile, his stalking, hourly phone calls became every other day chats with a warm, amusing guy who had a hypnotic phone voice, attentive and trying to woo me, like in our courtship. With every call, he charmed me just a little bit, creating "a reasonable doubt" like I was on jury duty. I wanted to believe that hope was love. Plus, he called and paid attention to me the way no one else did. I knew I needed to say, "Please, stop calling me." But I was afraid of what the silences would feel like.

And I wasn't willing to confront any of this, fearful I would find a part of me that was too ugly and desperate.

Meanwhile, Josie still retreated. Having had her fill of dining on stories of angst and marital woes, she told me in no uncertain terms, "We should get together, when you're ready to talk about anything else." I was alone and more vulnerable than I wanted to be—a seductive combination for Rupert, who had built our relationship on learning my weaknesses and desires, then worming his way into those needy unexplored places, not unlike some rat or other self-serving vermin. Woah – I harbored some pretty hefty anger toward this man.

On the other hand, he had found the neglected little girl in me and had taken her by the hand into the adult world.

A week after our call that left me crying in a heap, Rupert invited me to dinner, working hard at trying to re-win and woo me. He'd be cooking, he said. He never cooked when we were together, so he probably knew that was a sight I'd pay to see. I still had unanswered questions like—how could a smart woman be so stupid? So I figured that seeing him might help me understand how he'd fooled me. Also, having a blank social calendar, masochistic dinner theater seemed like a unique opportunity.

Visiting the apartment as a guest, to be served and waited on by my strange, estranged husband, I rang the doorbell. He greeted me, all smiles and cologne, dressed in my favorite shirt.

"Great to see you! Are you thinner?"

"Don't try so hard." I entered and looked around, curious, and not suspicious, for once. A big bowl was on the dining room table filled with salad. "You're using our good china? Who knew you set such a nice table?"

"This is a special meal." He served the salad and appetizers, while cooking the main course: filet of sole. His recipe? Fly by the seat of your pants. As we ate our salad, I noticed a strange odor from the kitchen.

"What's that smell?" I inquired.

"I'm cooking fish."

Alarmed, I flew into the kitchen. The frying pan was on a high flame. I grabbed a spatula and poked the filet. The paper that the fish had been packaged in was still under it, in the pan and on fire. I screamed at the stupidity and grabbed a dish towel, removing the pan from the flame. Rupert ran in. I took a deep breath.

"You left the packing paper on, under the fish, and put it in the pan."

Rupert surveyed the mistake. "That's why I need you here to make sure I do the right thing," he hugged me like a lost boy who'd just been found.

"Learn to do things right. I'm not a monitor or a mom." I released myself from the hug, irritated, trying not to show anger. "Let's just eat the salad." It seemed he'd do anything to please me—maybe even tell the truth. Impatient to seize that new honesty for my own healing, I said, "Now that we're not living together, you have nothing to lose."

Rupert nodded in agreement while chewing.

"We both know you went to prostitutes. Help me see your logic. What kind of women did you see? I could understand if you wanted a large breasted, six-foot-tall black woman to pee on you. What was your type?" I felt relieved and exhilarated, finally asking the questions that tormented me.

"Do you know how hard it is to find sweet women, who look like you?"

"You wanted women like me?" I was sickened. "Why not me?"

"You were so good and kind and loving. You were my wife; I could never do any of those things with you."

"But I wanted you," I pleaded. My stomach was knotting up.

"From the moment I met you, I feared losing you, I had to lie about everything…"

"Otherwise, I'd leave," I finished his sentence.

"Yes," he said reflectively.

"So the outcome was the same," I emphasized. "You didn't want exotic women to do disgusting things to you?"

"I wanted sweet women, like you," he repeated, seeking sympathy.

"To do what?" I demanded. "What turns you on, gets your dick hard, makes you come alive? Madonnas? Whores? Girl Scouts? I still have a uniform."

"Don't be disgusting."

"You don't like to lead in sex, maybe I should just do you, here and now." I stood from my chair, put one foot on it, and the other on the table.

"What are you doing?"

"We have a table cloth, I could do anything right now. Scoot your tushy onto the table. Maybe that's what you need to get a hard on."

"You'll fall and break the table."

"If I got a rise out of you it would be worth it. Come on, I'm here, I'm ready. You are withholding. Whip it out and shout!"

"Who are you?" he demanded.

"Who are you?! Why does someone pay for sex unless they want something unusual? I can't believe you wanted women like me—to do what? To be like me? To tell you jokes?"

"To hug and kiss and suck me," he mumbled, too embarrassed to say the words, let alone share the actions with someone who wasn't "working" for him.

I freaked. This was the weirdest thing I'd ever heard. My fantasy of his kinky call girls made sense to me. My fantasies were who I wasn't. His fantasies were who I was. A churning burned in my belly. I bolted from the table to the bathroom to puke my guts out. Looking in the mirror, I said to myself, "He's sick, it's not about you. Cancer is an illness too, like alcoholism. Would I walk away if his sickness was one of those?" I washed my hands and rinsed my mouth.

He had no empathy and no remorse, characteristics of a sociopath. I'd suffered sleepless nights thinking about where he'd been, whom he'd been with and what they'd done. He may have had an addiction that I was trying to help cure. But like all illnesses, the germs spread to other family members. How could I possibly heal him when I, myself, was so unhealthy? Thinking I could cure him had just made me obsessive, compulsive and tortured. Yes, his addiction had helped birth my own. Like most addicts, living in denial, I had been parading around, seeing myself as the healthier and saner one;

like the prettiest girl in Uglytown. My emotions see-sawed from feeling unlovable to being sternly superior. There was no sweetness in my life, never any ice cream cake—not with him, not with others, or even all by myself.

"The only thing my husband and I have in common is: we were married on the same day. He's so into masturbation, he thinks sex with a partner is a group experience. Now that I'm celibate I know why nuns are so mean. All I want to do is hit people with a ruler." A voice in my head said, "Save these jokes. Use them when you go onstage again." Walking from the bathroom, back to the table I broke the silence, "I should go."

"Please stay. I'm so glad you're here. Let's watch TV."

"I really should go."

He pleaded, "Please, please, give me another chance."

As if I still lived there, I plopped on the sofa. "If I leave now, I'm a quitter. We're finally starting to talk about some things. I want to heal my marriage," I said to myself as I picked up the TV listings. Finding two black video cassette boxes underneath, I opened them to see if we might want to watch them. Reading the titles, I saw they were—"Porno tapes? Porno tapes??" I raged. "Instead of prostitutes, what's this—a fuck party on a budget? Didn't we cut up your credit cards?"

"I used the fifty-dollar saving bond we'd gotten as a wedding gift from your uncle," he confessed, bursting into tears.

"You want me to feel sorry for you?"

"You don't understand," he persisted.

"Explain it to me."

"I can't. You just have to love me."

"I have been loving you—it hurts too much." That night I'd finally gotten the answer I'd been looking for: who he was fucking and why. Knowing didn't mean either of us was magically changed. He'd always need a secretive, sexual outlet: anyone but me or any other woman with feelings and thoughts (sanity optional)—that's what hurt the most. He'd never known how to include me in any aspect of his life; sex being the most prominent part of that exclusion. And, he felt no remorse. Pained to realize I was an omitted partner, the oxymoron of my marriage, my delusion made me stay—until now.

"You've been a bad boy. Enjoy the porno tapes. Mommy's leaving."

Rupert lunged to clutch at me. I moved past him, grabbing my purse, racing out, and slamming the door.

CHAPTER 21:

NEW PLANS

"Truth is, I've always been selling out. In the past, it looked like I had integrity because there were no buyers." —Lily Tomlin

Whenever I thought things were over, squashed, I'd be reminded that somewhere, hiding within Rupert's troubled self, was a man who still wanted to be married to me. That's why the final divorce dragged on. My attorney always told me that until our papers and divorce were final, I should offer an olive branch of hope.

I spent time with Rupert after our separation, still harboring the fear that no one else would ever love me. Meanwhile, my mom seemed to agree. This didn't help me.

Rupert and I excelled at bratty behavior. Every Friday around 3 p.m., one of us would call the other about the upcoming weekend. The one with the "good" plans would call the other and ask, "What are you doing this weekend?" The one with no plans or lonely feelings would respond, "Oh, nothing much, and you?"

In this strategic chess game of emotional manipulation, with a side of gut twisting jealousy, the partner with plans would say something like, "I have theater tickets, or a birthday party…" or something the other would find interesting. As soon as the planless partner's sighs of disappointment could be heard, the busy partner would say, "Got to go, have a great weekend." We were a magnetized matched set, as the master manipulator of the week became champ and the winner of the game, only to topple the following week, when the other won venomous victory. A tangled emotional web, both caught up, neither able to let go.

To combat my loneliness, I reached out to friends I hadn't contacted in years. One—Roberta—was managing editor of a women's magazine specializing in self-help and psycho-babble articles. Telling her of my angst, she helped me fashion it into themed stories and articles—writing about my painful experiences might prevent other women from having the same heartaches. So, I spent my extra time writing articles on women's issues: expert advice, given by a relationship misfit.

And so it came to pass that my torment became my bread and butter, as I fired off articles like: *"Is he cheating on you, 10 ways to tell."* Or *"Are you ready for a new relationship?"* and, *"The 30-day plan to get over him."* I was a guru, doling out advice to women desperate to change their lives and end their heartbreak. Maybe it was my own expertise that caused me to ignore every word of advice that I wrote for others—in any event, I continued to swim in my own ocean of misery, hoping I could turn the tides.

After a while, besides writing for Roberta, I pitched and wrote for other publications as well. Even though I was writing with greater frequency for an increasing number of magazines, I was still a struggling writer. Rupert, on the other hand, was a successful writer and editor—invited to the best parties New York City had to offer.

On one such occasion, Rupert had tickets to the hottest music and media event in town, mentioned in every newspaper and on every radio station. In his job as television editor at the *New York Daily News* he received two orchestra seats to the very first *MTV Music Video Awards*, to be held at Radio City Music Hall on September 14, 1984.

"I want you to be my date for a dazzling historic evening. Lots of celebs and champagne, and stuff you like," was the message he left on my home phone.

I told my roommate Tara about the event. She was packing to spend the weekend with her family. If I said no, I'd spend another weekend alone. In spite of Rupert's many offers, I had been doing that a lot lately. "Go! It should be fun," she counseled.

"What if it reminds me of good times I had with Rupert before we got married, and he tries to reel me back in?"

"It will be so packed with people you could get lost in the crowd and hardly notice him."

"Everyone in music who I ever wanted to see will be performing."

"Go! You get to dress up—we can pick out a dress for you from the closet of party clothes! Have a party night. It will boost your spirits."

It had been a long time since I had something fun to do on the weekend, and it would make for amusing stories to tell. Instead of renting boring videos to fill endless hours of time by myself, I'd see rock stars in tuxedos. It sounded pretty wonderful.

I told Rupert I was excited to go to the event, but he shouldn't get his hopes up. When the night arrived, I wore a vintage black velvet gown, off the shoulders, highlighting my long neck and small waist. As we stood in the lobby, celebrities walked by in their formal finery. Rupert looked at me with stars in his eyes.

Everyone was taking their seats, so Rupert and I walked down the aisle to the twelfth row. Lifelong music favorites were now onstage—just a few feet away from me. We saw Bette Midler, Tina Turner, Rod Stewart, ZZ Top and a host of others including some new girl who sang while crawling around the floor in torn crinolines: Madonna. This was the night that Madonna was discovered! For me it was a star-studded night filled with excitement, music and too much champagne.

Rupert was leaving the following morning to go to his weekend house. He suggested I sleep over and then spend the rest of the weekend in the apartment. I was tired, and tipsy; it sounded like a good idea. As we waited outside the theater for a cab, the wind whistled around my ears. I clutched onto Rupert for warmth, fending off the cold night. He leaned into me, kissing my neck.

Over at the apartment, I peeled off my party dress, put on something flannel and crawled into bed with Rupert. He felt so cozy and familiar that I curled up and spooned him, just like I'd never left. He seemed pleased. We both fell asleep and slept peacefully.

In the morning, I woke up with a new awareness of where I was and what I'd done. Was I giving him mixed messages, or was there a chance I might want Rupert back? A week earlier, I'd written an article, *Sex with your Ex: 12 reasons to say no.* There was also a sidebar: *If you're (occasionally) having sex with your ex.* That piece ran through my mind…

As long as your ex is in your bed, you're not moving ahead toward better, more fulfilling relationships. He's your ex for reasons. Whether it was your idea or his, the relationship as a whole didn't work out.

A woman has sex with her ex for any number of reasons. Ask yourself the following questions:

** Am I hoping for reconciliation?*

** Am I hoping that he'll realize what he's missing and fall in love with me again?*

** Am I having trouble letting him go?*

** Is he using me? Am I using him?*

** Am I just killing time until I find something better?*

** Is it really over, or do we still have a chance?*

If there is still hope for your relationship, sex is not the answer. If the sex is still good, then it wasn't the reason that things fell apart. Deal with and work on the problems. Keep sex out of it; it only clouds the issue. Do yourself a big favor and let him go. You may have a problem "kicking the habit." Do your best to get past him and move on with your life.

Many women wrestled with these feelings all the time, and I realized I was no different. Rupert woke up. I was so starved for affection. We cuddled and groped under the covers for a few minutes.

"Are you sure you want to go away this weekend?" I was testing him.

"People who live and work in Manhattan have to get away to save their sanity. Everyone I know has a weekend place. Poor people have smaller ones than rich people. But I'll go a little later so we can snuggle."

I was going to learn that I hadn't learned my lesson well enough.

I glanced over at the clock on my side of the bed. I saw something unusual there that caught my eye. I sat up to scrutinize it further: a pair of earrings for pierced ears and a necklace. They were not mine.

"Whose jewelry is this?" I demanded.

"What jewelry?"

"These earrings! Whose are they?" I welled up with rage. Going to prostitutes was one thing. But if he was missing me so much, and still talking about wanting me back, how could he sleep with other women and in our bed?

“Earrings? I don’t know,” he fumbled.

Even though it had been almost nine months, I wasn’t fully moved out yet. My clothes still filled at least one of the closets. “Whose fucking earrings are these?” I screamed, rubbing my arms repeatedly—half out of feeling dirty and violated, knowing I’d slept on the same sheets as some other woman, and half in an effort to soothe my rage, so wild and alien, I was certain it needed to be contained.

I was outraged, even if irrationally so, that he was having sleepovers with other women, in the bed that was a wedding present from my dad. I had compartmentalized his paying for prostitutes as being impersonal—a non-emotional detachment like playing tennis, as the non-athletic Rupert had once explained it to me. But it enraged me to think he was having girlfriend sex now. I needed to spin this into something sane on my part, but I was too devastated to think clearly. Angrier with myself than him, I had been falling for his song and dance yet again, like a battered wife who goes back for more. He was playing all of us, just to meet his needs.

I guess sex addicts don’t think about or notice things like clean sheets, or who is sleeping on them. I had been thinking that his steady sex diet was made up of prostitutes, not bringing women home. Churning with betrayal, and outrage, I blamed myself for not wanting to accept my reality. To make matters more painful, I realized that the night of the awards show would have been the night we'd celebrated our second wedding anniversary…if we were still together.

As if doused with ice water, that moment became the right time to bolt—leave with conviction, and a little drama. Yuck, repulsion. Where were my shoes?

Was going to a great show and glamorous party really worth the subsequent heartache I'd put myself through? Rupert was who he was – he would never change. Trying to find a sign of life in my marriage was as futile as trying to resuscitate road kill.

"You know, you fuck whoever you want, with me or without me. Doesn't matter to you, doesn't matter to me." Speedily collecting my clothes, dressing while talking, my voice rose into a scream, "I'm not staying here this weekend." I left, slamming the door.

I had to get all of my things out of the apartment, stay away from him, and jump-start my new life without looking back at him or who he was fucking. Where did he find these women? Was he dating and charming fresh meat into bed? Why was I thinking about his sex life? 'Cause I didn't have one of my own—and I desperately wanted one.

When I finally got home, to my dark, still apartment, I cried—and overate. Rupert was always having sex, with the effortlessness of breathing.

Seeing another woman's earrings on my own night table was a rude awakening, the slimiest realization of my husband's sex life. As for me, I hadn't dated all this time out of guilt and frustration that my marriage ended. Short on self-esteem, like a battered wife, my bruises were in my psyche. Whenever I felt better about myself, one needy, seductive call from Rupert could deflate my best efforts, not unlike calls from my mother.

In those last few months of frequent phone calls, his seductive voice was brimming with assurances, vowing devotion, reconciliation, and a stronger union—all wrapped in the ribbon of *I Love You.* It was a pretty package that never quite lived up to promises, yet it was presented adoringly for the taking. Yes, I wanted it. But opening the lid was like lifting the top off a box of candy, and seeing snakes jump out.

The poetry of his promises was a box of snakes. Still, my chubby snake charmer had a way of casting a spell on me and I'm assuming, by recent evidence, on many other single NYC women yet to cross his path, as well. I kept getting fooled and roped in, hoping he'd change. Looking back, as much as I felt emotionally tortured by his behavior, I spent too much time insanely peering into the microscope of his antics, and not enough time picking up the mirror to look at myself.

No self-reflection made for a bitter Arlene.

We weren't divorced yet but, Rupert's active pursuit of strangers churned in my gut, provoking me to have any sex life I could find—and now.

As a self-made, self-help expert, it was clear to me that I needed to get laid. But who? Someone who found me desirable.

Married women don't have a stockpile of sex buddies. For me, being the wife of a sex addict, rejected so often, I wasn't sure that if someone desired me, they wouldn't reject me the minute intimacy ensued. My newly minted PTSD disorder, coupled with my own sex drive and longing for the dance of seduction, was akin to burning an open wound, complete with the anticipation of pain, the scorching anguish, and the stinging relief.

In hindsight, I thought my hesitations were due to my husband's rejection/avoidance arabesque, coupled with my intense pre-Rupert, non-Raphaelite fat girl insecurities. When I was younger, I gained weight to hide from intimacy, believing only the kindest and most sensitive of lovers would see past my fleshy form to my true inner self—not exactly a plan for success. It kept me unpopular and virginal way too long. But that mindset only piggy-backed on my reluctance to see my own worth. A joke to myself that I never said out loud: *I was someone's third choice at an orgy.*

What I needed now was a sure thing. Plus, there's safety in familiarity: Paul? When Paul and I worked together, he mumbled about desire and wishing I was available. When I was still with Rupert, Paul and I had two groping sessions; he was the logical choice for my sexual re-entry. In truth, I was afraid to even approach him. Yet our connection was too intense to forget and move on. I needed to pull the thread of sexual tension and see where it would take me—and I needed to be confident it wouldn't break. We hadn't seen each other in months. He was busy with work, putting in a lot of overtime. I was figuring my life out, obsessing, regrouping. There were answering machine messages every week, back and forth, proof that some flicker of a fire still burned. So I invited him for dinner at my new apartment.

Friday night, I cooked, cleaned the house, bathed, and moisturized my freshly shaved legs—all in anticipation that now was the right time with Paul.

He arrived looking handsome, smelling freshly showered. Sharing a slow lingering hug in the doorway, my whole body tingled. It put a little lift in my step. Both eager to catch up on the changes in our lives, chatter was animated, a ping-ponging volley, talking over each other, gesturing wildly. All good signs. Showing him around the apartment, first the fire place, couch, then my room; the bed. I envisioned his head on those pillows, certain he'd be there soon. His eyes stared intently at my bed. I sensed we both felt a flicker of anticipation.

Back in the kitchen, grabbing pot holders, I bent down, opening the oven door. Glancing back, I saw Paul, standing right behind me, his eyes surveying my tight pants, as I checked the casserole dish. The heat from behind me seemed greater than that from the oven. At that moment, I was sure I felt his desire to do me from behind. I wanted that too, but only after downing enough wine to quiet my anxieties and insecurities.

I poured wine; maybe he didn't realize how much I wanted him, so I coyly tossed my hair like one of *Charlie's Angels.* A provocative move at the time, it suggested, "Come closer, I'm touchable, I'm wild for you."

"Nice apartment—I'm so glad you invited me for dinner," he offered like a toast, right before touching the glass to his lips, sipping. Paul seemed impatient, yet nervous.

"Hope you'll like my cooking." Fumbling for words, I tried to read his every glance and body language, while putting the salad on the table.

"It's great to see you," he said.

My chattering brain tormented me. See, he says he's happy to see you. You used to see each other every day, effortlessly. If we were so hot for each other then, did opportunity and availability make us stupid now? More wine, eager for engaging banter, but instead, quiet ensued. I put on soft, romantic music, served lasagna. We both chewed and smiled. Were we too hot for each other, like a pot of boiling water that just evaporates?

"Tasty lasagna." Paul smiled, eyes glimmering. I looked away—too shy to let on how hot I was, still waiting for a green light from him. "You know what I like."

Almost choking on my salad, was this the beginning of foreplay talk? Two people trying to be subtle. I think I got it right that he was hot for me. "More lasagna?"

When his azure eyes twinkled at me, instead of refilling his plate I wanted to sweep everything off the table—throw him down—climb on top of him and give us both what we really wanted. My desires were not my actions. Instead, I said, "Save room for dessert," teasing, part mom, part smutty bad girl.

Paul readily ate the second serving, his fork now moving slower, like a speeding car suddenly encountering traffic. "This is so good. I'm feeling full, but I don't want to stop." Plate clean, he leaned back in his chair, looked up, and smiled. Eyelids heavy, Paul curbed a yawn. "I don't know what's come over me, I feel relaxed, almost sleepy."

"Dessert?" I thought that the more I fed him, the more endearing I became.

"Kind of full. Couch?" He pointed. We moved, each sitting close to a sofa arm, then settling in wriggling closer together, legs touching.

I wanted to jump him, but I didn't have an ounce of confidence. I needed someone else to provoke intimacy and make me feel wanted—I had spent all my aggressor energy trying to get my husband to touch me. As an alternative to expressing deep desire, I subtly ran my lips along the side of his neck, like a kitten's endearment. When Paul leaned into me, my anxiety subsided, feeling secure enough to move closer. He put his arm around me, a warm, loving caress.

A minute later, Paul was snoring, eyes closed. Had I put him to sleep? I'm as sexy as a nap. Remembering my honeymoon, how a flash of passion was squelched by an overlooked instant, I verged on tears. Seconds later he woke, startled.

"Excuse me. Lasagna makes me sleepy, but I do feel cozy with you."

Cozy won't get me laid, I thought, moving my mouth so close to his he couldn't help but kiss me. Warm, familiar, now reclining, we wrapped around one another on the couch. Paul ran his fingers along the sides of my body as if tracing a memory he wanted to retain. This felt sincere and vulnerable. I knew *he* was capable of devotion and fidelity. I needed a taste of that with every pore of my being, not just my neglected sexual self. But now that he was here, I couldn't be here fully: my mind wanted to race to future times with Paul—he'd be so nice to see movies with, to walk arm in arm through the park with, or to wake up to.

Rewind. I forced myself to stay in the bliss of this long-awaited moment: enjoying a hot kiss in my cool, single girl apartment, with a sexy man, who'd already seen me naked. He was back for more. When the kiss ended, to catch our breath, I looked at him, his eyes still closed. At first, I was glad that he couldn't see the sign "Needy Girl" in neon letters imprinted on my forehead. As I rubbed his neck with both hands, his eyes remained closed, his face blissful. Desire weighed heavy in the air. As I opened the top two buttons of his shirt, his eyes finally opened. He moved my hand away, kissing me one more time, then sitting up from the couch.

"I should be going," he mumbled, unconvincingly.

Stunned, afraid to say, "Don't you want me?" or "I thought you came for more than dinner," I offered weakly, "It's early. There's chocolate pie."

"That's OK. I'm full and I need to go now." Paul grabbed his coat, kissed my forehead, reached for the door and flew away before I could say another word.

Why did he leave? I'd cooked a meal so heavy it put him to sleep. Laughably stupid. I felt emotionally dehydrated and burnt along the edges. I couldn't believe I'd put myself out there again, and orchestrated it with a three-course meal. Is this what men do when they care for me— race away like it's the leper Olympics?

Distraught, I grabbed a fork and picked at the leftover lasagna, still in the pan. First I nibbled a bite or two, tiny, slowly, sauce, and some cheese. My arms and legs heated up, heart pounding so fiercely; I couldn't taste what I was robotically stuffing into my mouth. Nor could I stop. Finally, I'd somehow inhaled half the contents of the pan. Mortified, I threw the pan into the sink as if angrily slamming a door, punctuating an argument, another confrontation too fearful to have. Then, I too felt sleepy—as well as angry, disappointed and still unfucked.

The next morning, Saturday, I awoke feeling kicked in the head by a bowling ball. Mixed metaphor, I know, but just go with me—that's exactly how I felt. Eyes swollen—maybe I had cried in my sleep—it took hours to make coffee, wash my face, and stop dragging myself around in a post lasagna haze. I wanted to call Paul.

No I didn't. I wanted him to call me and beg for forgiveness. I even wrote the speech in my head of what he'd say to me. He didn't call.

I begged Josie to meet me in the local diner. Sitting in a booth, I was a slouched bundle of need and frustration, wrapped in baggy jeans and a denim jacket, staring into my bowl of soup, wishing it were a Crystal ball.

"I know it's been difficult to be around me, whining about my marriage. But I have a new song to sing, that copywriter from my old job, Paul. He was at my apartment last night."

Josie perked up. "The guy who was hot for you when you were married? Please tell me you guys did it. If something good happened, you'd be shouting from rooftops."

Forlorn, I fumbled with the plastic wrapper on a tiny packet of oyster crackers. "A man rants with innuendoes for months. I invite him for dinner, which he enjoys. We kiss, lying on top of each other on the couch, heatedly humping. He leaves?"

Josie sat tall and animated, "That's not normal. What did you say?"

"He bolted before I could speak. I was amazed he could walk. I was afraid to talk to Rupert, and now Paul…I never say what I want or get what I want."

"Men suck."

"Paul knew how hurt and rejected I felt in my marriage and he behaved like this?"

"Do you really have feelings for him? Or were you using him as a scratching post for your unfulfilled needs?"

"You think I'm just a cat in heat?"

Josie said gently, "You are overeager and confused…wanting sex, with emotional attachment, yet too detached to see you're not there." Nailed it. She reached across the table and caressed my face. "You are fine. You just have bad taste in men."

"What do I do with that?"

"Regroup. Buy a vibrator. Go for a massage. That makes everyone feel better. Want to catch a movie? *Splash* is playing down the street."

"A romantic comedy about a guy who falls in love with a mermaid, when I can't even hook a human? Besides, Tom Hanks looks too much like Paul. Nah."

"Find out what his problem is. Something changed his mind. It's not you."

Josie's words, hot soup and a slow walk home boosted my spirits. Entering my apartment, I checked my answering machine—not blinking. "I can't call," I told myself out loud, wrote down what I'd say, dialed three digits, then put the phone down.

That evening, caressing a giant bowl of air-popped popcorn, I zoned out on the couch with music videos on MTV. Sunday morning, I did laundry, and vacuumed, still waiting for my phone to ring. No Paul call. Early evening, I took a breath and dialed… almost five rings. My heart would have burst out of my chest if the answering machine picked up. Instead, it was him, a distracted, "Hello?"

"It's me," I offered with barely an ounce of confidence.

"Hello," he repeated. Then, a moment of silence. "You called me."

"Yes, I called." My brain cells refused to fire, hoping he'd say the speech I wrote for him in my head. "This is hard for me. We've been close, and now I feel like I don't know you. You used to talk about how you wished we'd be together if I wasn't married. I've left my husband, I invite you over, and you run out? Please, tell me why you left."

Paul took the longest, most agonized deep breath and sigh I'd ever heard. "You're right—I owe you an explanation. I did want you; you're great. But I'm an honorable, old-fashioned guy. I just started seeing someone about a month ago. So I really feel I should give that relationship every opportunity. I'm sorry; this is a case of bad timing."

This moment felt worse than bombing onstage. "So if I didn't call you, I never would have heard from you."

"When it comes to you, I guess I'm just a coward." More silence. Then I heard his doorbell ring. "Chinese delivery is here. My dinner. Gotta go. You'll be fine, you'll see."

He hung up the phone and I thought to myself, "You're wrong, I'll never be fine."

CHAPTER 22:
THE BULIMIC AND THE SOFA BED

"It's hard to have a positive attitude...when you don't have one." — Arlene Schindler

About ten months after moving in, I finally unpacked the last of my things in Tara's apartment. Then she told me her rent was going up 20% and so she'd be vacating. I couldn't stay legally or financially. I had to apartment-hunt again.

Feeling like the poster child for displacement—Little Miss Rootless—I was too busy trying not to be homeless to even think about Rupert more than a few minutes a day. The upheaval of my living situation actually took my mind off my marital insanity—back to scouring the newspapers for roommate situations.

As part of the grueling, pavement pounding and interview process, one day I visited a spacious two-bedroom apartment with plush white sofas and a baby grand piano. It was walking distance from the Girl Scout offices and cheaper than living with Tara. The prospective roommate, Karen, was ten years older than me. She had curly hair that was wild and dry, yellow teeth and the looks and personality of an old maid—in the dictionary under spinster, they had her picture. But she said yes to me, so I moved in a few days later.

My child-sized bedroom was furnished with a hodgepodge of hand-me-downs: the dresser I'd moved from Rupert's, to Tara's, to here, my childhood desk from my uncle's garage and a plaid sofa bed that was so ugly, I left the bed open most of the time.

One night when I was watching television in the living room, my phone rang. I ran to my room, closed the door halfway and picked up the receiver. A split second later, Karen bolted out of her bedroom, closed my door shut, ran into the bathroom, and locked that door. Putting the phone up to my ear, I realized there was no one on the other end. The same scenario happened the following night. Phone rang, Karen bolted from her bedroom to the bathroom like a cockroach fleeing a bright light. When I picked up the receiver, there was no answer.

I realized Karen had called my line before her bathroom trip, because she didn't want to be seen half-dressed on her way to the bathroom. I waited until she returned to her room before venturing back into the rest of the apartment; her timidity was rubbing off on me. Now I'd contracted cockroach behavior too—environmental hazard. Cold and indifferent, she was the opposite of Tara, not wanting friendship or dinner, just someone to share the rent and stay out of her sight, nothing more.

On Friday night, Karen ordered enough Chinese take-out food to feed four people. She meticulously put the beef, chicken and rice into beautiful bowls on a regal platter and carried it into her room and shut the door. Earlier that week she'd sat me down for a talking-to, cautioning that I'd spent too much time in the living room while she was home. So that night I spent the evening reading in my room, with the door half closed.

An hour after flying into her room with the food, Karen bolted out and into the bathroom. She slammed, then locked the door, turned on the shower full force and the sink too. Then I heard horrible retching noises. I left my room, glanced at the bathroom door and then peered into Karen's room. The platter was on her bed. The bowls, once brimming with food, were now licked clean. I moved to the bathroom door, concerned.

"Are you okay?" I queried, trying to be helpful.

"I'm fine, go away," she demanded, while flushing the toilet. I went back to my room. The rushing waters stopped, and Karen scurried back to her room, slamming the door behind her. I thought about the strange events I'd just witnessed, coupled with my roommate's dry hair and yellowing teeth—The realization hit me like a lightning bolt: Karen was bulimic and had just thrown up her Chinese feast. In a flash, this moment portended what being single in my thirties would be like if I didn't take responsibility for my life and work hard to fight my bitter-divorcee demeanor.

The foreshadowing was inescapable. Was Karen the mirror of my future?

From deep within myself, I heard a voice – *my* voice, "Learn the lesson now! Don't be like her. Life makes her so sick she's throwing up. What's your excuse? Sure, you're a magnet for crazy. You've been through terrible things, but let's find a positive side to all of this, soon, so you—*so I* don't become a dried-up, closed-off lonely old woman, resembling yellow-toothed, witchy looking Karen."

"I'm a procrastinating bulimic; by the time I'm ready to purge, it's already turned to fat." It always did get a laugh. Now I knew up close the gut-wrenching agony of the disease. Overeating gave me an initial pleasure in fullness—it provided a relief from emptiness. Many lonely nights I was comforted by a warm belly that induced a deep trancelike slumber. I couldn't imagine violently rejecting all that food to feel good.

My life was filled with great comedic material, *if only* I could step out of my own way, write and perform it—Big "if." I wondered: *Is bulimia contagious?*

CHAPTER 23:

The Boy from L.A.

"Men in LA are different than men in NY. Their lies have back stories." —Arlene Schindler

Every time I witnessed Karen's cockroach scurry through the apartment, my skin crawled with the fear of becoming a spinster. Believing I was officially ready to date, how would I meet people? What kind of people? People who read. Perhaps the newspaper could help me. I responded to seven personal ads. Getting no replies, I decided to place my own.

In the era before internet dating, or sophisticated matchmaking/dating services, all that was available for a proactive dating search was creating and placing personal ads in printed publications like *The Village Voice, New York Review of Books,* or *New York Magazine.* Writing a personal ad was like polishing a diamond. It took painstaking hours of refinement to capture the brilliant cut, color and clarity of my "female seeking male" creation. Every word mattered and had infinite meanings, both negative and positive. I spent hours with a thesaurus. "Adventurous" meant "into threesomes." "Entrepreneur" meant "does not work well with others." My favorite, "looks younger" meant "insecure and lying about hair plugs."

I agonized and was finally satisfied with the following:

ARE YOU THE REAL THING? I am. Fiery redheaded writer, emerald eyes, ivory skin, vivacious, bright and funny, seeks unpretentious, intelligent, honest, film buff, with sense of humor and zest for life.

After the ad had been printed, I raced to the newsstand to get the publication and see my gem of a personal ad on the printed page. I stood on the street corner like a jittery junkie, waiting as the papers were delivered. When I heard the stack of papers slam to the ground, I breathed a sigh of relief, anticipating the high that came next. My eyes raced through the personals column to find my ad, hopeful to be assured it was easy to find and featured prominently.

I waited a day or two for the letters to arrive. When the first plump pouch filled my mailbox, I was elated. Frantically I opened the large manila envelope, shaking its contents over my living room coffee table. More than two dozen letters floated to the table like confetti. A surge of energy flowed through me, a jolting buzz, like turning on the lights for a Christmas tree. I changed out of work clothes into comfortable house clothes, poured a tall drink with lots of ice, turned on music and settled in for an evening of letters to ME, from strangers who wanted to meet ME. Many phone calls followed, a dozen first dates, and a few new friends. I was brimming with hope and opportunity.

Important to note, in this pre-internet era that photos were seldom if ever used. Wit, personality and penmanship ruled in this pre-swipe left or right on an image world.

The week between Christmas and New Year's would normally be the loneliest time of the year for me. This year it was filled with voice mails and parties from new men I'd met, thanks to my ad in the *Village Voice*. Last year at this time I was planning to vacate my marriage. Now I was preoccupied with a flurry of new men—too busy dating to think about who my husband was humping for the holidays.

I had a bunch of first dates: friendly and cordial, but without chemistry. During these get-togethers, I learned what to look for, what to talk about, and how to politely exit a lunch, coffee, or cocktail hour that lacked potential. Then there was a guy, raised in New York City, who'd spent the last six years in California. He'd just completed his Master's degree and moved back two weeks earlier.

I liked the fact that we were the same age and exploring new starts in our lives. Over the phone he sounded sweet and warm. I pictured him with long blonde hair. In person, Warren was a 6'4" vegetarian with piercing brown eyes, full sensuous lips, and a shaved head. He was kind and gentle with a deep, warm laugh—the first person I had enough rapport with to go on more than one date. We took long walks through Central Park. He asked me out for New Year's Eve. I was thrilled to have a date and not be in the cootie club of datelessness this year. He planned to cook dinner and give me a massage afterwards. Considering we'd had a few dates together, I'd hoped this would be our sex date—to start the year on a new foot, relaxed and well fucked.

New Year's Eve, I arrived at Warren's apartment, a one-room studio, third-floor walkup. He proudly announced that his apartment was 500 square feet. I think it was more like half that—we're talking tiny.

His apartment was so small, you had to go outside to change your mind. It was so small you couldn't laugh ha-ha-ha you had to laugh he-he-he, or your cheeks would hit the walls.

We ate dinner cross-legged, sitting on the floor, spitting distance from every piece of furniture in the apartment. He played Indian music. We laughed a lot. Right after downing his last morsel of food, Warren kissed me, gently moving my body to relax under him as he moved some giant pillows for comfort. With confidence and grace, he guided my body, caressing me close to his tall, strong physique—a refreshing change from the fading memory of Rupert.

As soon as I was relaxed, wanting more of him, Warren turned me on my stomach for a massage. My shoulder aches melted. The rest of me was melting as well. If he was trying to seduce me, he was succeeding at high speed. I moaned softly into the pillow, trying not to sound too eager. I loosened my blouse so he could rub my back. Then, when he was rubbing my neck, he he began rubbing with his mouth, teeth and tongue right where his hands had been. It had now been almost two and a half years since I had sex. Hot and ready, both still fully clothed, but that changed soon, as he removed my shirt, then pants, caressing and kissing my legs. After he'd kissed me all over, he quickly undressed himself, then speedily slid us both over to the futon mattress, where we gloriously kissed and caressed for an endless amount of time. He poured more champagne. We sipped. Then he touched my mouth with his finger, to grab the last droplet of champagne. He drew it to his lips and then, slid that same finger between my legs, gently at first, then probing, seeking the moist places and sensuously stroking until the wetness increased.

"This is the sex date," I thought, sighing. "Finally."

I reached for his cock, bigger than large, it was gargantuan. Delighted and frightened, could my born-again virgin self take him inside me? I thought about how wonderful his naked body felt, how sensuously he tried to please me. After what seemed like hours of touching and licking he inserted himself inside me—or at least he tried to. As turned on and wet as I was, my vagina was like a locked steel gate to him. Breathing deeply, "Keep trying," I insisted, as if he banged on a door and no one was home.

Was he too large, or was I too out of practice? To relax, I told myself jokes. "*His penis is so large, it needs its own pair of pants. Remember the cartoon Beanie and Cecil? How about Cecil with a yarmulke? Warren's dick is so large, it's a space capsule for a Barbie doll. His hands are so big, his cock could apply for statehood.*"

"Wait, let me get something," he wriggled to the side of the futon and produced a tube of lubricant. "This should help," he offered, easing the tension. He squeezed some of the clear gel onto his hand, rubbed some on himself and onto me. He tried again to penetrate me, only able to barely get inside me. I felt so much pain I wanted to scream, but I was thrilled to be experiencing something I had missed since my honeymoon. We thrusted together. Pain turned to numbness. Relishing his passion and hard cock, my breathing increased, but I couldn't deny the pain.

Praying for this moment to end, "Please come, please come," I screamed silently. A few minutes later, after what felt like an eternity, he did. We kissed.

"Happy New Year," Warren said, collapsing on top of me. I was delighted that my New Year, 1985, began with my first sexual experience since my marriage. I decided that the only way to heal myself after a sex-starved marriage with a deviant husband was to have as much sex as possible. I hoped that this would be the beginning of my most sexually charged year ever.

New Year's Day, I woke up to Warren breathing on my naked shoulder. I looked forward to the new morning, new relationship and New Year, with hope and with a swollen, throbbing vagina. So sore I thought I wouldn't be able to walk, I knew I wouldn't be able to greet Warren as he was hoping when his hardness rubbed against me minutes later.

"If it's not one thing, it's another."—Roseanne Roseannadanna

"Be careful what you wish for."—Anonymous—AKA every wise man ever

Now I had a hot hard man who wanted me. But I was on fire from pain! Maybe in time this would be funny, but now it was sadly pathetic. I made excuses. I touched him and, as he moaned, I stroked him over and over with my hands until I satisfied him.

My celibate body and fantasizing brain had made plans my vagina was clueless in keeping. Our sex parts fit together like threading a needle with a jump rope. What did Warren think of me now? I was embarrassed to tell him how sore I was, thinking he'd find me problematic, and reject me. It would be quite a few days before the swelling subsided. After breakfast, I excused myself to go home and take a hot bath. While soaking my mind replayed our passionate night. I tried to touch myself in the tub, but it hurt too much.

We spoke on the phone the next day, talking about getting together, (once I could walk comfortably). He called again, days later. "How are you feeling?" he asked, concerned.

"Much better."

"Good. I enjoyed our time together, and ringing in the new year. But, um, uh…my old girlfriend from San Francisco is moving to town in a few weeks. I think we're getting back together then."

"Oh," I said, disappointed.

"If you ever want to get together for brunch, or a walk through the park, *as friends,* let me know," he offered. "I've got to run." Warren hung up the phone.

I cradled the receiver close to my heart, like a dagger.

But at least I would forego any further piercing.

#

Rupert and I were still legally separated, not yet divorced. Both frustrated by the time, energy and money it cost for our attorneys to sever our relationship, we talked on the phone periodically, or had a quick drink after work, to iron things out and speed the process along; a poor justification for continuing our competitiveness, and the obsessive behavior.

Whenever we met, I made sure I looked fabulous and desirable, to make him want me, to see what he'd lost, for my own sex starved ego, and because my attorney Herbie said, "Seduction greases the wheels of compromise and negotiation." He had lots of snappy comments. When I showed him our wedding photo, he said, "You're beautiful. He's a troll. I see this marriage as your reaction to a fat adolescence." Herbie served as my attorney, school of life teacher and therapist, all for one billable hourly rate that was greater than a day's pay at Girl Scouts.

Rupert usually called me on the weekends, either before or after he'd had phone sex with some anonymous stranger. That had been his pattern in the past. I knew that because in my super-obsessive phase (not to be confused with my now moderately obsessive phase) I steamed open the phone bills and the charge bills and saw that the calls for phone sex and the calls to me from his weekend home were always back to back.

Sometimes he sounded boyishly guilty, as if he'd just done it and wanted to be punished or found out. Or else his voice sounded masculine and horny, as if I was the warm-up to the cool climax. Knowing this sickened me, and festered in my mind for hours after each call, as I raced to the faces, places and sounds of his potential sex life. I saw him grunting, pig-like, beads of sweat on his forehead, whining in climax, socks still on. I let myself get sucked into the opera of his sordid scenarios, killing any seeds of growth I tried to plant for myself.

If Caller ID existed at this time, I wouldn't have taken the calls. But it didn't; the ring of an unknown someone had a hypnotic stir, and I would rush to the phone. Rupert's after-call aches fed my insanity as frustration swirled around my squandered sexuality. Feeling sexually rejected post-marriage by both Paul and Warren (who'd both moved on to other relationships) pierced more profoundly than the fat-girl rejections of adolescence—a time when no one wanted me, and shared their reasons why: because of how I looked. I had barely healed those wounds when Rupert and I first met. Our celibate marriage ripped into those old scars, leaving me all the more exposed and vulnerable to these most recent pains. Would I ever heal, or ever be whole? Now I'd encountered men who liked the way I looked, but didn't want to sleep with me, because they were honorable and faithful to other women. Wounded as I was, I viewed the world through my eyes as rejection, believing no one would want me in the ways I sought to be desired.

I used to joke that people could "smell" when you were chronically unemployed, and it perpetuated your joblessness. My insane sexual neediness sparked the aroma of my own dysfunction. Smart seducers must have smelled that I was too dangerous, clingy or volatile for even a passing intimacy. I'd replaced fat-girl body armor with crazy-girl guardedness.

My attorney advised me to behave "nicely" to Rupert, repressing my rage to strangle him, and my voice from screaming, "Fuck off!" This was probably prudent advice. Meanwhile, Rupert was screwing everyone in his path. I knew this because whenever I visited the apartment I became a buzzard, swarming and picking through his bills, mail and anything on the desk I could snoop my nosy beak into. Frenzied curiosity, the thrill of the forbidden, coupled with the heartbreak of discovery was a dizzying emotional merry-go-round, probably comparable to what Karen felt during her bulimic episodes.

The very fact that I was still returning to that apartment kept me entangled, crippling my own future. Plus, when I focused on his insanity, I didn't have to look at my own—that was convenient. I was a champion at making myself feel miserable. If there was an Olympic sport of self-sabotaging behavior, I'd surely be a gold medalist.

During one of my (obsessive) visits to the apartment, I'd found letters from women responding to his ad in the classical music lovers dating newsletter. I saw their photos too! How dare he succeed in the dating world, where I was struggling? The need to know any nugget of information regarding his life without me burned through my veins like acid on open wounds. I wished I could stop being an obsessive nosy hole. I wanted to fuck fearlessly and frequently, like I was sure my sick dick ex-husband was doing in every spare moment.

In hindsight, I realized Rupert's sex life never really changed from the time of our first lunches. Even then, we barely had an emotional relationship, while he was fucking lots of other people. Now, he wasn't relating or having better relationships. He was just experiencing the world dick first, as always. While Rupert was having sex, I obsessed about NOT having it—more lack of self-reflection that devoured my sanity.

Still, seeing his appetites in action made me hungrier, and more desperate—as needy as an abandoned child—grasping to fill a gaping hole I thought was between my legs, but was really in my heart. It had now been four months since my night of painful passion on Warren's futon. Sure, I was meeting people, but never connecting. Yet I hungered for my sex life to feed me, because then I'd feel normal, like I believed other women lived—in the magazines I read and wrote for.

Looking back, I did not understand what intimacy was—an interaction that sparks closeness. Rupert couldn't have sex with me. I couldn't talk to him about our lack of sex. I married someone incapable of getting close to me. Mirroring that behavior, I couldn't get close to anyone either.

But I blamed him.

I began to realize that I didn't really want to just fuck around. That would have filled an empty place, but exacerbated a different kind of agony and loneliness. I needed to experience healthy intimacy, someone to hold and love me—a well-rounded relationship, with sex being the frosting on the cake. Only then would my Rupert interactions would be easier to deal with. On a night after drinks with him, talking about our settlement, we stood on a street corner and just when I thought we'd agreed on everything, he coolly said, "I'm not done with you yet."

"Not done with me? What am I—a pair of shoes you haven't worn out yet?"

Rupert smiled eerily. "I don't want a divorce. I haven't replaced you yet."

"You mean like when a pet dies, and you get a new, one just like it?" Really pissed, agitation bubbled through me. As we both stepped off the curb to cross, I tried to push him in front of a passing car. In that moment, I realized I needed professional help of an illegal kind.

#

Growing up in Brooklyn, there were a perpetual supply of "wise guys" who could "do you a favor" for a price. I contacted someone who knew someone who knew what those prices were. My friend Joyce had an Uncle Johnny, who owned a moving company. They schlepped furniture from one house to another, six days a week. In between, they were in the business of moving *people*, as in having them change their minds. Joyce and I went to Sunday dinner with Johnny and his family. After dessert, the three of us sat in the living room.

"My niece tells me you're having a problem she thinks I can solve."

"She's got a man she can't get rid of," Joyce offered.

"Somebody is bothering a nice girl like you. It's good you came to me. I'll take care of anybody who's bothering either one of youse."

"It's my husband," I started. "He won't give me a divorce. "

"Would you rather be a widow?" he suggested. "That's doable."

I looked at Joyce, as my request was calmly considered, like an order from a drive-through menu. Raising my eyebrows to her, I hoped she'd ask about smaller stakes.

"What else do you offer besides widowhood?" she responded, acting almost as my translator.

"I don't want to kill him—just maybe a big scaring," I added, trying to soften the request.

"Broken leg? Broken arm?" he suggested, almost like saying, "How 'bout some fries with that?"

"What about breaking windows, maybe car windows?" I returned, as if casually getting renovation estimates. In reality, this was quite an unsettling conversation. "Someone told me the only way to hurt rich people is through their money."

"That's pretty deep," Johnny nodded.

"Can we just mess up his car?" I was getting the hang of Johnny's world.

"A broken window or two, sugar in the gas tank, a slashed tire," Johnny brightened.

"Now you're talking," Joyce and I answered in unison.

"What's the price for this, Uncle Johnny?" tested Joyce, the deal closer.

"A couple hundred—the price of a nice new Sony TV. But I'll make sure you are well taken care of. Any friend of my niece Joyce is a niece of mine."

"Thank you, Uncle Johnny," we both replied in chorus, hugging him.

"I'll sleep on it," I added. I didn't really want to hurt Rupert or his car; I just wanted to know that I could. If Rupert refused to give me a divorce, I had a tool to play hardball: Uncle Johnny and his pals.

I was pretty disgusted with myself. Had I reached a new low? Or would I get myself into an even more appalling situation?

#

I never did have to call on Uncle Johnny to make something bad happen. Bad things seemed to happen all on their own.

"Honey, I had a car accident. I'm at Lenox Hill Hospital," was the phone message I came home to one day after work, mere weeks after dinner with Johnny. I called the hospital, spoke to a groggy Rupert, and visited him the next day.

On the best of days, Rupert was a soulful, sad faced Germanic cherub resembling Peter Lorre, if Lorre was cast as *Underdog*. Seeing him at the hospital was like a scene from some avant-garde French film without the subtitles or the popcorn. I expected a swollen face, legs in traction—basically someone who looked more like Oliver Hardy in a piano moving mishap.

When I arrived, Rupert looked like a transvestite the morning after, wearing a woman's ratty pink chenille robe, and resembling a less attractive version of Jack Lemmon in *Some Like It Hot*. He was unscarred except that the middle two fingers on his left hand were bandaged in a splint, akin to a penis in a cast. He looked laughably off balance, and I clasped my hand over my mouth to hide my smirk. He was trussed up in a hospital bed, so I tried to force some concern.

"What happened to you? Who was driving? How did they hit you?"

A tear came to his eye after he took a good look at me. "How are you?" he asked.

"I'm not in a hospital bed, in a woman's pink robe," I blurted. "Tell me everything. And where'd you get such an ugly robe?" I sat on the side of the bed.

"We were going away for the weekend, packing the car for the trip and Debbie closed the trunk. Only she slammed it on my hand and broke two fingers. My hand turned black in five minutes. The doctors were afraid it was infected. That's why I'm here."

"So you weren't in a DRIVING accident? It was a PACKING accident?"

"You could say that," he answered weakly, very weakly.

"That's different." My mind raced for an emotion somewhere between annoyed and confounded. I resisted the urge to jump up and leave the room.

"I'm glad you came to see me," he mumbled, medicated by painkillers. He reached for my hand with his undamaged one. "You never would have slammed a car door on me."

Little did he know that just weeks earlier I had priced accidents with hit men, like a sleek gangster's moll in a Warner Brothers B-movie. In this instant I realized that in times of crisis or great irony I step out of the moment, liken it to a film I've seen, then jump back in—much like the actors in the film *The Purple Rose of Cairo.*

"I can't believe the mess my life has become," he sobbed. "I should have been so much nicer to you; I don't know what I was thinking. I wish…"

"Honey, how are you?" said Debbie from the hospital room doorway. Rupert and I both froze. His hand moved from mine. I stood up. This was the woman who'd slammed the door on his fingers, the woman he was seeing now, who'd given him the pink robe. She was a chunky, manly looking woman, wearing a flowered blouse and tight jeans, sort of resembling a chintz sofa, with a head, not unlike the butch matron in every prison movie ever made. Even a small child had the "gaydar" to see she was a lesbian. Debbie was accompanied by a younger, smaller woman, Hope. Rupert introduced us all. Debbie and I scrutinized each other judgmentally, and then each feigned a polite hello.

My mind left the scene and the accident that brought all these women here together. "How would I cast this moment?" I pondered. "Was I the Norma Shearer of the group? Or more of a Joan Crawford? Maybe a Meg Ryan? Sandra Bullock?"

Rupert told me just last week that he and Debbie were spending weekends together, nothing too serious. He complained they were seldom alone because she always had an entourage of young, athletic women at her side. I x-rayed Debbie, mystified she was Rupert's squeeze du jour. I couldn't quite visualize the "squeeze" part.

"This is my tennis partner, Hope," she said. Tennis. Hmmmm.

The room suddenly felt hot and small. Perhaps too much testosterone was making me woozy. Rupert seemed so girly, goofy and tiny in the bed. Debbie looked so big, bossy and so different from me. The moment was disturbing and becoming increasingly uncomfortable. I needed to flee—immediately, yet gracefully.

I was glad that I'd seen Debbie, because her being in the picture made my divorce possible. Maybe now that he'd found someone, he'd replace me. But how could he be with someone so unattractive, so unfeminine, and so clearly not even heterosexual? Did he ever notice any of the women he was with, including me?

"I've got to run. Feel better, Rupert. Take good care of him." Exiting swiftly, fleeing to the elevator on the verge of laughter and tears, I wiped sweat from my brow.

Walking the fifteen blocks home, evening breezes cooled my cheeks. Bernard Hermann's score from Hitchcock's film *Marnie* filled my ears, especially when she said, "I'm just some kind of wild animal you've trapped!"

My mind raced with thoughts of sadness and relief—and then to the taste of pizza. Popping a piece of bubble gum into my mouth, I hoped to chew and bubble my thoughts and anxieties away. Stopping on a corner, waiting for the light to change, I looked up at the breathtaking sunset as the sun crept behind the clouds, transforming their color and shape before disappearing beyond the horizon. In this moment of beauty, I felt my breath rise and fall throughout my body with a tremendous sense of peace.

Crossing the street, I replayed Rupert's voice in my head, "I'm not done with you yet, I'm not done with you yet. I'm not granting you a divorce until I have someone to replace you." Then I saw Debbie's face. With her in his life, my future was possible. If she was bucking to be the next wife, then I could be free! I blew a bubble with my gum, then burst it with my tongue. Salivating at the thought of freedom, I wouldn't have to be polite or take his phone calls any more like my attorney always said I should. I'd spent so much energy trying to end this mess. I could taste closure in my immediate future. Did I still remember what would make me happy?

Throughout my life whenever I'd had freedom, too many choices and too much happiness, the only way I'd found to cope was to gorge until numb. Then I'd feel fat and sad—familiar footing. I saw myself as lost and alone, in a black and white Ingmar Bergman film, like a seashell on a beach, hoping to be swept up and away by a wave of someone's passion. Knowing me, I'd try to build a sand castle on that wave.

Finally, home, there was a Humphrey Bogart double feature on cable: *They Drive by Night* and *The Two Mrs. Carrolls*. I turned on the set, put on a nightgown, and crawled into bed. Knowing freedom was in my future, my emptiness and heartfelt aches of failing as a marriage partner were somehow soothed by snuggling in, and enjoying the first film. I never felt alone watching movies. The best remedy for my frustrations of a contested divorce was cinema therapy.

Continuing my affair with Bogie, readying for the second movie, I considered the similarities between the story lines of my life and those found within classic melodramatic films. In *The Two Mrs. Carrolls,* Bogie wanted to get rid of Barbara Stanwick, but not before he had Alexis Smith to replace her, just like Rupert with Debbie and me.

Except Bogart wouldn't be caught dead in a ratty pink robe.

CHAPTER 24:

ROBBED TWICE

"There's a country western co-dependent song. It's called, 'If you leave me, can I come too?'"—Kate Clinton

My life revolved around going to work and getting out of my marriage—a mirthless merry-go-round. Since I'd accrued vacation time at work, I planned a few days in Atlantic City, reconnecting and gambling with Bob. It had been too long since our adventures at the race track. These last few months I'd put any kind of fun on the back burner. I needed to be my old self again, like before I became Mrs. Santo.

Planning for my trip, I took my lunch to work every day for a month. Each day I'd put the five dollars saved into an envelope in my underwear drawer. The Friday before our Saturday departure, I raced home from work, to find the front door of our apartment unlocked. I cautiously raced inside, to find my room ransacked. All drawers were opened and picked through.

Karen came home minutes later. Nothing of hers was stolen; there was nothing to take. Her only jewelry were crafts pieces she'd made in summer camp. The fact that her stuff was too crummy to be robbed, and that I'd lost all of my valuables escalated the tensions between us. Gone were my diamond engagement ring, wedding band, and the money envelope for my trip. I felt violated, angry and broke. Losing my rings from Rupert felt like the only tangible remains of our union were now gone.

My skin crawled in the picked-over room, still smelling the stench of the body odor of whoever ransacked it. I didn't know where to turn. Devastated, and needing to flee, I thought the one who would most understand my lost wedding jewelry was the guy who gave them to me. I called Rupert. We both cried, talking about the rings being gone. He offered to replace them.

"Get in a cab and come over here right now," he said, taking charge. This made me feel cared for. After calling the police, I did go to Rupert's. After I entered the apartment, he held and consoled me like there was a death in the family. Since he'd recently called me to visit him in the hospital, my insanity had conjured a new layer of sensitivity brewing between us, one where we could turn to each other in tough times. My self-delusion, coupled with his, was comforting and familiar. I didn't want to be alone; I needed to belong to someone. When I was with Rupert, it felt like family. In that moment, I belonged to someone. Reeling from the robbery, I indulged an old tape, not unlike gorging until numb: if Rupert really wanted me, he'd use this last window of vulnerability as an opportunity to climb back into my life.

Together on the couch in a half recline, I rolled into him, clingy and needy, like Madonna in an early music video, hoping that in holding me closely, his heart would surface, and he'd take me in his arms for a love affirming kiss. Instead, he held me clumsily, stroking my head, like I was his dog. The phone rang. He answered it on the second ring, as if expecting a call.

"Hello…. yes…can you give me half an hour?" he said to the caller. "Me too."

"You're not going to stay with me?" Now was my turn to be the pouty, traumatized child.

"I wish I could, but I can't," he explained, seeming a bit torn.

"You're an adult, you can do whatever you want," I shot back, quietly but pointedly.

"I have a car load of people I'm driving to the country this weekend, but I should stay here with you," he said, trying to soothe me, and to half-heartedly convince himself.

"I wish you'd stay with me. I need you," I implored, devastated, and powerless.

"I hate to leave you. I have all these people," was his excuse.

Feeling empty, insane and desperate to connect, I blurted, "You can leave your wife when she needs you most. This could be a life changing night, and you bail on me." I was angry now. "We're not divorced yet. This isn't about obligation. This is about new pussy and you don't want to screw it up. Get out of here, go. Go!" I screamed, now throwing pillows from the couch at him. I mercilessly manipulated Rupert to choose me, and stay, to provide a last fleeting stronghold of crumbling stability—unrealistic expectations dashed again. The emptiness in my core, still unfilled. Now I was the dried-up unlovable old shrew I'd feared I'd become.

The weekend I was robbed was a pivotal weekend in Rupert's life, as well. Although he said he regretted abandoning me at my moment of need, he went off for the weekend with Debbie, who thereafter became his live-in girlfriend.

CHAPTER 25:
ZOMBIE DATER

"Whenever I want a really nice meal, I start dating again."—Susan Healy

Rupert had moved on to his next significant relationship, and I hadn't. Jealousy of his "success" engulfed my every waking breath (that is, those not spent romanticizing or objectifying food, or getting over heartache via transfusions of pizza—or éclairs from the bakery two doors down from the pizzeria).

Debbie was his impetus to speed the divorce. Since he owned both homes before we'd married, and plowed through our savings during our marriage, all I received upon signing the papers was eight thousand dollars. Once the divorce was final, I decided to do two things: have a divorce party and place a new personal ad. At first I wanted the party to be a dozen friends at a Chinese restaurant, with comedians to "roast" the occasion. But as the date of freedom drew closer, the celebration that felt best became a cozy dinner at home with just Josie and Bob, coupled with the best bottle of wine I could scavenge from Rupert's collection.

As a free woman, I dove into dating like it was my new job. My newest ad garnered lots of responses, a dozen phone calls, and nameless, faceless, two-or three-date experiences. On every first date, there was a "get to know you" phase where conversation swept through family background, childhood, and the Rupert years. If I had to tell one more new person I'd never see again about where I went to high school, I was pretty sure my head would explode. My ad ran in *New York Magazine*. It was 1985 and rumor had it that dates from *NYM* were better educated and more affluent than the *Village Voice* audience. They were—and they were weirder too.

Meeting so many men and having so many first dates, I had to write them down. I entered each name, age, occupation, interests and salient characteristics like: "occasionally witty," "has twin daughters," "likes Indian food." I was nothing if not methodical.

Charlie, 32, Bronx	Copywriter, divorced	Goofy laugh, Hitchcock
Dennis, 30, Queens	Investment banker, twin	Talks about cars and ex
Mark, 29, Manhattan	TV news, never married	Loves Chinatown, skiing

Dressing carefully for each date, just like when I was doing stand-up comedy, no one knew—least of all, myself—that I was not mentally present or emotionally available. If Mr. Right actually stared me in the face, I wouldn't have seen him. That didn't stop me. I believed a new relationship was the elixir to cure my ills and heal my wounds.

"The definition of insanity is doing the same thing over and over and expecting different results."—Albert Einstein (one of my favorite comics)

Blind dates were once the exclusive terrain of the geek, dweeb or socially inept. But with personal ads, blind dating was as easy as ordering take-out food. I plowed through blind dates like a hot knife through butter: two a day, three on Sundays—all as unremarkable as a single French fry. The parts of the dates that kept me coming back were the kisses. I came to learn that, whether or not we connected on the date, if we kissed, that would seal the deal for a second date.

A good kiss tastes like hope. I didn't know a lot of things, but this much I did know: a sensuous kisser was someone I could grow to like. But for the first time in my life I experienced something painfully creepy to me: with each man I kissed, I felt absolutely nothing.

"Zero, zilch, zip, nada." — Anonymous

You'd think I'd closed my eyes and was kissing my own arm, like when I first learned how to kiss as a curious 12-year old. After kissing the first two or three men and feeling a stony iciness, I assumed I had just met New York's worst kissers. But after puckering up for five or six more lip-smacking disappointments, I turned the lip of blame to myself.

I was a dating zombie, a social sleepwalker who kept dressing and reapplying lipstick and leaving the house no matter what was going on inside of me. How could I ever possibly "see" anyone? I wasn't even there. These men were having drinks alone with a soulless mannequin in tasteful clothes, and a face that somewhat resembled me.

Writing about emotionally ambivalent or unavailable men, I built a reputation as a relationship expert with articles like: "*The Blind Meeting the Blind:*"

The worst blind date I ever had committed suicide three hours before the date. The best was with a handsome actor with a southern accent who wanted to take me back to Kevin Kline's apartment, supposedly to watch an Elvis television special. After over 60 of these "relationship crapshoots," the best way for me to meet men is still blindly.

Not all of my dates were pleasurable. One guy got claustrophobic in a restaurant and ran out after the fruit cup. There was a rock musician who insisted I listen to all 75 of his demo tapes and admire all ten of his tattoos. There was the banker who casually stated, "I want someone down- to-earth to enjoy my estate, my pool and my Porsche." There was the ex-Marine who said, "You're put together pretty well, know what I mean? Do you think I really care if you want dinner, know what I mean? I wouldn't throw you out of bed, know what I mean?" I got the picture pretty quick. Know what I mean? Next.

Surprisingly, I could remember enough to write about my experiences, but I was immune to learning what I did and didn't want in a relationship or in another person. Bad dates or good ones, dating became a more self-destructive behavior for me than over-eating. I gorged on first dates like devouring a family-sized pizza by myself. As such, I stayed utterly clueless about the Arlene I was bringing to the table.

Sometimes it was all about "dating for meals" or trying new cuisines. Was I in it for the meals or the masochism?

#

"When someone breaks up with me, they race right out and lose their virginity," said a comedian ex-boyfriend after we ended. Now whatever I was selling, no one was buying.

One Saturday, early evening, after a happy hour date that was over in 45 minutes, I was home, exfoliating. *Never go on a blind date on a Saturday night.* The phone rang. It was Rupert. *Never answer your phone on a Saturday night.* We hadn't spoken in five months. The sound of his voice took me aback like a slap in the face.

"Hi honey," he murmured, followed by a deafening silence, as if it was my job to carry the conversation.

"What's up?" I finally said.

"I wanted to hear your voice," he mumbled.

"Are you alone?" I knew the answer. I'd held the receiver for too many calls like this—Rupert reaching out, trying to cope with his phone sex compulsions. "Is mommy out?" As if talking to a child or pet, I guess I was playing his game, painfully sad and co-dependent.

"Yes, she went with her friends and promised to come back an hour ago," he whined, like an abandoned child. "You sound great," he cooed back. "Am I going to see you soon?"

"Why would you want to?" I asked, fishing and hungry for an ego boost.

"You know I still think you're special."

"What would your girlfriend say?"

"She wouldn't know."

"What's new with her?" I asked, kicking myself for getting involved.

"She moved in," he said hesitantly. "She wants to have a baby."

"You never wanted a baby," I was now hooked, giving my opinion, as if I was watching an interactive soap opera.

"She wants a baby; I said yes."

"It's a big deal," I emphasized. "It's not like when you want Chinese food and she wants Italian and you compromise to eat Italian. It's a lifelong commitment to another human being."

"It hasn't happened yet," he ended the line of conversation impatiently, trying to change the subject. "So when can I see you?"

"How about next weekend?" I dared.

"I can't," he mumbled, regretfully.

"Why? You never have firm weekend plans." I was now biting my nails.

"I do. I'm getting married then," he mumbled, embarrassed.

"Newsman buries the lead! When were you going to tell me?"

"Eventually. It's no big deal."

"That's a good attitude," I answered, curtly.

"You're being mean."

"Are you going to make this one work?" I dared. Now I was pacing the room.

"I try to be a good husband," he said, not convincing me.

"What can I say? Best of luck. I've got to go." Hanging up, numb and nauseous, I had wanted to know what was new. I didn't want it to be so happy.

CHAPTER 26:

THE WOMAN IN THE GLASS BOX

"I'm in therapy now. I used to be in denial, which was a lot cheaper."
—Robin Greenspan

Feeling boxed into a long-gone world that I wouldn't let myself get away from, I knew I needed help. A friend suggested a therapist who specialized in sexual trauma, including childhood incest, rape, and other sexual distress. I knew my experience was a lot less violent, but it still needed special attention. The therapist, Patricia, told me she was the victim of domestic abuse. She'd divorced that husband and recently celebrated her 15th anniversary with her second husband. If she could do that for herself, I had high hopes. With my problems painfully close to the surface, I was determined and hopeful I could work through them.

"I had a little husband for a little while," I began, wrapping my pain in humor. "He was a sex addict who frequented prostitutes. We lived on his salary, and he used my paychecks as his play money, or fuck money."

"That was funny, but what are you really feeling?" asked Patricia.

"I felt that if I was a good, loving wife who stood by my husband, I could make his problems and addictions go away." I rattled off the Rupert years with speedy, detached words, like reading someone else's book report. Biting my nails, I crossed and uncrossed my legs. I tucked my hair behind my right ear, then slipped my fingers behind that same ear and fluffed my hair forward.

"Then I became addicted to shadowing his life. I steam-opened credit card bills and collected crumpled receipts from his pockets," I reported. Then, I paused to take a sip of water from a tall, clear glass. "I found charge slips for 88 visits to prostitutes! Why didn't I leave him after I'd found 44 charge slips?"

We both took a breath and stared into the silence.

"Why?" Patricia repeated. She was a somber 40-year-old redhead; her skin was sun-kissed with freckles and showed crinkly lines whenever she smiled.

"That's why I came here." I found a piece of lint to pick off of my sleeve. More silence. "I didn't want to fail at being a wife." I blurted. "I thought if I behaved differently, I could change the outcome. Why would someone marry and then ignore me? I made a mistake. I saw it as my failure."

"Do you think you're a failure because your marriage ended?"

"Yes, I'd failed at jobs before; I didn't want to fail at my marriage, so I stayed. I didn't want to look like a quitter. Looking back, I moved too quickly going into it. Then, I twisted myself inside out, trying to make things work. I gave it my best."

"What made you leave?" she asked, pointedly.

"I left when I hated myself. I'd hoped marriage would make me feel less lonely," I reflected. "But *this* marriage was the *loneliest* time of my life." I started to cry.

"What did you want going in?" She handed me tissues.

"I wanted a partner, a companion. I got a scam artist who wanted me for window dressing as he screwed prostitutes. I didn't challenge him or speak up for myself because I'd never learned how. In the household where I grew up, we had that, 'Don't talk back to your parents' rule. So, I didn't mouth off in my marriage, either. I never voiced my frustrations, dissatisfactions, or feelings. Instead, I pouted like a moody little girl who stuffed down her emotions with food. I wanted to be loved and cared for. But mostly, I kept believing him even when there was evidence to the contrary. I allowed myself to be manipulated." I started sobbing and took another tissue.

"How can we work together so this won't happen again?" Patricia asked, after I calmed down.

"I have to trust myself more—take responsibility. If something feels crazy I need to stop and examine it—not forge ahead. Neither of us were adults here."

"You two fed each other's immature behavior." She classified Rupert as a sociopath, explaining he used sex with prostitutes as a coping behavior. Had he been born to a less affluent family (with no money to indulge such habits), she said, his coping behavior might have been to molest family members, especially a daughter if we'd had one. Disturbed and relieved I'd dodged that bullet, the thought of having a child—a daughter—with him, made me shudder.

Every Monday night, I spent my 50-minute hour releasing my anguish. Patricia looked visibly shocked by my stories. After each tale of Rupert's behavior, she'd probe, asking, "How did you feel then?" knowing full well my difficulties in accessing my emotions at the time I experienced them. I struggled to find my feelings and give her answers. The results were a lot of painful silences punctuated by crying then mumbling something like "I couldn't" and ending with "I don't know."

I was so exhausted after these sessions that I'd subway home, linger in a long shower, slither into bed by 9:30, and fall asleep. In the mornings, I'd wake, renewed and refreshed, somehow hopeful that I was closer to stepping outside my pain and trauma. Happy that I'd taken the all-important first step to find help.

As I worked with Patricia, I learned to look ahead.

"You're too rough on yourself—too self-blaming," Patricia would explain.

"I stumbled into marriage, fell on my face, and became a cast-off like the books and records he'd collected then ignored."

"But you're not there anymore, and you're not with him. He has a new life; so do you. That's where you need to focus. Look ahead—not behind you."

Thinking about the future produced another waterfall of tears.

"Have you ever heard of battered woman syndrome?" Patricia asked. "It's where you stay with someone who is abusive because you think they need you, thus perpetuating your own continued abuse."

"Is *that* what I have?" My eyes widened, transfixed on hers. I couldn't quite accept that, so I continued, defensively. "He chased after me, asking me to marry him. I trusted that commitment. He knew I was a secret-teen fat girl, and accepted me. I knew of his perverted addiction and I had to take care of him. Our sicknesses made us need to take care of each other."

"You just had a powerful realization," she said, smiling. "I'm proud of your willingness to dig deep. You're not a fat girl anymore. No one sees that in you, but you."

To experience the sensation of touch and the feelings it created, Patricia suggested I find a massage therapist for monthly massages. Three blocks from my apartment, I found a masseuse and went to her studio. During each session, with the nurturing of intuitive hands, I became reacquainted with the sensation of feeling pleasure from my body. I was still the woman in the glass box, but the glass was getting thinner.

CHAPTER 27:

WOMEN WHO LOVE TOO MUCH

"I figure the only time I really need a man is about once a month—when it's time to flip my mattress." —Pamela Yager

As part of sensory exercises suggested by my therapist, I dated occasionally, to rebuild my abilities to interact and trust again. But those dates were usually dinners bound for disaster.

Seeing me taking out the garbage one day, my neighbor Camille called out in her colorful, forthright way, "What's with the all dressing up and going places alone thing you do?"

"I have blind dates."

"That's it? No second dates? No relationships? You enjoy this?"

"Like a trip to the dentist," I assured her.

"Tuesday, six o'clock—come with me. There's a meeting for women like you above the *99 Cent Store*. We'll go together. Trust me—it will be good for you."

Tuesday evening came and Camille and I strode together up a flight of stairs to a dusty room above the discount store on Broadway.

When we entered, there were already 10 other women in the room, sitting in chairs in a circle—women of all different ages, shapes, and sizes. They all greeted Camille. I knew there were meetings like this for overeaters that I'd always meant to attend, but I was too busy snacking. The women began by reading an agenda for a 12-step meeting. A lot of people I knew went to 12-step meetings to stop drinking, overeating, or using drugs. I listened, still not certain what this particular group was all about.

That night, Camille led the meeting. Her eyes greeted people around the circle and then she read from a sheet of paper in her hand, *"Welcome to the women who love too much meeting,"* she began. "A woman who loves too much turns loving into loving too much by focusing all her time, energy, and attention on a partner who may be unavailable or uncaring or unable to love her back. She thinks about the relationship to the exclusion of other interests, tries "to figure him out" in order to change him, gives up her activities and friends for him, and feels empty or panicky without him. This group is for women to explore and discuss their patterns, to focus their energies on growing and developing their own lives, becoming stronger and healthier partners along the way."

There was a group to deal with the issues that had come to fill every part of my life? These women all had the same problem I did? Who knew? I guess Camille did—she was my new savior.

A woman with dark glasses and an ornate diamond wedding band started the discussion.

"I'm a buyer for a department store. I travel for my job to the same five cities each month. I have a lover in every city." She continued. I sensed she sounded equally attached and aloof to each one of them. "I know this is wrong. I love my husband. I enjoy these men too, but I can't stop." Professing heartfelt feelings for all of them, she said she saw herself as an attention junkie, not a sex addict.

Then Camille shared: "I met this guy in an English literature class. I knew I had to go out with him. We'd speak for a moment or two before or after class. He told me he was going to a retreat, an ashram upstate, to take a vow; did I want to go? I thought wow, he's asking me away for the weekend—this should be great! Well, it turns out it's a spiritual retreat, and the vow he took was one of silence. No talking. I mean, no talking at all. Worse than a fire drill in fifth grade. Men and women on separate sides of the chapel. We're not allowed to speak—not even to say 'bless you' after someone sneezes. I'd see him at prayer meetings every few hours. I tried to get him to hide behind a building for a quick clandestine sentence or two. He'd have none of it—not even a knowing glance or an encouraging head nod. So I'm 300 miles from home, speechless at an ashram, still trying to get a guy to like me. That's when I realized I had a problem."

The others nodded knowingly at Camille. I listened to every word everyone shared about her behavior and though each woman had a different set of experiences, they all gorged on relationships, just like me. I went to meetings every week, listening intently, wide-eyed, in jaw- dropping amazement, trying to glean life-altering knowledge. By the third meeting, when all eyes were on me, I spilled forth my Rupert rant like a Sunday church meeting revelation.

"I *married* a sex addict, a master seducer, a tortured soul, nestled inside an otherwise normal appearing man. That's how they get you. He was smart, successful, well mannered. The only red flag of the situation was that for one evening or afternoon during the week, he'd disappear for a few hours. I thought this was just a person's need for privacy and I didn't think much of it. During our marriage, he slept with 88 women, but *never me.* He got me hooked on a drug during our courtship and then cut me off. That drug was his cock."

All eyes were on me and I felt validated by how riveted in disbelief everyone appeared. "The rejection, deception, and hurt chewed through my guts like a flesh-eating disease, demonizing my self-esteem. He used sex for problem solving; going to brothels the way some people go to their local bar." Some women nodded knowingly. "Since the marriage ended, I've abused dating in an effort to heal my hurts, hoping the next kiss from someone new—from someone who desired me—would soothe my burning sense of rejection."

Baring my burdens, venting vitriol, bitterness, frustration, and pain, I felt a sense of release and relief. After I spoke, I looked around the room. Even the woman with five boyfriends was stunned. The others nodded sympathetically. I exhaled with the exhilaration of a bulimic flushing a toilet after a really good purge.

Thereafter, I contributed at every meeting, sharing something of my own story and listening intently as others shared theirs. In so doing, I began to release my pain, and ungirdle my pent-up angst. One night, I wanted to end with a joke or a punch line to leave them laughing, but something inside me said, "No, not this time. You're not onstage. Don't tell them—keep it for me." I passed, took a breath and whispered, *"Life is short and so was my ex-husband."*

Sitting in this circle, looking at these women, I really saw myself. I learned that whenever I viewed dating as reaching out for someone, I was really pulling inward, beating myself up inside. These women were other faces and other phases of my disturbing, self-destructive behavior, if I didn't change it now. I needed to save *myself*—take care of *myself*, not look to a man to save and take care of me. Finally.

I'd stopped obsessively dating and replaced it with going to these meetings. If I needed extra support, Camille and I went for coffee, which started leading to cheesecake and crullers. So instead we put on sneakers and took long walks through Central Park. Walking together was blissful and freeing. I got out of the house, out of my head and into fresh air, admiring trees and sunshine. Breathing deeply, I people watched, noticing women my age pushing strollers. I tried not to delve too deeply into their lives and joys. With every step and every exhale, I was relieved and pleased to not be snooping, spying, or concerning myself with Rupert.

With all of this walking, my stomach, butt, and thighs got slimmer. My clothes fit better, I felt prettier and my self-esteem increased. I started to believe that good times were just around the corner. However, it was just a very long block, a windy day, and I was walking very slowly.

#

My personal experiences helped me charge ahead in writing articles for women's magazines. Health, beauty and relationships was my expertise. My big achievement: I got women from trailer parks to townhouses eager to moisturize their faces and apply eye cream by gently tapping with their ring fingers. Soccer moms without crow's feet have me to thank.

By the mid-1980s, no longer a Park Avenue wife, stand-up comedy became the new rock 'n' roll. Everyone worth seeing was mike-in-hand in front of a brick wall, telling jokes. When entertainment reviewer of *The New York Post* Curt Davis passed away, the newspaper split his job into two reviewers positions— one for cabaret and one for comedy. I landed the comedy reviewer job becoming the originator of the comedy column! I was excited because I was not only a writer well versed in comedy history (thanks, Dad!), but I'd done stand-up. Because of this, my reviews were informed by my knowledge of the process and the performance, from both sides of the stage.

In 1986, I originated the Comedy Review column for *The New York Post*. It was the first of its kind in the country, devoted to stand-up, helping spur comedy's greatest growth period. I interviewed my comedy heroes and got to see young up-and-comers.

I saw 19-year-old Chris Rock perform in his red leather "Thriller" jacket in front of 12—that's right, 12—people, when his joke was "I used to work at McDonald's making minimum wage." Audiences got a sense that it was a fresh experience. Lovable opener Jon Stewart talked about how he couldn't get a date. Meanwhile, every woman in the audience elbowed her friend and whispered, "I'd take that cute little guy home, wouldn't you?" During a lunchtime interview I almost made Gilbert Gottfried choke while he sipped tea when I said, *"A shpsik yung mantsbil nite nos inem lokshen."* Yiddish for, "A funny young man doesn't sneeze in the noodles." Yiddish words make people laugh, especially if it's a quote from Mel Brooks. So I learned to say, while Gilbert was drinking, "I'll wait. You'll spit."

"I ran into an old boyfriend on the street. Now he looks like a loser. I can't believe I talked baby talk to that man for three years of Friday and Saturday nights," said Susie Essman, decades before Larry David plucked her to be an insult queen on *Curb Your Enthusiasm.*

One night I brought an aspiring comedy writer friend to see a show with me.

"I could do your job. It's not so hard," she said. That took the smile off my face.

That night, the headliner was Bobby Slayton, a California comic, who seemed under the radar, but was not quite a TV name. His set began to tepid response, followed by a sweaty brow. Next he said something like, "I heard the New York Post reviewer is here. That's a job, reviewing comedians…they'd be better off milking cows."

My friend turned ashen.

"You still want my job?" My friend recoiled. Now the club owner was ashen too, anticipating a bad review.

I found Bobby to be brave and a master in timing. In my review I wrote, "Bobby Slayton is sexist, racist, yet endearing." This quote was his introduction on his first HBO comedy special.

Five years after I had been onstage for the first time, my world was comedy, again. Enduring friendships were with comedians and comedy writers, some rekindled from stand-up, others in my new reviewer role. Writing about comedy for *The New York Post* for two years was a delight. When the entertainment department of the paper underwent editorial changes, I found myself looking for new writing assignments, anywhere I could.

CHAPTER 28:

PLAYGIRL

"When it comes to sex, those who can, do it. Those who can't, talk about it. Those who can't do it and can't talk about it, write for Playgirl."—That was me.

At the time in my life when I had felt the loneliest and most desperate about my lack of physical intimacy, I was a writer and sex expert for *Playgirl* magazine. "What Your Taste in Men Reveals About You," "The Lover I'll Never Forget," and "How Many Dates Before Sex?" were some of my titles. The irony was too much.

I'd interview men on their seduction secrets, learn their innermost thoughts and desires, while I was untouched by human hands. I felt like a born-again virgin, dried up inside, and fearful of exuding the rancid scent of a bitter divorcee. While "sexpertly" enhancing others' intimacies, I was incapable of my own. At least when life was sexless with Rupert, I had someone to hold through the night and to kiss in the morning.

Now, other than monthly massages, my life was devoid of cuddles or physical touch. I worried I'd lost my ability to be sexually responsive. When you don't drive a car or even warm the engine, everything freezes. Untouched for so long, I thought I was incapable of thawing.

"I've dated every man in town. Maybe I'll have better luck if I change teams and start dating women," I'd joked to myself in the mirror, as I put on "Cherries in the Snow" lipstick. Were my musings the beginning of comedy bits I could sell to a friend, or did I mean it? Rupert was with a lesbian now, so maybe it was a hip trend, like nouvelle cuisine or short skirts. Dating men had been disastrous by the dozens. What if I did switch teams? Could I be that brave? Dating a woman was a thought that I'd filed in the back of my mind, on that "to do" list that never gets done, along with losing 10 pounds and spending a summer in Tuscany.

#

My latest article for *Playgirl* entitled, "Are You Ready for a New Relationship?" was a big success. Now a monthly contributor, I used my own dilemmas to bring comfort to thousands of readers. Who were readers of *Playgirl*, a monthly magazine that featured self-help articles and photos of naked men? I found out, in a most surprising way.

One night a friend from Girl Scouts, Maryanne, invited me out for cocktails. A few years earlier, my Girl Scouts job ended when the organization made 10% staff cuts, due to decreasing troop memberships. It seemed girls were veering away from the cookie selling troops, joining the more progressive and co-ed Camp Fire

Girls. Maryanne insisted on taking me to *Catch a Rising Star*, the uptown comedy club where the city's best comics tried out new material. I'd always aspired to, but never performed there. Besides, after being in comedy clubs night after night as a *Post* reviewer, I now dreaded going to clubs. But Maryanne encouraged me, "One drink, two comics and we'll leave." She offered a digestible amount of comedy and booze, so we went.

The performers that night included three regulars from *Saturday Night Live:* Chris Rock, Adam Sandler, and David Spade. They were pretty funny, so we stayed a while longer. However, the funniest comic of the evening was the MC, my old pal from the days of stand-up, Barry Brickel. We knew each other from long nights at the bar at *Pips*, a club in Brooklyn. Barry had become a comedian's comedian, and writing jokes for other comics. He rivaled Robin Williams with his humorous rants that ping-ponged back and forth between genius and insanity. Or, as Barry would say, *"You think your mom's crazy? I have paperwork."*

In the old days when Barry laughed at my material, I took it as a big compliment, because he wrote the wittiest jokes. Tonight, between sets I visited him, near the bar.

"Barry!" I exclaimed, uncertain if he'd remember me.

"Arlene, great to see you! Are you performing these days?"

"No, that was another lifetime," I replied, my voice trailing off.

"You were good—better than most."

"Thank you, I appreciate that," I smiled. "What about you? Where else are you performing besides here?"

"I'm doing colleges and corporate gigs. Corporate is big money. What about you? Wait—I know what you're doing: you write for *Playgirl!*"

"How do you know that?" I was shocked.

"I have a subscription. I loved your piece in the March issue. Do you get to meet the guys? Mr. March—now that's some piece."

"You're a subscriber?" I laughed, surprised on so many levels.

"Honey, I thought you knew—I'm a big old queen. I read it cover to cover so many times; I should get those issues laminated. I've got to get back to the stage. Working here beats the no-necked monsters in the burbs at Uncle Knuckles Chuckle Hut. Give me your number and we'll do lunch."

Whenever someone says to me, "Let's do lunch," they mean, see you later in life…much later. We exchanged numbers. I thought I'd never hear from him.

I was wrong about Barry. He called the next day for lunch that Friday. Sitting in an outdoor café, we each had large salads. He removed the avocado and put it to the side. I removed the yolks from my hard-boiled eggs and placed them on my bread plate. He took my yolks and motioned for me to take his avocado.

"Take my yolks, please," I quipped. He laughed. "Remember that comedian with the comb-over who used to steal jokes?"

"Earl Brown. I heard he'd been in jail."

"Yes, for armed robbery," Barry added. "He stole from people's homes. Then he made license plates. Now he steals jokes from other comedians."

"Didn't he do that grape nuts bit? 'What are grape nuts? No grapes, no nuts!'" I said. "Like no one would know it was vintage Seinfeld, from The Tonight Show."

"Remember the bowling alley in Queens with comedy on weekends?"

"And you had to get your punch lines in between strikes?" I laughed too.

"On league championship nights, no one heard a word you said."

Reminiscing about crummy clubs, crazy club owners, and bad comedians, I made him laugh a lot. This was the most enjoyable meal I'd had with a guy in months.

After lunch, Barry dragged me to go clothes shopping with him on Columbus Avenue. He needed a jacket for a TV appearance he was making the following week.

"May I help you?" asked the saleswoman.

"Can you help me lose 60 pounds by next Thursday?" Barry quipped.

The saleswoman's jaw dropped. "I can find you something that's figure-flattering."

"How about figure-flattening? Or something that makes me taller…five or six inches taller would do it."

I helped Barry find a jacket. Exiting the store, he turned to me, "I had the best time with you today. You're one of the funniest women in New York. If you won't perform, at least write with me—your wit can really make a difference."

I was honored and flattered, having a good time, and connecting with another human being. "Sure, I'll give it a try," I grinned.

"Come to a show with me next week," he implored. "Help me rehearse my set tomorrow? You might have a new joke or two for me." He hugged me close and kissed my cheek.

Walking home that afternoon, *I felt happy.* When I was with Barry, I didn't feel lonely. It was nice to know I could feel relaxed and comfortable with a man and know exactly where the relationship wasn't going.

Throughout the following week, Barry and I were inseparable, like two freshman girls in high school. We laughed a lot, talked about boys, and compared moisturizers. I was writing comedy again, and working with a gifted comedian who respected and encouraged my talents.

The night of Barry's show, he was nervous. I calmed him. He held my hand before and after the show, like a spouse at a business dinner. At the end of the evening, he walked me home.

"Good show tonight!" I said to Barry.

"I couldn't have done it without you," he added, squeezing my hand. "You don't know the half of it."

"What do you mean?"

"They said the set went so well, they want me to go to LA in two weeks to do it again. That's not the best part," he added. "I said I couldn't go anywhere without my writing partner. I asked for two plane tickets. YOU and I are going to LA in two weeks."

We both jumped up and down like winners on *The Price Is Right.*

#

As I packed for my trip, I thought of Rupert, still furious with him. But then my mind shifted to Barry and all the laughing we'd be doing together in LA. Nothing can take your mind off uncomfortable things better than a free trip. After a hundred blind dates with most of the single men in NYC, I was now a fag hag having a bi-coastal weekend. I'd found a safe, hilarious haven to help me forget my man worries, yet I still felt like a lovable woman—and a funny lovable woman, at that. Barry provided an abundance of acceptance.

I decided that during our cross-country flight, Barry would help me solve my sexuality issues. Surely, decades of relationship turmoil could be solved by a gay man at 35,000 feet.

So as we sat on the plane, side-by-side, I read a fashion magazine, and Barry filled in the little boxes in his *Big Book of Crossword Puzzles*.

"Barry, how's that puzzle?" I inquired, trying to distract him.

"I need 27 down, five letters. Shirley Booth was the lead character on this show."

"Hazel."

"Very good!" He smiled gratefully as he filled in the boxes.

"Now, can you fix my life?" I asked.

"I didn't know it was broken."

"Dating issues," I replied.

"You're a relationship expert for *Playgirl!* I was hoping *you* could fix *my* dating life."

"I'm serious. You know about men."

"Not that my mother knows."

"Just the Marines, Navy, and Con Ed service guys," I quipped.

"You left out the cable repair men on the East Side, but we're trying to focus on you. By the way, since we're switching coasts, have you considered switching teams?"

Since we were going far from home, I thought I'd ask, "Would I have a better chance of having a good relationship with a woman? How many women would it take to make me a lesbian?" I whispered.

Barry looked me up and down, surprised. "Are you mad for the muff? Would you explore? Sort of a Lewis and Clark of the labia?" he laughed.

I laughed too. "I'm just inquiring. How did you know when you were switching teams? How do you know when it's right?" I whispered.

Barry looked me up and down, surprised. "Everyone is different," he smiled. "If it feels right, then that's where you belong."

"Nothing and no one feels right. That's my problem."

"You're young, you'll find your way," he said. "Hey, if you ever wanted a roommate, we could be like Laverne and Shirley. I'll be a big old queen, and you could be the fix-it gal. We'll get you a wrench set and a tool belt. Oh look, they're starting to roll out the food carts. I hope it's not turkey tetrazzini like the last flight. The sodium made my ankles swell up for three days."

"I think you've made sense."

"My job is to be amusing and colorful," he laughed.

"You're like a VW bug crammed with clowns."

"Oh, you charmer. See, words with "C's" are always funnier…I'm gonna use that for one of my bits."

"Glad I could be of service," I nodded.

Barry looked at me seriously then started laughing. I hit him on the head with my magazine. Five minutes later, the food came. I gave him my dinner roll. He gave me the tomato from his tiny salad. We were behaving like a comfortable old married couple.

We arrived at the hotel to a beautiful room with two big beds. One wall had floor-to-ceiling windows. When I pulled the blinds open, there was a glorious view of the Hollywood hills and smack in the middle was the famed "Hollywood" sign.

"Hey Barry, look at this view. By the end of this weekend we might want to move here."

"Yeah, right, and monkeys will fly out of your ass."

"Keep it down, bitch," I fired back.

"So far I'm having the best time with you."

Later that evening, Barry and I put on our colorful evening clothes and drove to the *Ice House*, a comedy club in Pasadena. We had a light dinner with the other performers for the show that was being taped that night. Barry's jokes were polished and sharp. In fact, he killed it. As his set ended and he bade the audience, "Thank you and goodnight," he smiled and looked straight at me. When he got off stage, Barry made a beeline for me. He gave me a lingering hug. "You are my lucky charm. I'm taking you everywhere."

"Great set, man," said the comic who preceded him.

"Killer jokes," said another comedian, who patted him on the shoulder.

I'm a success with a gay man, I thought to myself, riding back to our hotel. Later that evening, driving through the neighborhoods of Los Angeles, Barry and I were high on adrenaline mixed with jetlag and the hypnotic smell of roses whirling through the car's open windows.

"So far, this is a great trip," I said. Back at the hotel, we wandered around the bar area and the pools, and strolled back to the room at 4 a.m., New York time.

Next morning, while Barry was asleep, I got up and took a shower. When I exited the bathroom, he was lying on his bed, drinking coffee and reading the sports pages.

"Finally, she emerges, sanitized," he quipped.

"I didn't realize you were a jock faggot. Or is it faggot jock?"

"I ordered breakfast. Eat darling, you need to keep up your strength."

"Bitch. What's on for today?" I fired back.

"I want to sit by the pool and work on my tan. Afterwards, meet me under an umbrella—we could bang out some jokes for an hour or two. My friend Dan invited us for brunch tomorrow at his home in the Hollywood Hills."

"Is that what people do here?"

Barry nodded, "They work on their tan, and they brunch. The tan and the well-fed are the unemployed. The scrawny and pale are the successful actors, too busy to eat or sit in the sun."

"How would we fit in?"

"The cachet of writing comedy in Los Angeles is that once you work on one television show, you could be hired for another. And, no matter how good or how long that show is on the air, it builds your track record. Comedians from the clubs in New York have moved west and became affluent homeowners with fancy cars in no time. They're not smarter or funnier than us."

"How do we get one of those lottery tickets?"

"We have to take some meetings."

"Where do we find these meetings?"

"If you're hot, they find you!"

"Are we even lukewarm?"

“I had a great set last night, I’ll make some calls,” said Barry. “Tanning and calling for work—those are my best skills. I’ll drum up something.”

“Thank you, my little drummer boy.”

While Barry tanned, I shopped at the *Beverly Center*, a mall within walking distance of the hotel. In New York, we walked everywhere. Here, no one walked. I watched the cars driving by, each filled with just one person. When those cars stopped at red lights, drivers put that moment to use. They applied lipstick or brushed their hair. I saw one guy take out an electric razor and give himself a shave. This new world was very sunny, and wackier than I’d expected.

Early that evening, we dined in Beverly Hills near Rodeo Drive. Afterwards, we window- shopped the extravagant stores.

“Glad we’re here when stores are closed,” I laughed. “It saves me the heartache of trying on things I can’t afford and spares me the scrutiny of salesgirls thinking I’m a shoplifter.”

Looking in a window, spotting a mannequin, Barry turned to me and said, “That dress would look *lovely* on you….pretty, pretty!”

“And it only costs…a week’s pay!” I exclaimed.

“If we had more pretty things, we’d be much prettier people,” he reasoned. “If we were prettier, we’d attract prettier people,” Barry was only half-joking. “Then we could be rejected by a whole new, better class of people.”

Next we strolled past Tiffany’s. I tried to change the subject. “Here we are, ‘Breakfast at Tiffany’s’…isn’t it glamorous?”

"It's more like '*Brisket* at Tiffany's.'" He struck a pose. "Only *I* want to be Audrey Hepburn. *You* can be George Peppard. He was supposed to be playing a big old queen, and she was his long-necked fag hag."

"I've got that role down pretty well."

"In LA, you could be fag hag to the rich and famous," Barry wrapped his arm around me and nuzzled my neck. "You know, as a team, you and I could be so successful—money, money, sitting by the pool writing jokes."

"Better than standing in the subway, seeing some guy pee on the wall while you're waiting for a train," I added.

"I like the way you conjure penises in your stories," Barry exclaimed.

"Is that all my charm is to you, dick references?"

Barry held me close and kissed my forehead. "Your charm means the world to me." He looked me in the eye, "Together we could take this town."

Throwing my arms around Barry, I said, "May these brisket nights in Beverly Hills be considered our hungry years."

"Amen. You know, they have the cutest salesmen at Gucci and Prada…and sometimes they deliver," he added, chuckling.

"From your mouth to Neiman Marcus," I said.

Sunday, we visited Barry's friend Dan, brunching on his patio, high in the hills, with a view of "swimming pools and movie stars" in the canyon below. His ultra-modern house had high ceilings, big windows, white furniture, and impressive contemporary art, including a David Hockney painting above the fireplace. Dan cooked amazing vegetable omelets and the fresh fruit he served was mouth-watering.

"Dan, everything is delicious," I smiled.

"That's California organic produce," he replied.

"If California was a cult, Arlene would be its biggest devotee," Barry chimed in. "She'd be making potholders out of her own hair, just like those Manson girls."

As the sun set, we bid goodbye to Dan. We were flying back to NY in the morning, both of us sad our adventure was ending.

"Dan has a fabulous place," I breathed, taking in the warmth of the evening air.

"And a fabulous life," Barry added. "Everything here is fabulous." The car cruised through the sprawling mansions of Beverly Hills, with endless well-manicured green lawns. Jasmine was in full bloom, wafting through the air. "So, cookie—could you be an LA woman? A whole new state for you—for dating, mating and sexual rejection."

"All I need is a new body and a tan," I laughed in agreement.

He cackled. "If you are going to dream, dream in Technicolor."

"Look at these beautiful homes! I bet each of their bathrooms is bigger than my entire apartment. Even the air is beautiful…smell that jasmine."

"Is that what that is?" Barry asked. "I thought it was you."

"Why do we live in a city that smells like urine?" I demanded. In that instant, our eyes met. There was a long, knowing glance.

"I don't know," Barry responded.

"Small cramped apartments, subways, rain, snow, cold…" I rattled off.

"Why do we live in New York?" Barry whined.

"Maybe we should move here?" I blurted, shocked by my own statement. We stared at each other.

"Maybe we should."

CHAPTER 29:

Last Licks Lunch

"Things are going to get a lot worse before they get worse."—Lily Tomlin

"I can't wait for the sun," I said as I watched the dreary gray sameness of New York slowly fog over as our plane descended into clouds. Shortly after we landed back in NYC, Barry arranged two weeks worth of work for us, in California—a writing gig on a late-night variety show, "*Into the Night.*"— ABC Television's first stab at comedy/variety in years. Barry and I envisioned this great life in LA, where it never rained, we laughed all the time, and wrote for television. It sounded like a dream.

Meanwhile, in Manhattan, I realized that nothing in my life fit there any more—like a pair of jeans left too long in the dryer. Feeling uncomfortable in my apartment, I couldn't stand the putrid smell of the city. Subways I'd been riding my entire life were now unbearable. In my mind, I was already preparing my move to California with Barry, queen of comedy, as my companion. Together, we'd be the new golden duo, working non-stop, laughing all the way from one big paycheck to the next. A move across country would change my luck, change my life and, with any luck, change my sex life.

Cleaning out my closets, I got rid of my flannel nightgown collection, most of which had threadbare elbows and food stains. And I gave away my snow boots and wool skirts—no need for them in a place where it didn't snow and never got cold.

My thoughts focused on the future, packing for my new life. Then there was Rupert—I had to tell him I was leaving town. In leaving I hoped I'd sever the inexplicable feeling of being tethered to him. After 10 months of not speaking, I finally had good news, so I called. "Hello Rupert, how are you?"

"Arlene, it's always a pleasure to hear your voice."

"What's new by you?" I asked, wanting to temper my news.

"Nothing much, and you?"

"I'm moving," I tried to be provocative.

"Uptown? Downtown?" he quizzed.

"Out of town," I blurted. "California."

"You're kidding me!"

"Would I kid you?" I answered a question with a question.

"I have to see you before you go," he insisted.

"Don't think I'll have time," I stammered, realizing I hadn't thought this through.

"No time for me? I was your only husband," he begged.

"What would your wife say?"

"Who cares? Why should she know?"

"That's the Rupert I know. Just wanted to give you my headlines."

"Please see me before you go… at least say good-bye to me."

"I'll think about it. Gotta run." I hung up.

I'd see him one last time and be over him. Look fabulous and make him want me. "See him, cut the cord, and it will be done," I thought. Besides, lately, I looked really good and wanted him to see that I'd blossomed into a much lovelier flower than the one he'd first picked.

How and where would we meet? My mind raced with cheesy scenarios straight out of a Joan Crawford movie.

Since we both loved opera, I allowed myself the indulgence of a farewell swan song/aria as the *denouement* for our divorce. I was in the mood for a "Sunset Boulevard" Norma Desmond farewell moment: cinematic high-drama and emotive facial expressions—to make sure I was over him. And yeah, I wanted to tease him—see if he still had a spark of interest, so at least I'd walk away with some satisfaction.

We agreed on lunch at a dimly lit restaurant within walking distance of my apartment: I chose it in case I felt like choking him, then I could make a mad dash home. I meticulously styled my hair and put on make-up with greater care than any first date or job interview.

Our relationship began with him impressing me with expensive lunches in tasteful locales. We'd come full circle. But unlike a lunch kicking off the marriage, the goal of this meal was to say what had gone unspoken. This was, as we say in Brooklyn, "the last licks lunch."

It was a cold day in April. As I entered the restaurant, a gust of wind swirled around me, blowing my hair and making it hard to pull the door open. Arriving at the table flustered, the graceful, serene entrance of my fantasy was instead a Laverne DeFazio (from the 1970s sitcom Laverne & Shirley) slapstick struggle. Rupert was seated in a booth, facing the door—waiting. He appeared chubbier. I loved seeing his extra chins and sensing that mid-life complacency had made him seem older and duller. As we also say in Brooklyn, he looked like shit and I looked marvelous. I felt redeemed; this was a good start.

Rupert's new fat belly struggled to shimmy out of the booth, to stand and greet me. Both uncertain whether we should hug or kiss, we danced a bit until he lunged towards me, planting a peck on my half-frozen cheek.

"Well, you certainly look fabulous," he exclaimed. "You're glowing! And your cute nose is red from the cold."

"That won't happen in California."

"I can't believe you're really going. I'll miss you. Stay in touch."

"Why?"

"I know you'll be successful. I always thought you were great." He smiled.

"Who are you, and what have you done with Rupert?"

"You know I wanted the best for you, in my own clumsy way. I always thought your talent would land you great success."

"You never said anything like that to me before."

"I mentioned it to your mother."

"We both know she'd never tell me."

"I hope you'll think nice thoughts of me when you're famous in LA."

"I don't think nice thoughts of you in NY! Why would I think them in LA?"

Rupert half chuckled.

The waitress took our order. He stared at me, smiling. I looked around the room, at all the high-backed black leather booths. How many couples broke up in booths like these, in this very restaurant? Then I addressed my curiosity. "So, how's it going with your fourth wife?"

"I still think of you, and miss you. I wish things between us had been different."

"Sure. Are you saying your marriage sucks?"

"You know," he mumbled.

"No, I don't know, tell me."

"You punished me for being a bad boy." He's blaming me? I thought.

"What are you, 12 years old?" Both sides of my brain bolted into battle. Scream, make a scene, throw water in his face, and run out," said my inner drama girl. The other side told me to sit quietly, take it all in, be serene and charming.

Forcing myself to contain my rage and appear polite, my hands trembled. I rearranged the silverware, but my knife slipped off the table, hitting the floor, under the table, irretrievable. Lucky for him, I thought, A fork could be just as violent if you cut the right vein.

"Rupert, there's something I really need to know." I began. "What was it like for you when I left? Do you understand why I left?"

"I felt badly that you'd felt hurt. I tried to get close to you. I guess I didn't know how."

He said it tenderly. I wanted to believe this was a breakthrough moment—where we'd shared an ounce of togetherness and Rupert had offered something from his heart.

I was on the verge of speaking, really using my voice, to finally put him in his place, when the waitress bellowed, "Who gets the corned beef?"

The intimate moment flickered away, like a candle that had been blown out, leaving us in the darkness and din of the crowded restaurant, estranged again.

I'd entered this marriage full of hope, believing love would grow. I could see now that I'd squandered my twenties, living in a fairytale, too fearful of being alone to speak up, to claim my part in our relationship. I devoted myself to someone who wasn't emotionally available to me, then or now. I got a lot of hope kicked out of me. As I ate my lunch, I chewed on this realization and my stomach became too twisted to eat. I'd rather daydream about the future—sitting at a pool in Los Angeles with Barry, writing jokes and laughing. Yet I sat there, my mother's gracious daughter, fork picking at my salad, completely closed off to my true rage and to the world around me.

Years ago, when I dreamed of what marriage would be, I never thought I'd be divorced, especially before thirty. Once I'd made the commitment, I didn't think I'd be able to let go. These last few moments of slime bucket memory lane helped me cut the cord—with a machete. I took a sip of water—step one of my exit.

Rupert touched my hand. I almost jumped.

"You always had the sweetest, softest hands."

"The better to strangle you with, my pretty," I half smiled.

"You've become so mean. What happened?"

"I married you." I couldn't sit there a minute longer. "You fucked all those women, and you still want to be chatty?"

So much I wanted to say, yet once again I sat paralyzed, unable to access my feelings, my mother's daughter: still polite, raised never to cause a scene in public or in life. Heart racing, vision blurry—the room got hot. All sounds around me became muffled, as if I'd fainted, but my eyes were still open. The next few minutes seemed like a slow-motion sleep-walking blur—a stop-frame pieced-together montage of what I had wanted to happen and what really occurred.

Rupert leaned in. "Listen to me," I heard him say, as if from a distance. "I missed a great opportunity with you. I did love you. I didn't know how to show you. I was a jerk with my own demons and fears. You are precious. Know that you were deeply loved, but by a fool. I didn't know how to be a good husband to you. I do now, but I'm too late. You're leaving. I lost out."

"You're married, and you're asking for a do-over? What we had was not special. It was kind of sad and sleazy. Take your love and give it to your new wife."

Dazed, as if those words were summoned up in a trance-like state, and not from my mouth, the room cooled down. My senses returned, as did my better judgment. Seeing Rupert's pudgy, aging face, I felt all charm vanish, replaced by sadness and pity. It was official: I was done—fully sickened and ready to let go.

"I'm not feeling very well. I'm going now."

"You haven't finished your lunch. Will you be okay? Should I go with you?"

"No, you've done enough. I'm finished here, really." I said. Energized by the power of my words. I stood to leave. Rupert helped me on with my coat. He was bursting to say something. He took a step closer and put my collar up.

"It's cold out there," he said, sadly.

"More than you know," I mumbled, pained and exhausted.

I exited the restaurant to another gust of wind and a sprinkling of snow, which I now welcomed as a cold blast of reality. Striding home, my cheeks were wet with snowflakes and tears. Yes, I'd walked out on Rupert yet again—but this time I had somewhere to go.

CHAPTER 30:

WHO KNEW? THIS IS WHAT A HEALTHY RELATIONSHIP LOOKS LIKE

"Without deviation, progress is not possible."—Frank Zappa

On a recent Los Angeles morning, I left my TRX suspension class, where I held a plank position as long as classmates half my age, and then got into my car. This is LA, where we might hate traffic but are slaves to our own modes of transportation—no crosstown buses for us.

For me though, driving came quite late, in my mid-thirties. And even later, finally, at 53, I met a man who didn't reel me in only to leave me waiting at the airport at midnight, like an old suitcase or broken box, both from the same flight and both unclaimed (another story for another time). I ponder this as I drive. I might have gotten a late start, but the fruitless running in place now feels worth it.

Part of my mission post-Rupert had been to get my life "back onstage"—by writing about the people who literally were on it. My gig at *The New York Post* helped me get other entertainment assignments for various publications including theater reviews for *Daily Variety*.

But something was still missing from my life, a romantic partner. After hundreds of blind dates—including four *produced* screenwriters and three *unproduced* (there's a big difference between produced—rare—and unproduced—every waiter and their dentist) along with three architects, two chefs, and one psychic—I met a man whose voice soothed me—but he was the polar opposite of Rupert's velvety slick seduction.

After great conversation on our first dinner date—the kind where we're feeling exhilarated, brimming with intense banter, and losing track of time until the moment of breaking our gaze and realizing that waiters are sweeping and putting chairs on tables, and we're the last two left—came our next date, two days later. He insisted on seeing me perform in a spoken word show—similar to stand-up in that it is storytelling, which can be humorous, but different in that memorization or reading is optional, and the emphasis is on being in the moment. After the show, over cocktails, we confessed things that brought us even closer together: We each did not like what the other wore on our first date. For me, he wore too much black, with white sneakers. For him, I was dressed too colorfully, in a burnt orange jacket over a brightly printed dress.

But what he said next stayed with me.

"You're too pretty, you don't need black eye make-up," he mused. "I just broke up with a woman very different than you. Her idea of a night out was going to dungeons."

"Did you like that?" My spidey senses anticipated a land mine.

"It's unique once, then it's like performance art that's a little too close."

"I know what you mean."

"You do?" He leaned in, intrigued.

"I just dated someone who also liked dungeons," I said. "But the guy told me, 'before I take you there, you need to meet some of my sexual community. If *they* like *you*, then I'll take you."

"How did *you* like the dungeon?" Perry asked with a smile.

"I told that guy I didn't think my sex life needed a community and that I preferred one-on-one intimacy. Basically, game over. We didn't go to the dungeon together, or anywhere else."

Perry took my hand over the table and kissed it.

It turned out we were a great match in other ways. He'd had a long career as a music editor, catering to rock musicians and film composers, and is now a composer in his own right. He excels at helping creative people flourish. When I developed a one-woman show called *The 56 Minute Relationship*, billed as "a wonderfully horrible tale of love, marriage, betrayal and how to get an estimate on a reasonably priced mob hit" with a flyer featuring my wedding photo with my ex-husband's head cut out, Perry organized a crew of sound, lighting, and camera people to film and edit the show. Instead of flowers or jewelry, this was his love letter to me.

Before and after the filming of the show, the dirty laundry of my marriage—the lies, deceits, and addictive behavior of my life with Rupert—was laid bare for Perry to view, on the page, on stage, and in the editing room. And after all of that, Perry still wanted to be with me. But I had more healing to do. Simple courtesies, like Perry's need to excuse himself to make a phone call, reminded me of my ex-husband's phone sex secrecy. I had been through a lot, and I still had what they call "trust issues."

"Where are you going with your phone?" I asked suspiciously.

"I'm calling my mother."

"Really?"

"Yes, really. Would you rather I sit in here and you can talk to her?"

Perry genuinely cared about me. He was patient, willing to work through my fears and doubts to get us to a more hopeful place—something I'd never had with a partner.

"If something is bothering you, don't walk away," he mentored me. "Sit with me and we'll talk about it."

This communicative approach to our relationship has helped us both face our own personal battles, including food and yo-yo dieting. As someone who has struggled with body image and weight all my life, I have finally met my match in my all-black-clothes-all-the-time dude whose hedonistic eating habits led him to gain 100 pounds over the course of two years.

Now, together, we are on a supportive weight-loss mission further fueling our trust in each other. We believe in being silly, kind, and goofy whenever possible, especially after grocery shopping. One carries, one puts all the food away. One puts the grocery bag on their head while serving the other a cool beverage when they're parched from shopping.

Happiness still feels a little uncomfortable and unfamiliar, like breaking in a new pair of shoes. It's a long way from Brooklyn to Park Avenue, to a cramped single-woman apartment in LA, to living with a man who owns almost as many pairs of shoes as I do.

But not so far from my beginnings. This time, though, I'm onstage on my own terms, telling tales of women's secrets and desires in LA's spoken-word circuit—a raucous romp through the hidden lives of today's "mature" woman.

"Why do women live longer than men?" I will ask an audience. *"All that time spent in ladies' room lines, they get back at the end of their lives."*

My friend, Deb, a comedian I met in the 1980's who I'm still close with, she and other comics still jockey for club spots, gigs on cruise ships, and features on social media. We support and encourage each other's writing and performing. We see the new generation of funny women coming up, especially the real, relatable and far-from-Hollywood-ideals of Nikki Glaser, Tiffany Haddish, Amy Schumer and others, admiring how they're not afraid to grab on to their self-esteem and protect it—even as they fight against norms expected of women: to be thin, submissive, and careful to not discuss things that make others uncomfortable.

"All my friends are getting married. I guess I'm just at that age where people give up," says Amy Schumer.

Schumer is the hero of her joke, a world away from what had been my take on marriage, with me as the victim in my own joke: "When I turned 25 and wasn't married, my parents put a sign in front of their house: Last girl before freeway…plus salad bar."

Laughter demands attention. It's the opposite of being invisible—which is what it feels like to be a woman over 50 in Los Angeles. The city's focus on youthful beauty makes one feel like there's a bus waiting for you, in front of your house, to take you far away—to the land of the menopause invisibles—a zombie city that serves free coffee in the wee hours of the morning—the time when menopausal women are wide awake.

All in all, performing in Hollywood clubs at age 55 is different than New York at 25. Performing spoken word now, I can read or hide in the pages of my stories if I feel self-conscious or afraid of forgetting a line. Plus, there's more real life, less shtick.

One night, as I strode to the stage at a story salon I frequent, the audience applauded me. I hadn't said a word, yet they were already giving me love. They know my painful, laughable goofy truths and were ready for more. This minute was better than dozens of nights in comedy clubs.

"For a woman my age, there's so much hormonal change and memory loss, I'm not sure if I'm having a hot flash or a flash back."

"What do you call a 50-year-old woman buying a 40-count box of tampons? An optimist. Who here married their boss from a one-week temp job? Oops, only me. I became vulnerable to the siren song of marriage, thinking it would bring normalcy to my otherwise out-of-step life. Ha. The joke was on me. I didn't see the humor in it till 30 years later. But that's okay: life is short and so was my ex-husband."

I'd always heard that tragedy plus time equaled comedy. I'd tossed it off as an over-rated cliché. My painful Rupert years had finally set me free. Audience applause at the end of the show felt better than sex with an understanding, unconditional lover.

I never thought that those support group meetings back in the days—where going up those stairs to that little meeting room felt like failure—would ever yield positive outcomes. It turns out, they boosted my courage and self-esteem so much that I had faith in myself again.

Being with an addict takes away a belief in yourself—whether it was doubting that I had what it takes to make an audience laugh again or to find a partner who wants me as I am—that can take years to regain. And if I hadn't had a group of women to bolster me, I might still be sleeping on a fold-out futon with a crazy roommate as far away from where I am now as I can imagine. That's why it's important to seek help to get back to the person you were before you got swept up in the addictive drama of an addict.

It took years to heal that pain of being the partner of a sex addict, but with the help of friends, lovers, therapists, support groups, and lots and lots of laughter, I no longer feel alone.

About the Author

Arlene Schindler, born in Brooklyn, N.Y. is an author and speaker sharing humorous tales of women's secrets and desires. She originated the comedy column for the *New York Post*, writing reviews and profiles of comedians appearing in New York City. It was the first of its kind in the country, helping spur comedy's greatest growth period. Her writing has appeared in the *Los Angeles Times*, *Daily Variety*, *Purple Clover, Huffington Post* and many other publications. She's also a contributor to the anthology *Women Under Scrutiny*. Her novel *The Last Place She'd Look* is a raucous romp through the hidden sex lives of today's mature women.

Contact Arlene

Twitter @SmunnySchindler
Website: http://www.arleneschindler.com/
Goodreads: Arlene Schindler

Like Arlene's Facebook Author page and stay up to date on all things Arlene:

www.facebook.com/ArleneSchindler/

For The Reader

Thank you for purchasing and reading this book. If you enjoyed it please leave a short review on book-related sites such as Amazon and Goodreads. Readers rely on reviews, as do authors.